THE BLUE COLLAR
INVESTOR
presents

D0885711

Cashing in on covered calls

Investing with stock options

Alan Ellman

S
P
AMR
PRODUCTIONS
Long Island, NY

Special thanks and recognition to *Investopedia, Chicago Board Options Exchange* and *Zachs Investment Research*, whose online definitions were utilized, in part, in the development of the Glossary for this book. Global footnotes thereto, include:

- Investopedia.com, http://www.investopedia.com/terms/o/optionchain.asp
- Chicago Board Options Exchange, http://www.cboe.com/LearnCenter/Glossary.aspx
- Zachs Investment Research, http://www.zacks.com/help/glossary/?id=v_z&PHPSESSID=c761

The Blue Collar Investor, and all logos, images, and graphic reproductions associated thereto are pending registered trademarks on behalf of The Blue Collar Investor, Ltd.

Original *The Blue Collar Investor* logo design: **David B. Greenberg**, Vice President,
  Success By Design, Roslyn Heights, NY. www.successbydesigns.net.

Book Jacket, *About the Author,* and *ESOC* order form photographs of Dr. Ellman: **Angelo Caruso**,
  Visions Video & Photography, Long Island, NY. www.visionsvp.net

Associate Editor:	**Jamie Ellman**	Book Jacket design:	**Barbara Karnes**
Contributing Editor:	**Barbara Karnes**	Original *CCC* Logo design:	**Barbara Karnes**
		Original *Eltoon* design:	**Barbara Karnes**

Library of Congress Cataloging-in-Publication Data

Ellman, Alan
  Cashing in on covered calls : investing in stock options / Alan Ellman.
  p. cm.
  Includes index.
  ISBN: 978-0-9774233-5-4   2 0 0 7 9 4 1 7 8 1

Except where noted, all photographs, images, illustrations, and "figures" in this book were provided courtesy of the authors and/or owners, or as part of the public domain, To access full-sized versions go to **www.thebluecollarinvestor.com/vip.** Use of this document repository is available with your BCI-VIP code* provided at the time of sale, or directly from the aforementioned web address, with proper proof of purchase information, as defined therein.

BCI-VIP code: acronym for The Blue Collar Investor's Very Important Person code, an alpha-numeric, multi-digit password used to access a secure, electronic document repository established to further support the continuing educational needs of all book purchasers.

Special Discounts on bulk quantities of this book are available to corporations, professional associations, institutes of learning, and other organizations - for educational, gift, promotional, or other purposes. For details, contact Special Sales Dept., **SAMR Productions**, 77 Arkay Drive, Suite K., Hauppauge, NY 11788.

Dedication

Dedicated to three members of my family who left us much too soon:

My first wife, Wendy.

My father, Jack.

My brother, Ronald.

They contributed immensely to my life and to the person I have become.

It brings tears to my eyes that they are not here today to see what is happening in my life.

I'm hoping this book is available in heaven!

Table of Contents

Preface

Sixteen years prior to the penning of this book I decided to learn about the stock market. My experience with the stock market prior to that moment was limited. My parents invested in the market but it was their broker who made all the decisions. Buy this. Sell that. And, they usually went along with it. Sometimes they made money. Other times they lost.

I knew that this type of investing was not for me. I like to understand what I am doing, and why. I need to be in control. I also recognized that I would have to educate myself to an extremely high level to accomplish these goals.

So, one Friday, on a day off from my dental practice, I went to Borders and purchased my first stock book, One Up on Wall Street by Peter Lynch.[1] The following Friday I bought a second book. A pattern was emerging. By Thursday of every week I'd be finished with last Friday's book, anxiously waiting the purchase my next one. This mania continued until I'd voraciously devoured over 100 books.

Between hardcover chapters, I'd be reading the Wall Street Journal or Investors Business Daily, (aka IBD); two staples

---

1   Peter Lynch, One up on Wall Street (New York: Simon and Schuster, 1989).

in the financial universe. Eventually this led to a taste of Baron's on the weekends, and a smorgasbord of magazines, seminars, educational CD's, TV programs, radio shows, and more. I was a kid in a candy store of fundamentals, charts and calculations. I simply couldn't get enough!

The ritual began. Whenever I was home, I'd find myself with pen, paper and a yellow highlighter in hand, eagerly making my way upstairs to the sanctuary of my office. I finally understood how a nerd felt about his pocket protector, as the world of stock option investing began to unfold. My goal was simple: to uncover the untold secrets privy only to the top Wall Street insiders, and utilize this information to create a winning investment strategy for the blue collar investor.

To accomplish this, I even called the Investor Relations department of many publicly traded companies to obtain financial statements and balance sheets before they became readily available online. Despite the fact that some of the data would prove inaccurate, due to the creative accounting methods employed behind closed boardroom doors, I found, overall, this education was paying dividends. My investments were regularly outperforming the "market" by 2% to 3%, using the S&P 500 as my benchmark. On the surface, the results may not have seemed dramatic. To the savvy investor, however, they were significant.

The success continued for about seven years. I was buying and selling stocks, making money, and finding myself inspired by the results. It was around that time I read an article on self directed IRAs. Suddenly, one sentence caught my eye that would change my investing strategy for years to come.

YOU"RE ALLOWED SELLING STOCK OPTIONS
IN A SELF-DIRECTED IRA ACCOUNT!

I thought to myself. How could this be? The government never allows you to do anything risky in an IRA. Options are risky. Aren't they?

What I discovered was that I could begin Cashing In On Covered Calls, selling options within a government approved IRA account. This realization would now allow me to substantially pump up my profits.

The timing of this discovery was significant, as my first wife was seriously ill, and my two sons were still enjoying the benefits of their higher education; Craig in private college, and Jared in medical school. Between the hospital bills and the kid's tuition payments, cashing in on covered calls was about to alleviate a tremendous financial burden.

The ritual continued. Off to Borders I went.

There were several books on stock options, with only a few focusing on the niche of covered calls. I bought them all! Three books, two pens, one pad, and four yellow highlighters later, I started selling covered call options. Although I was very much an options neophyte, I found myself procuring higher returns than I received from trading stocks.

Was this beginner's luck? A temporary fluke?

Admittedly, I was a newbie. I made some mistakes. Unequivocally, I was a pro. I corrected them.

My returns went even higher. It didn't take me long to come to the conclusion that this was for real. Perfecting and enhancing my system became a main focus. Selling covered call options represented more than 90% of my stock investing portfolio, simply because I was able to generate returns higher than any other strategy.

The ritual expanded. In 2005 I decided to conquer real estate investing. (my local Borders is doing quite well!). I succeeded. Subsequently, in August of 2006, I was asked to speak before a group of real estate investors about some financially rewarding deals I had been involved in. At that presentation, I mentioned the fact that I purchased my first real estate investment property with profits generated from selling stock options. I was surprisingly inundated with requests to explain how I did it. So...

First I conducted some seminars. Now I wrote this book.

This book is for the average investor. The person who may have a family member who is ill. The parent who may have children in college. The employee who may be working 60 hours a week to make ends meet. The client who may have an advisor telling him how to make a lot of money, but who is really more interested in procuring income for himself. The baby boomer who may have a mother struggling to enjoy her golden years. The guardians with young children for whom they want a better life. This book is for YOU.

I also wrote it for me.... If I can make the lives of some families better by sharing the system that I have developed, then I have enhanced my life, as well!

Acknowledgments

I found this part of my book the most difficult to write. The truth of the matter is that having a great support system makes the road to success much easier to navigate. The first person who comes to mind is my beautiful wife Linda. She has endured many hours of watching Oprah and Dr. Phil all by herself while I typed away in my business office (hunt and pecked is a better description of what took place). When Linda did approach me it was always as a source of support.

Can I get you a cup of coffee? Is there anything I can do?

I always thought to myself as I was penning this book.....*how lucky can one man be?* In addition to my wife, my sons Jared and Craig have always been a source of inspiration to me. No matter what I do, they admire and encourage every bit of it. Sometimes I think that they overestimate their father but that just motivates me even more.

Another person who may overrate me is my Mom, Minnie Ellman. I always found her motherly admiration a motivating influence in my life. She is also a good sport about the *fake* testimonial letter I credit her for during my seminar series[2].

THANKS MOM!

---

2   See Appendix VI, *Commendation,* 258-259.

My stepson David Kaplan has assisted me with computer related issues, as my technical abilities are still in the nurturing stages. David has been an incredible asset in this regard as has been my brother-in-law, Glenn Shapiro.

I am also pleased to acknowledge the great work of Linda Simon and Roseann Rachlin. I met these women at a spousal bereavement group in 1999 and they have been close friends since. Linda and Roseann were invaluable assets at the registration tables during my filmed seminar series. I can't thank them enough for their contributions.

I also want to recognize Barbara Karnes, the woman who is responsible for getting this started. Barbara is the Founder and COO of the LIREIA (our local real estate investment club). She invited me to speak at our filmed *Deal Panel* meeting in August of 2006. During the course of my real estate presentation, I mentioned that I purchased my first investment property with the profits I earned from selling stock options. After that the phone calls and emails began questioning how I go about selling these options.

It was this unexpected interest in my system that inspired me to write this book, and then to do my DVD and CD series. Barbara has been a source of encouragement, motivation, and guidance throughout this journey that has turned me into an author, a speaker and a teacher, and I must admit that I love every minute of it.

Finally, many thanks to my beloved New York Yankees who have endured (without complaint) countless innings of baseball without my irreplaceable support. Now that this book is finished I will once again be a dedicated fan ensuring the New York Yankees another trip to the World Series.

Play Ball!

Alan G. Ellman

Preview

Many of my fellow *blue collar stock investors* have little knowledge as to how stock options work... I certainly didn't when I started my exploration into this fascinating and rewarding arena. That's why I have decided to start this book with a *preview,* to give you a flavor of how the investment strategy works.

Since most investors are more familiar with real estate than the stock market, I will begin with a property example, and then spotlight a stock example.

Real Estate Example:

You have done your due-diligence, and located a great property in a great location. You paid $100,000 for the parcel. You feel there is a tremendous opportunity for the value to appreciate and would have no problem holding on to this property for the long haul. However, if someone should offer you $120,000 at any time during the next 6 months, you would take it for a quick $20,000 profit.

Now, another investor sees your property and feels its value should accelerate to $150,000 during the next 6 months. He is willing to pay your asking price of $120,000, but doesn't want to commit this amount of money to the deal at the present time. He prefers to tie-up your property with an Option to Purchase, and act only after the appreciation has occurred.

The investor offers you $10,000 for the right, but not the obligation, to purchase your property for $120,000 at any time over the next 6 months. This fee is yours to keep whether the property is purchased from you or not.*

There are two possible scenarios that could follow:

1. *The value of the property does NOT exceed $120,000 during the next 6 months.*

   In this case, the investor will not buy your property. You have made a 6-month, $10,000 profit on a $100,000 investment. This represents a 10% return, or 20% annualized. You still own the property, which you were happy to keep for the long haul anyway, and are free to work out a similar deal with another investor for the next 6 months.

2. *The value of the property DOES exceed $120,000 during the next 6 months:*

   The investor will buy your property for $120,000. Now you have made a total of $30,000; $10,000 on the sale of the option, and $20,000 on the sale of your home. This represents a 30% profit, or 60% annualized.

Stock Market Example:

You have done your homework and located a great performing stock. You are more than willing to own this stock

---

*   In most Real Estate deals this premium is applied to the purchase price, but not so in the case of stock options for the long term. However, if you can leverage this equity into a significant profit in the short term, you would be willing to sell your shares. Here is how this works:

Hypothetical

You purchase 100 shares of company XYZ @ $48 per share. Your investment is $4800.

Next, you sell a call option, offering someone the right, but not the obligation, to purchase those shares from you for $50 per share at any time during the next month. In return for assuming this obligation, you will be paid a premium. In this case, you will be paid $1.50 per share, or $150 per contract. This fee is yours to keep whether the stock shares are purchased or not.

There are two possible scenarios that could follow:

1. *The stock value does NOT supersede $50 per share, and the option is not exercised* (shares are not purchased).

   You have made a $150 profit on an investment of $4800. This represents a 3.1% one month return or 38% annualized.

2. *The share value goes beyond $50 per share, and your stock is sold at the $50 agreed upon price.*

   Since the stock was purchased at $48 per share and sold at $50 per share, you have generated an additional $200 profit for a total of $350. This represents a 7.3% one month return, or 87% annualized.

This is just a brief overview of how the investment strategy works. This book will walk you through all the steps necessary to master covered call writing. For the best results, use in conjunction with its companion DVD and CD series** .

Let's show those Wall Street Insiders what we're made of!

**   visit www.TheBlueCollarInvestor.com for more information.

part 1

The Basics

of Selling

Covered Call Options

Full-sized, versions of all charts, graphs, forms, photos, and other images contained in this book are available at

www.thebluecollarinvestor.com/vip

Chapter 1

Why Sell Options?

When I was in High School I worked hard BECAUSE I wanted to get into a good college. When I was in college I studied endless hours BECAUSE I wanted to get into an outstanding dental school. I *gave up* four years of my life in dental school BECAUSE I wanted to have a profession that would allow me to support my family and feel positive about being a productive member of society.

When you put time, effort and money into something you should know why you are doing it! What is the *BECAUSE*?

So, why should you consider selling stock options? What is the *BECAUSE?*

BECAUSE...

    1. **You can get a higher rate of return on your investment, while at the same time minimizing the corresponding risk.** This is accomplished with a system that guides you to select the GREATEST STOCKS in the stock universe which are *optionable*. Then you must calculate the returns you receive from the sale of the options so you can determine which options will give you the best returns. Finally,

the system must have several *exit strategies* that will allow you to minimize loses and maximize profits.

MAXIMIZING PROFITS AND MINIMIZING RISK is what my system is all about.

2. **You can create a great and profitable strategy for moderately bullish, moderately bearish, and neutral market conditions**. SEE FIGURE 1. This encompasses most market situations. However, if the market is accelerating exponentially, or dropping precipitously, then you don't want to be selling options. In the first scenario, you want to own the stocks and not cap the appreciation by selling the options on those stocks. In the latter, you want to own real estate and bonds, or simply keep cash in reserve, and avoid owning stocks.

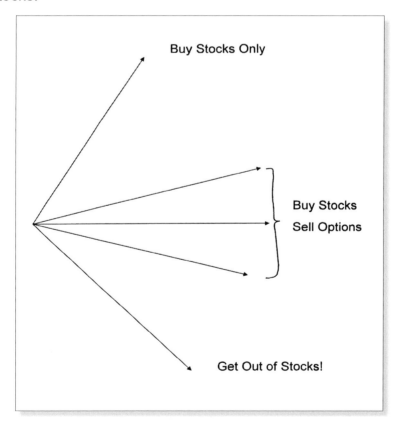

Figure 1

3. **You can earn money from the comfort of your home**. It's you. Your brains. Your computer. And, THE SYSTEM. Imagine two feet of snow outside. Everyone's life is at a standstill. But NOT YOURS! You simply go to your computer, and start generating cash. There is no traveling. No speaking to other people. And, no waiting for your profits. The option premiums are generated into your account in a matter of seconds!

4. **You can compound your profits in a matter of minutes!** You sit down in front of your computer and sell a series of options. You can then use these funds to purchase more stock, and then sell the option of that newly acquired equity. What other investment allows you to instantaneously compound your profits?

5. **You can control your profits, and results, through a series of EXIT STRATEGIES**. This is an integral part of my system. If a stock is dropping unexpectedly, you can take action. You will be able to minimize your loses, and even turn loses into gains. You will seize control.

6. **You can create DOWNSIDE PROTECTION for your investments**. Should you purchase a stock for $48 per share, and sell the option for $2 per share, you will not lose money until the stock price drops below $46 per share ($48- $2).

7. **You can develop an investing skill that you can pass on to your next generation** and utilize to assist the previous one.

8. **You can capture all corporate dividends** as opposed to an option buyer who does not realize any of these profits.

There you have it…. my *BECAUSE LIST*.

Does it sound too good to be true? On the surface it does. I was not a believer at first but have become one over the past eight years.

Is there risk? You are in the stock market, my friend, and by its very definition there is risk. But the risk is in the STOCK, not in selling the option.

This system works very hard to maximize the profits, and tries even harder to minimize risks.

Chapter 2

The Three Golden Rules

Not everybody should be selling options!

That's right. Despite the earnings potential and the limited risk, there are some of you out there who should avoid trading options. During my fifteen years of trading stocks and options I have experienced many emotions. Mistakes have been made, and then corrected. I have learned to control my emotions and not repeat my mistakes. That is the formula for success.

In this chapter I will set forth three golden rules that are essential for your success as an options seller. All three must apply to you....two are not good enough. If you know that one or more of these rules cannot, and will not, apply to you, look for another strategy.

If you find that all three rules don't apply to you, and who knows YOU better than YOU, close this book right now, and accept my thanks for your purchase. If, however, you continue on, you will succeed. Failure is not an option.

The three simple rules are:

1. **YOU MUST BE ABLE TO TOLERATE SOME RISK**

Historically, the stock market goes up 11% per year. If the market went up consistently the same every year, and we could precisely predict the future, options would cease to exist. There is volatility to the marketplace. Some people are betting that the market will go up, others that it will go down. You sell a stock at $48 dollars because you think it has reached its price potential, while another investor buys that same stock for $48 dollars because he thinks it will appreciate dramatically. This is the nature of any marketplace.

We need to understand the workings of the stock market and its inherent volatility so that when it fluctuates, we are able to make informed, unemotional decisions. To demonstrate, let's compare a one year stock price chart with one that runs 30 years. In the short run, (see figure 2)[3] the market has more volatility than in the long run (see figure 3)[4].

In the one year chart of the S&P 500 (a commonly used market benchmark of 500 large cap, US companies) we see numerous shifts in the market, both up and down. If we were to get physically and mentally ill every time there was a dip, and euphoric every time there was a rise, our health could become compromised. In addition, we may find ourselves overreacting to the situation and making a poor investment decision.

We must let this volatility work in our favor. Let's collect our significant option premiums, the value of which is partially related to this volatility. If the market movement turns against us, then we will react appropriately by initiating one of our well thought out exit strategies. Tolerating risk means that you will

3   Investools, www.investools.com.
4   Ibid.

not get sick on market downturns, you will stick to the system, and you will let your brains - not your heart do the talking.

Figure 2

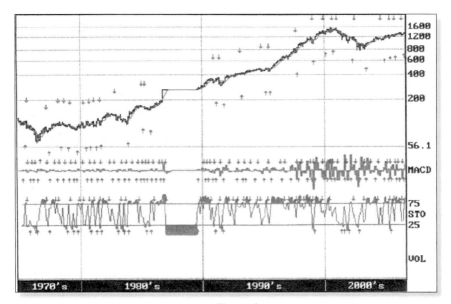

Figure 3

Hopefully you have passed the first requirement for options selling so we can move on to Golden Rule # 2.

2. YOU MUST ONLY SELL OPTIONS ON STOCK YOU WOULD OTHERWISE LIKE TO OWN

Don't make the same error I made early on in my options selling career. As structured as I am, I would, from time to time, be tempted to buy a stock and sell the corresponding option simply because I would get an incredibly high premium return.

This happened to me several years ago with Taser, a company that produces stun guns. It seemed that every week a new report would come out regarding the efficacy of using this product. The market would move the stock dramatically up over a short period of time. I could get 7% per month, or higher, selling Taser options. VERY TEMPTING. But these prices were *news driven*, not sound fundamentally-based increases.

I collected my great premiums and watched Taser go from the thirties to under $10/share. This was a great learning experience for me and gave birth to Golden Rule # 2. In essence, you must promise yourself that you will never buy a stock and sell the corresponding option solely based on the premium return.

In fact, it works in the opposite order. First you must identify stocks you would love to own, regardless of the option premiums. Then, from this pool of stocks we will decide which ones to select for the sale of options. Remember, 40% of my system is designed to increase your investment profits. The remaining 60% is to limit your risk and loses.

If you have qualified yourself as having passed the first two golden rules, we move on to the third and final one.

3. **YOU MUST HAVE A PLAN WITH MULTIPLE EXIT STRATEGIES**

See if this sounds familiar to you:

You hear that company XYZ had a *blowout* earnings report. Not only that, but it announced a stock split, and a dividend increase. You rush out to buy 1000 shares. Sure enough, two weeks later the stock is up $3 per share and you have made a neat $3000!

Now what? Well, maybe it'll go up even more!!

Nope. Instead it drops 50 cents in a week.

No big deal. You're still up $2500. It'll go back up.

Wrong again. Two weeks later, the big boys (mutual funds, hedge funds) are taking profits, and the stock plummets $3. Now you're losing money!

Got to get it back..

You wait a little longer… Then longer… Then its too late, and you're down $5000! You went from up $3000 to down $5000 because you had no exit strategy.

When you buy a stock or sell an option YOU MUST KNOW WHEN TO CLOSE THE DEAL.

In stock trading *lingo*, when you sell an option it is called **selling to open**. You've created an open contract, and need to determine how and when to close it. In options selling, this means setting up a system that will allow you to determine if, and when, to get out of a *position*. This means spending some time watching over your portfolio but not a lot (of time) if done correctly.

You must promise yourself that after buying stocks and selling options, you are willing to watch over these investments and institute an exit strategy when indicated.

If you still have your book open… Congratulations! You have met the requirements of the three golden rules, and have not just made a donation to the Alan and Linda Ellman Book Fund!

Chapter 3

Option Returns vs.
The Market and Mutual Funds

It's time to talk dollars and cents!

The returns I have been receiving from selling options will become more apparent as you read on in this book. Suffice it to say, the range is between 2-4% per month and 25-40% per year. This is more impressive than any other *low risk* investment I have ever come across.

Real estate investing is right up there, but requires travel and involvement of other team members such as lawyers, accountants, property managers, lenders, appraisers, just to name a few. Furthermore, it is difficult to liquidate these investments in comparison to stocks and options.

That being said, I am of the firm belief that all investors should be well diversified in all three asset classes: stocks, bonds and real estate (four if you include cash).

I have done quite well with my stocks/options and real estate while my bond portfolio creeps along at a snail's pace. The bonds are the extremely safe and conservative portion of my portfolio. They are guaranteed by the U.S. government. Just for the record, I purchase I-Bonds which are inflation protected. No tax is paid on the interest until you redeem these bonds, and they can be purchased online without paying any commissions:

Go to www.treasurydirect.gov for more information on this subject.

So how do these stock option returns stack up against *the market* and against mutual funds? Let's use historical numbers for our comparison. It doesn't make sense to use any one person's personal experience or opinion. People lie, numbers don't! Historically the stock market appreciates an average of 11% per year. This number is corroborated in FIGURE 4 [5]. on the next page   This information is from the Motley Fool web site which is a highly regarded site for stock information.

Is 11% per year satisfactory for you? It's not for me, so I sell options. The bond market historically returns 5-6% per year and there is virtually no risk in many aspects of bond investing (certainly not in I-Bonds). If I'm going to incur risk, I want a bigger prize at the end than 11%.

What about actively managed mutual funds? Here we have some of the smartest and most savvy stock minds in the world managing our money. Surely, the returns from our mutual funds will far surpass those of the market in general. WRONG!

Let's refer back to figure 4 of our *Motley Fool Mutual Fund Center* page. On the top I have underlined an amazing statistic: **80% of mutual funds UNDERPERFORM the market**. How can this be? These mutual fund managers are really smart. They are experienced. They are very well paid! Does this mean that the proverbial monkey throwing darts at a chart of stocks can outperform most mutual funds? I wouldn't go that far but I think it's important to recognize some of the obstacles that these managers are up against.

---

5   The Motley Fool, www.fool.com.

If you and I want to sell our 300 shares of Dell Computer, we can do so with the click of our mouse in a matter of seconds.

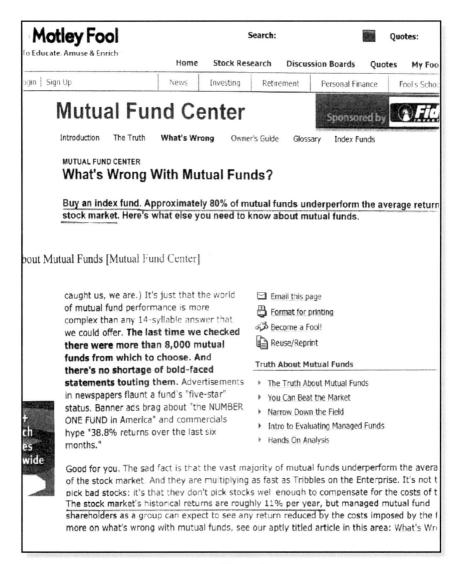

Figure 4

If a large mutual fund wants to sell its 250,000 shares of Dell, they will have to do so in small increments (small being a relative term). This is because if the fund manager put in a sell order for too many shares, the price they would receive would decrease because of the rules of supply and demand.

By the time they are finished selling all the shares, some of them may have been sold at a less favorable price than you and I sold ours for. Also the funds have administrative fees. Furthermore, these folks who manage your money are entitled to get paid. You pay them from your profits (hopefully profits... either way you pay them).

As these fund managers buy and sell stocks in hopes of making you lots of money, there are also transaction fees... the market makers have to get paid as well. You pay the transaction fees. When a stock is sold at a profit, there are tax consequences. You pay the taxes unless you are in a tax sheltered account. This is why many accountants recommend placing actively managed mutual funds in tax sheltered accounts, and passively managed (Index) funds in non-sheltered accounts.

What all this means is that there is an 80% chance you will under perform the market if you are in actively managed mutual funds. Will you be happy with less than 11% per year? I can answer that one for you: NO!

What about passively managed mutual funds? You can at least get your 11% per year by investing in an Index Fund that mirrors *the Market*. Index funds are required to contain those stocks that make up the sector it reflects; such as, the S&P 500, or the Wilshire 5000 (Total Stock Market). I own both. There is no stock selection involved since the fund is tied to a particular market sector and the number of shares is based on market capitalization (number of outstanding shares times the price per share). IBM, for example, will carry more weight in the fund than a small company that just went public. This type of *stock selection* can be handled by a computer. No guru needed. So the administrative and transaction fees are less, since there is virtually no trading, which also results in lowering capital gains tax.

All this adds up to more profits for us. For the record, I invest in the Vanguard family of funds since they have the lowest expense ratios. Vanguard S&P 500, or Total Stock Market Index Funds, will get you close to the 11% historical market returns.

The decision is yours. History tells us, if you *Dollar Cost Average* over the years, an 11% return is quite realistic (to be discussed in a later chapter).

What all this means is you can mirror the market with passively managed mutual funds. Will you be satisfied with these conservative returns? If 11% per year will make you happy, the answer may be to purchase a Vanguard Index fund.

If, however, you are looking for greater returns and you are willing to put in some time and effort, read on and allow me to share with you my system for selling stock options.

Chapter 4

Definitions

(Terminology you must know before getting started)

When you sit down at a blackjack table in a casino (not one of my investment strategies!) there are terms you need to know and understand or you will get crushed. Split, double down, hard seventeen, soft nineteen, and insurance are all essential terms to know when participating in this game.

In a similar fashion, when you sell stock options there are a few terms that are critical to your success that you must know and understand. They should become part of your everyday vocabulary. Fortunately, the list isn't that long and can be broken down into three categories:

1. Option Defined

A- **OPTION** - the right, but not the obligation to buy or sell 100 shares of stock at a fixed price (called the **STRIKE PRICE**) by a specified date (called the **EXPIRATION DATE**). It is the right to execute a stock transaction. When you sell a call option, (which is what my system is all about) you are selling someone (who you will never meet, speak with, or have anything to do with) the right, *but not the obligation* to purchase 100 shares of stock at a certain price, by a certain date.

B- **CALL OPTION** - the right but not the obligation of the owner (buyer) to BUY 100 shares of stock at a fixed price, by a specified date. That option can be exercised any time from the date of purchase until the date of expiration. As the seller of a call option you are undertaking an obligation to sell 100 shares of your stock to the option buyer by a certain date, at a certain price. For taking on that obligation, you will be paid a *premium*.

C- **PUT OPTION** - The right to SELL 100 shares of stock at a fixed price by a specified date. We will not be dealing with put options.

2. **Option Strike Price as it relates to the Stock Price**

A- **AT-THE-MONEY** - a market condition in which the value of the underlying stock is identical to the strike price of the option (see *1A above*). An example is when you sell the $50 call option (see 1B above) on a stock that is currently trading at $50.

B- **IN-THE-MONEY** - a market condition in which the current value of the stock is higher than the strike price of the option (see *1A above*). An example is when you sell the $50 call option (see 1B above) on a stock currently trading at $52.

C- **OUT-OF-THE-MONEY** - a market condition in which the current value of the stock is lower than the strike price of the option (see *1A above*). An example is when you sell the $50 call option (see 2B above) while the stock is trading at $48.

3. **Option Value as it relates to Strike Price**

> A- **INTRINSIC VALUE** - the dollar amount that the option premium is In-The-Money (see *2B above*). (At-The -Money and Out- Of- The- Money options have no intrinsic value) (see 2 B &2C above).

> B- **TIME VALUE-** the option premium *above any intrinsic value.*

Here is an example to clarify these last two definitions (see figure 5 on next page)[6]:

- You purchase a stock for $56 per share.

- You then sell the $50 call option for a premium of $8 per share (or $800 per contract of 100 shares).

- This option is $6 In-The-Money ($56 minus $50).

- We now know that of the $8 premium, $6 is from intrinsic value.

- Since we received an $8 premium, the remaining value of $2 is time value ($8 minus $6). The longer the time until expiration, the greater the time value of the premium.

To Summarize:

- Intrinsic Value = Stock Price – Strike Price

- Time Value = Total Premium – Intrinsic Value

---

6   Options Industry Counsel, *Covered Calls,* (circa 2004).

(8)

Intrinsic Value And Time Value

Stock Price = $56.00
Price of 50 strike Call = $8.00

Stock Price
= $56.00
 ] Time
Value = $2.00

Total Option Premium
(or Price) = $8.00

Strike Price
= $50.00
 ] Intrinsic
Value = $6.00

Intrinsic Value (call) = Stock Price – Strike Price
Time Value = Total Premium – Intrinsic Value

For a 60 Call at $2.10

What is the intrinsic value? _____

What is the time value? _____

(9)

In / At / Out For Calls

- In-the-Money Calls:
  Stock price is above the strike price

- At-the-Money Calls:
  Stock price and strike price are equal

- Out-of-the-Money Calls:
  Stock price is below the strike price

Figure 5

Referring to the chart, in the second example (figure 5), the Intrinsic Value is zero because the $60 call option is Out-Of-The-Money, (stock is selling for $56) and only In-The-Money option strike prices have Intrinsic Value. Therefore the total premium of $2.10 is represented by Time Value.

Once you've mastered these definitions, you're ready to head off to the black jack tables of options selling!

Chapter 5

Components Of An Option Contract
AND NEW OPTION PRODUCTS

This chapter is being updated for the fifth printing of Cashing in on Covered Calls. Since this book was first published in January of 2008 the options symbology has changed. The option ticker symbols in this book will reflect the original symbology although an explanation of the new option ticker symbols (as of February, 2010) will be explained in this chapter.

First let's look at the original ticker symbols as you will view them throughout this book in figure 6 below:

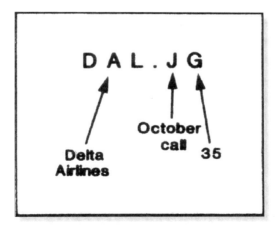

Figure 6 [7]

7.   Thomsett, Michael C. *Getting Started in Options.* New York: John Wiley & Sons, 1993: 46-47.

- The first few letters to the left of the dot, dash or space represented the underlying security and oftentimes were different from the stock ticker symbol

- The first letter to the right of the dot described the expiration month and identified the option as a call or put option

- The last letter represented the strike price

As you can see, the previous system was confusing and far from user-friendly so it was enhanced in February of 2010. Figure 7 highlights what the current option symbology looks like:

Figure 7

- AAPL is the ticker symbol of the stock

- 05/22/2010 is the expiration date, the third Friday of April

- "20.00" is the strike price

- "C" represents a call option

As you can see, the updated ticker symbols are much more intuitive and self-explanatory.

Non-standard contracts

These are options that don't have the standard terms of an options contract, namely 100 shares as the underlying asset. They are normally created as a result of a specific event such as a merger, acquisition, spin-off, extraordinary dividend or stock split. As a result of the changing circumstances, the contract is adjusted to be equitable to both the option buyer and seller by equating the new underlying asset(s) of equal value as the owner of 100 shares. The Depository Trust Company (DTC) determines how the shares will trade pre-event while the Options Clearing Corp. (OCC) decides how these changes will be reflected in the options. Each situation is unique and therefore non-standard. This makes them difficult to understand and therefore risky to most investors. As an example, when Bank Of America Corporation (NYSE: BAC) took over Merrill Lynch, the owner of 100 shares of Merrill received 85 shares of BAC stock plus $13.71 in cash. NS contracts of BAC now would deliver 85 shares of BAC + the cash as opposed to the standard contracts which represented 100 shares. The obvious rule is: avoid all non-standard options. Let me add another: if an option value seems too good to be true, it is.

Weekly expiration options contracts

At the time this book was being updated a relatively new options product was becoming popular called Weekly Options Series or Weeklys. These weekly expiration options are listed on a Thursday or Friday and expire the following Friday. The exception is that weeklys are not traded the week of expiration Friday and therefore do not list new weeklys on the second Thursday of the month. The next new weekly series is then listed on the Thursday prior to expiration Friday. An investor needs to carefully examine the option symbols which will display the precise expiration date of an option and that will identify the option as a weekly. It is yet to be determined if these new products will have a place in our world of covered call writing. For more information on these products go to the following link:

http://www.cboe.com/micro/weeklys/introduction.aspx

Quarterly expiration options contracts

There are a few heavily traded ETFs that, in addition to the standard monthly expiration contracts also have quarterly expiring contracts. These unusual contracts will expire at the end of the month in March, June, September and December. Many of the strike prices in these months will show different premiums for the same strike prices. For example, QQQ may have two $45 strikes, one expiring on the third Friday and the other at the end of the quarterly trading month. The latter will show a slightly higher premium due to the added time value. Other ETFs that have quarterly contracts include SPY, DIA and IWM and others are expected to be added in the future. For more information on these products go to the following link:

http://www.cboe.com/micro/quarterly/introduction.aspx

Chapter 6

What Is Covered Call Writing?

The definition of covered call writing is the purchasing of stocks and selling the corresponding call option on a share for share basis. What this means in layman terms is we are obligated to sell our shares to the option buyer at a certain price by a certain date.

You must own 100 shares of a particular stock for each option contract you sell.

For example, assume you purchase 300 shares of Company XYZ @ $17 per share. You then sell the next month's $20 call option for $1 or $100 per contract. Since 300 shares allow you to sell 3 contracts, you will have $300 (minus commissions) added to the cash in your brokerage account virtually instantaneously.

Since you paid $17 per share and received $1 per share for selling the option, your breakeven is $16 (see figure 8 on next page)[8]. Any further drop in the price of the stock now represents a loss to the investor. As you can see, selling the option *does* give you downside protection. In this case that protection is $1. There is also a cap on the profits an investor earns when selling a covered call option. By selling the $20

---

8   Options Industry Council, *Covered Calls,* (circa 2004).

call, you have undertaken the OBLIGATION to sell your shares @ $20. No matter how much higher than $20 the share price achieves, you must sell at $20. Therefore, as figure 8 depicts below, your profits are capped at $21. This represents the total of the $20 sale price plus the $1 option premium. In this scenario, you have made a $4 per share profit since the stock was purchased for $17 per share.

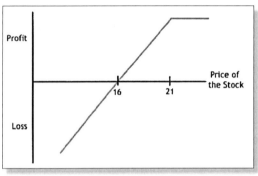

Figure 8

Let's now discuss the RISKS involved in covered call writing. Perhaps you have uncovered them yourselves by reading and understanding the concepts discussed thus far in this book:

1. STOCK PRICE BREAKS BELOW THE BREAKEVEN CREATING A LOSS
   However, we have lost less money (the value of the option premium) than we would have, had we not sold the option. If the stock value is dropping unexpectedly, we will initiate one of our exit strategies to minimize losses…or perhaps even create some gains.

2. PROFIT POTENTIAL IS LIMITED BY THE STRIKE PRICE OF THE OPTION
   As shown in figure 8, we are obligated to sell our stock at $20 per share. This gives us a $3 profit on the sale of the stock plus a $1 profit on sale of the option; but no more, no matter how high the stock price goes. *Don't Get Greedy*! If you can earn 2-4% per month with this strategy, focus on those returns. Don't worry about the occasional stock that takes off like a rocket ship. Just pat yourself on the back for selecting a

top stock and be satisfied with the great return you achieved on this deal.

3. POSSIBILITY OF ASSIGNMENT
   Once the current price of the stock surpasses the strike price of the option, there is always the possibility of assignment. We are dealing with **American-style options**. These are contracts that can be exercised at any time between the date of purchase and the expiration date. Most exchange-traded options are American style. All stock options are American style. This is opposed to **European-style options** which can only be exercised on the expiration date.

That being said, it is quite rare to be called out before expiration. Assignment has only happened to me three times in the last eight years and that was when the stock price had catapulted way above the strike price. In most cases, when we want to avoid assignment we can do so by initiating one of our system's exit strategies. Be aware, however, that in the rare cases of early assignment, we will *lose* our shares, as they will be sold at the strike price. This is not a major problem for us as we can use the cash to purchase another equity or buy back the same one.

That's about it as far as risks go. In a market that is neutral, slightly bullish or slightly bearish, these risks are far outweighed by the monetary advantages of selling options. If the market conditions are right for selling covered calls and you have the appropriate exit strategies in place, these risks should not discourage you from enjoying the tremendous benefits of selling call options.

part 2

THE YTEM:

How To Make Lot$ of

$,$$$,$$$,$$$

Full-sized versions of all charts, graphs, forms, photos, and other images contained in this book are available at

www.thebluecollarinvestor.com/vip

Chapter 7

Creating A Watch List
of the Greatest Optionable Stocks

Now that we have an understanding of how selling call options work, it's time to get started. Remembering back to our *Three Golden Rules (see Ch 2 above)*, we are first concerned with selecting only stocks that we would want to own independent of selling options....the greatest performing (optionable) stocks in the stock universe. You can sell options on about one out of every three stocks.

Since there are between 7,000 and 8,000 stocks to choose from, we need to shrink our list to a manageable number. This has to be done in a way that will be both accurate and time efficient. Most software programs, brokerage houses, and stock websites have stock screening mechanisms where you can use the default screens or even customize your own screen to arrive at a smaller list. Many are excellent vehicles capable of locating outstanding stocks for your watch list.

After having tried many different stock screening options, I have decided to use the *Investor's Business Daily 100 (IBD 100)* (See figure 9[9] on next page), because of the tremendous success it has achieved since its inception. This list runs in each week's Monday edition which can be purchased on Saturday. This allows you to utilize your weekend time to

---

9   *Investor's Business Daily*, "IBD 100," September 11, 2006.

go through the list and be prepared to take action when the market opens on Monday.

Figure 9

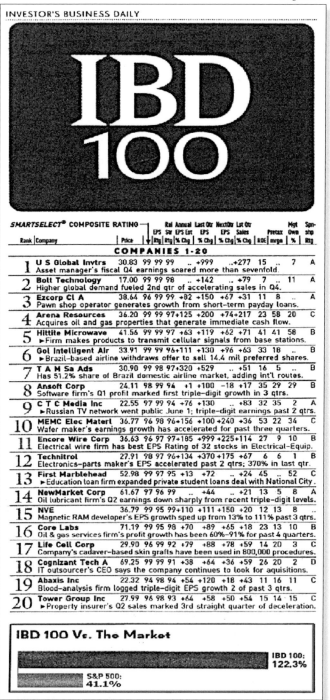

INVESTOR'S BUSINESS DAILY

IBD 100

SMARTSELECT® COMPOSITE RATING

Rank	Company	Price	EPS Rtg	SW Rtg	EPS Est % Chg	EPS % Chg	EPS Sales % Chg	Pretax ROE	Mgt Own %	Spn-shp Rtg
1	**U S Global Invtrs** Asset manager's fiscal Q4 earnings soared more than sevenfold.	30.83	99 99 99	.. +999	..+277	15 ..	7	A
2	**Bolt Technology** Higher global demand fueled 2nd qtr of accelerating sales in Q4.	17.00	99 99 98	.. +142	.. +79	7 ..	11	A
3	**Ezcorp Cl A** Pawn shop operator generates growth from short-term payday loans.	38.64	96 99 99	+82 +150	+67 +31	11 8	..	A
4	**Arena Resources** Acquires oil and gas properties that generate immediate cash flow.	36.20	99 99 99	97+125 +200	+74+217	23 58	20	C
5	**Hittite Microwave** ►Firm makes products to transmit cellular signals from base stations.	41.56	99 99 97	+63 +119	+62 +71	41 41	58	B
6	**Gol Intelligent Air** ►Brazil-based airline withdraws offer to sell 14.4 mil preferred shares.	33.91	99 99	96+111 +130	+96 +63	33 18	..	B
7	**T A M Sa Ads** Has 51.2% share of Brazil domestic airline market, adding int'l routes.	30.90	99 98	97+320 +529	.. +51	16 5	..	B
8	**Ansoft Corp** Software firm's Q1 profit marked first triple-digit growth in 3 qtrs.	24.11	98 99 94	+1 +100	-18 +17	35 29	29	B
9	**C T C Media Inc** ►Russian TV network went public June 1; triple-digit earnings past 2 qtrs.	22.55	97 99 94	+76 +130	.. +83	32 35	2	A
10	**MEMC Elec Materl** Wafer maker's earnings growth has accelerated for past three quarters.	36.77	96 98	96+156 +100	+240 +36	53 22	34	C
11	**Encore Wire Corp** Electrical wire firm has best EPS Rating of 32 stocks in Electrical-Equip.	36.63	96 97	97+185 +999	+225+114	27 9	10	B
12	**Technitrol** Electronics-parts maker's EPS accelerated past 2 qtrs; 370% in last qtr.	27.91	98 97	96+134 +370	+175 +67	6 6	1	B
13	**First Marblehead** ►Education loan firm expanded private student loans deal with National City.	52.98	99 97	95 +13 +72	.. +24	45 ..	52	C
14	**NewMarket Corp** Oil lubricant firm's Q2 earnings down sharply from recent triple-digit levels.	61.67	97 96 99	.. +44	.. +21	13 5	8	A
15	**NVE** Magnetic RAM developer's EPS growth sped up from 13% to 111% past 3 qtrs.	36.79	99 95	99+110 +111	+150 +20	12 13	8	..
16	**Core Labs** Oil & gas services firm's profit growth has been 60%-91% for past 4 quarters.	71.19	99 95 98	+70 +89	+65 +18	23 13	10	B
17	**Life Cell Corp** Company's cadaver-based skin grafts have been used in 800,000 procedures.	29.90	96 99 92	+79 +88	+78 +59	14 20	3	C
18	**Cognizant Tech A** IT outsourcer's CEO says the company continues to look for aquisitions.	69.25	99 99 91	+38 +64	+36 +59	26 20	2	D
19	**Abaxis Inc** Blood-analysis firm logged triple-digit EPS growth 2 of past 3 qtrs.	22.32	94 98 94	+54 +120	+18 +43	11 16	11	C
20	**Tower Group Inc** ►Property insurer's Q2 sales marked 3rd straight quarter of deceleration.	27.99	96 98 93	+64 +58	+50 +54	15 14	15	C

IBD 100 Vs. The Market

IBD 100: 122.3%

S&P 500: 41.1%

The *IBD 100* is a computer-generated ranking of the leading companies trading in the United States. These rankings are based on a combination of each company's profit growth and relative price strength in the last twelve months. Factored into these parameters is IBD's Composite Rating, which includes key measures such as return on equity, sales growth, and profit margins.

Figure 10

To the right of the list are the corresponding charts (see figure 10^{10} on previous page). These allow for a convenient look at the price patterns for those interested in technical analysis. Some of these charts have highlighted borders to indicate that they may be approaching a *buy point,* my phrase for the point at which technical indicators are suggesting a purchase.

WHY THE IBD 100? If you look at the bottom of figure 9, there is a bar chart comparing the returns of the S&P 500 (a key market benchmark) to those of the IBD 100. Since its inception, the IBD 100 has nearly tripled the returns of the S&P 500! To me, this is a great starting place! With this decision to use the IBD 100 as our starting pool of stocks, the number of stocks to choose from has diminished from 8000 to 100!

Figure 11

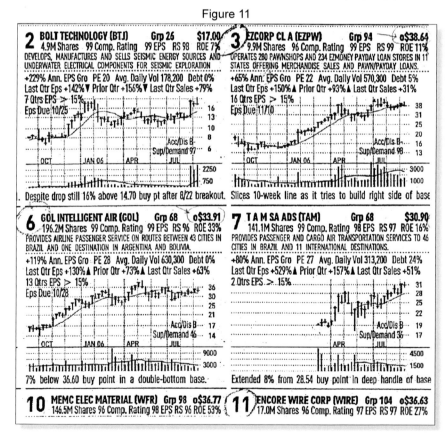

Now let's cut *that* in half.

Referring to figure 11[11] on the previous page, note the two stocks at the top of the page: *Bolt Technology* and *Ezcorp*. These are the number 2 and number 3 ranked stocks in the IBD 100 this particular week. I have circled the number three stock but not the number two stock. The reason has to do with the letter *"o"* that appears before the $38.64 price of Ezcorp. Note that an "o" does not appear before the $17 price of Bolt. The significance of that "o" is that this stock is optionable....we can sell options on Ezcorp but cannot on Bolt. Since this system is all about selling options, Bolt is out of consideration.

I have found that going through each week's list and circling the stocks that are optionable, will bring the list down to about 50 stocks. Quite manageable, wouldn't you say?

I have an annual subscription to IBD's Monday special wherein the Monday edition is delivered to my home every Saturday. The *special* also gives you complete access to the IBD website which I find extremely useful.

Later in this book, I will give you examples of other ways of locating the greatest stocks in the stock universe although the IBD 100 remains my primary locator.

So now we have about 50 stocks.
Are they on our watch list?
NOT SO FAST.

We have to put them through more screens.

We want the best of the best.

---

11   Ibid.

As I said, IBD has a terrific web site. I highly recommend you sign up for their service. At the time of the writing of this book, the cost of the *Monday Special* (52 newspapers and access to website) is $189 per year. It is money well spent.

Let's go to the IBD web site with our fifty stocks.
www.investors.com

Figure 12

Assuming you are a registered user, you must first log in to continue the screening process. At that point look for the phrase *Enter Symbol / Keyword*, and type in the ticker symbol for the stock you are researching. Then highlight the circle that reads *Get Quote*. Next, click on the *Magnifier Icon* to get to the *Quote Page*. Now, scroll down to just below the price chart of the equity being screened where you will see a list on the left hand side of the page that reads *SmartSelect Ratings* (see figure 12[12] on preceding page).

Smart Select Ratings: Definitions

1. Composite Rating: The IBD *SmartSelect* Composite Rating combines all 5 *SmartSelect* Ratings into one easy-to-use rating. More weight is placed on EPS and RS Rating, and the stock's percent off its 52-week high is also included in the formula. Results are then compared to all other companies, and each company is assigned a rating from 1-99 with 99 being the best. A 90 rating means that the stock has outperformed 90% of all other stocks in terms of its combined *SmartSelect* Ratings.

2. EPS Rating: Exclusive rating found in Investor's Business Daily's *SmartSelect*® Corporate Ratings. Stocks are rated on a 1 to 99 scale (with 99 being best) comparing a company's earnings per share growth on both a current and annual basis with all other publicly traded companies in the William O'Neil & Co database. Stocks with EPS Ratings of 80 or above have outperformed 80% of all publicly traded companies in earnings. The EPS Rating combines each company's most recent two quarters of earnings-per-share growth with its three- to five-year annual growth rate.

3. RS Rating: This IBD *SmartSelect*® Corporate Rating is a measure of a stock's price performance over the last twelve

months, compared to all stocks in its database. The scale ranges from a low of 1 to a high of 99.

4. Group RS Rating: A percentile-based version of Industry Group Rank, a proprietary number obtained by calculating the least-squares curve fit of summed prices on certain stocks within that industry. Another calculation is then done using all companies in the group. Separate weightings are used for different time periods. *Industry groups are ranked in value from 99 (highest) to 1 (lowest).*

5. SMR Rating: A proprietary rating pioneered by Investor's Business Daily to help investors identify companies with superior Sales Growth, Profit Margins, and Return on Equity ratios. Parameters are combined into one simple A through E ranking system.

6. Acc/Dis Rating: Exclusive rating in Investor's Business Daily. One of the IBD *SmartSelect*® Corporate Ratings, it tracks the relative degree of institutional buying (accumulation) and selling (distribution) in a particular stock over the last 13 weeks. Updated daily, stocks are rated on an A+ to E scale.

The six circles under the Checklist heading must all be green to pass the Green Alert Screen. **If all six are green, the stock is still under consideration.** Any yellow, reds or NRs (no ratings) eliminates that stock from consideration.

Please note that this quote page shows the stocks sector, not its industry. To get the industry group, hit the link that says "Get IBD Stock Checkup", and the industry group will appear on this checkup page under the heading that says "Performance within Industry".

Thus far, we have started with a pool of the 100 top rated stocks by Investors Business Daily's computer generated ranking system. We have then selected only those stocks on which we can sell options. This will usually reduce our pool of stocks down into the fifties. That number is then further reduced by going to the IBD website and checking the technical, fundamental, and attractiveness ratings of the remaining stocks. We then also check the group technical rating of that stock's industry.

As the number of stocks decrease, we are also decreasing the risk of a losing investment and increasing the possibility of higher profits.

We will do one more fundamental screen before we move on to technical analysis and calculating option returns:

7. MAR and OBV

Update to The Weekly Stock Screen and Watch List

The Blue Collar Investor Team has upgraded the Weekly Stock Screen And Watch List by adding 2 new institutional screens and removing the original risk/reward screen.

After months of research, we have made the decision to incorporate the Mean Analyst Rating or MAR and On Balance Volume or OBV to enhance the quality of our screening process and our Premium Member Stock Reports. We feel the MAR and OBV institutional components will strengthen the screening process for several reasons:

MAR

- The metric is non-proprietary and is the mean rating from multiple analysts…that is, not from a single perspective or model but from several independent viewpoints.

- It is available at no cost from multiple well-known financial websites such as Yahoo Finance, Finviz, and others.
  www.finviz.com
  www.finance.yahoo.com

- We will be able to update the MAR every week vs. every two weeks as we currently do with risk/reward, so the data will be more current.

- The MAR comes from the views of institutional analysts who follow the specific stock in question. As we always mention, the market is driven by the "big boys", that is, the institutions. So, we are taking advantage of this body of knowledge.

- The MAR is a more intuitive metric than the risk/reward metric, and as such, we believe that it will assist us in our personal stock selection. There won't be any interpretation necessary.

OBV

For years, the BCI methodology has stressed the significance of the institutional investors (the "big boys") in impacting stock performance. This explains why we require a minimum average stock trading volume and option open interest before entering our option-selling trades. By incorporating OBV, we are factoring in the trend of institutional interest or lack thereof in each security and adding another dimension to our stock screening process.

The absolute value of the OBV indicator is less important than the direction of the OBV. The relative direction (▲, ▶, ▼) of the indicator is what we are looking for…are the institutions accumulating shares and supporting the stock (▲ & ▶) or are they exiting from the stock (▼).

The OBV indicator is non-proprietary and is available in virtually every charting platform, including the following free platforms:

www.stockcharts.com

www.freestockcharts.com

www.barchart.com

www.tradingview.com

OBV is typically available in the charting packages provided by your broker as well.

As always, we're there to answer any questions that you might have with our improved screen.

***Detailed explanations of these 2 metrics can be found in the appendix section of this book.

Running List Symbol	Company Name	Wkly Rank or Other Source	Price ($ US)	Industry Segment	Segment Rank	Pass Fund'l & Analyst Tech Screens	Mean Analyst Rating (MAR)	OBV	Chart: PRICE BAR above 20 EMA above 100 EMA (Y/N/C)	Tech Ind. OK: MACD & STOCH. (Y/N/T)	Chart Comments	Beta	Div. Yield	% (Tentative Unless Bold)	Next ER Date (Tentative Unless Bold) SEE NOTE IN KEY	Wkly Avail	NTM OI >100 Contr	# Wks Run On List	Comments (The last or next Ex-Div date is shown)
									PASSED PREVIOUS WEEKS & PASSED CURRENT WEEK										
BA	BOEING CO	BC20-20	386.47	Aerospace	A	Y	2.00	▲	Y	?	MACD ▲ / STO ▼	1.35	1.90		10/24/18	Y	Y	1	08/29/18
ABMD	Abiomed Inc	3	415.71	Medical	A/A	Y	1.70	▼	@	?	Price @ 20 EMA / MACD ▲ / STO ▼	1.32			10/25/18		Y	4	
SVB	SVB Financial	15	319.71	Banks	C/C	Y	2.00	▼	@	Y	Price @ 20 EMA	1.42			10/25/18		Y	2	
MED	Medifast Inc	PRW	212.33	Consumer	A/A	Y	2.00	▲	@	?	Price @ 20 EMA / MACD ▼ / STO ▲	0.90	0.90		11/01/18		Y	2	09/20/18
OEC	Orion Engineered	26	31.38	Chemical	B/B	Y	2.30	▶	@	?	Price @ 20 EMA / MACD ▲ / STO ▼	1.13	2.60		11/01/18		Y	5	12/17/18
RP	Realpage Inc	33	61.03	Software	A/A	Y	1.90	▶	@	?		1.01			11/01/18		Y	15	
SHAK	Shake Shack Inc Cl A	Other	61.18	Retail	B/B	Y	3.00	▶	@	Y	Price @ 20 EMA	0.96			11/01/18	Y	Y	2	
ZTS	Zoetis Inc	BC20-16	91.85	Medical	A/A	Y	2.10	▲	Y	?	MACD ▲ / STO ▼	1.37	0.60		11/01/18	Y	Y	6	07/19/18
CPE	Callon Petroleum Co	Other	12.06	Energy	A	Y	2.00	▶	Y	?	MACD ▲ / STO ▼	1.17			11/05/18		Y	1	
FANG	Diamondback Energy	50	136.35	Energy	A	Y	1.70	▲	Y	?	MACD ▲ / STO ▼	1.14	0.40		11/07/18		Y	1	08/17/18
NVDA	Nvidia Corp	22	269.06	Chips	B/C	Y	2.00	▶	@	?	Price @ 20 EMA / MACD ▲ / STO ▼	1.90	0.20		11/15/18	Y	Y	2	08/29/18

Figure 12a - Location of MAR and OBV in Stock reports
Beginning November 2018

Those stocks still remaining have withstood the test of the *screens.* Survival of the fittest, if you will. These securities will be added to my watch list unless they are trading below their 20 day moving average (to be discussed in the next chapter) or if the option returns are unacceptable (discussed in Chapter 9).

Next it's time to unleash the secrets hidden in the charts.

It's time for TECHNICAL ANALYSIS!

Chapter 8
Technical Analysis

Thus far we have been analyzing stocks *predominantly* via FUNDAMENTAL ANALYSIS (a small percentage of the aforementioned screening criteria, however, were technical in nature). This is the process of determining whether or not a particular company is a good, sound investment. By doing this type of screening we are reducing the amount of emotion that comes with an investment decision. Either it's in or it's out. Fundamentals tell us the positives and the negatives of the financial health of a company, thereby reducing risk. Risk reduction is what this system is all about. Great fundamentals provide the foundation for our all-important watch list.

The next step in the process of systematic evaluation is TECHNICAL ANALYSIS. This will help to determine buy and sell points. Technical analysis is helpful in forecasting potential price direction to better time your entry and exit points.

There are many sophisticated investors who rely exclusively on fundamental analysis and others who depend only on technical analysis. My philosophy is why not utilize both? Once you have developed a list of fundamentally outstanding stocks that are optionable, why not further screen your investment decisions by doing technical analysis?

The only drawback that I can think of is the additional time involved. But what if we can develop a system whereby these screens, both fundamental and technical, can be evaluated within a manageable time frame. In that case, there can be no argument against doing both.

There are a myriad of technical indicators. When I first started my education of stock investing, I tried to evaluate way too many of these indicators. It was overkill... gave me a headache!

I have streamlined my system to include four of these indicators: *Moving Average, MACD (pronounced MAC-D), Stochastics and Volume.* Keep in mind that one indicator by itself is not enough to base your buy/sell decisions on. That's why I use four indicators. Call it a confirmation or **consensus of indicators**. In essence we are putting our investment decisions through a series of fundamental and technical screens. As we do so, our risk is diminished (but not eliminated) and our reward potential is enhanced.

Before we discuss these four categories of technical analysis, I need to say a word about the **PRICE BAR** (see figure 13).

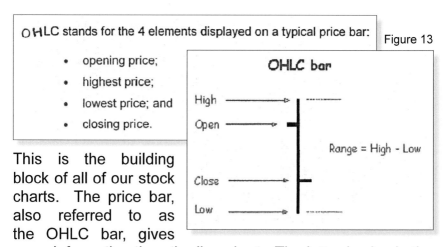

OHLC stands for the 4 elements displayed on a typical price bar:

Figure 13

- opening price;
- highest price;
- lowest price; and
- closing price.

OHLC bar

High
Open

Range = High - Low

Close

Low

This is the building block of all of our stock charts. The price bar, also referred to as the OHLC bar, gives more information than the line chart. The latter is simply the closing prices connected by a line. The former, gives five bits of information: The high, low, opening, and closing prices of the day (or week for longer term charts). Since we know the high and the low prices, we therefore can compute the trading range (high minus low) which is the fifth piece of information. If, for example, we see that a stock has closed near the high of its trading range, we can take that as a positive sign of upward momentum going into the next trading day. I would suggest that if you are using a charting service that shows a line chart as its default, and you can customize to a bar chart, you should do so. *Yahoo Finance* and *stockcharts.com* are two such sites.

MOVING AVERAGES

Moving averages are one of the most popular and easy to use tools available to the technical analyst. They smooth the graphic plotting of a data series and make it easier to spot *trends*, something that is especially helpful in volatile markets. It visually shows you the average price of a stock over a set period of time and is used to determine the path of least resistance. Stocks tend to follow their trend. As heard on Wall Street each and every day, *The trend is your friend*. This knowledge can help you become more accurate in your forecasting, and more successful as an investor.

Moving averages are trending indicators, meaning they will be more accurate and provide more useful information when a stock is in some sort of trend. They oftentimes act as **support** for stocks that are temporarily pulling back in the midst of an uptrend. For stocks experiencing a downtrend they act as **resistance**. Stocks tend to bounce off their moving averages in the direction of the trend. Once broken, they help to identify when a trend is probably ending.

When a stock is trading sideways, (known as a trading range) this signal is not as useful as when a stock is trending, and should only be used in conjunction with other indicators. False signals can occur in this scenario.

So let's make this information come alive. If we look at Figure 14[13], the 20 day moving average (red line) is in an uptrend from March to May; it's in a downtrend in July and August; and it's trading sideways in December.

Figure 14

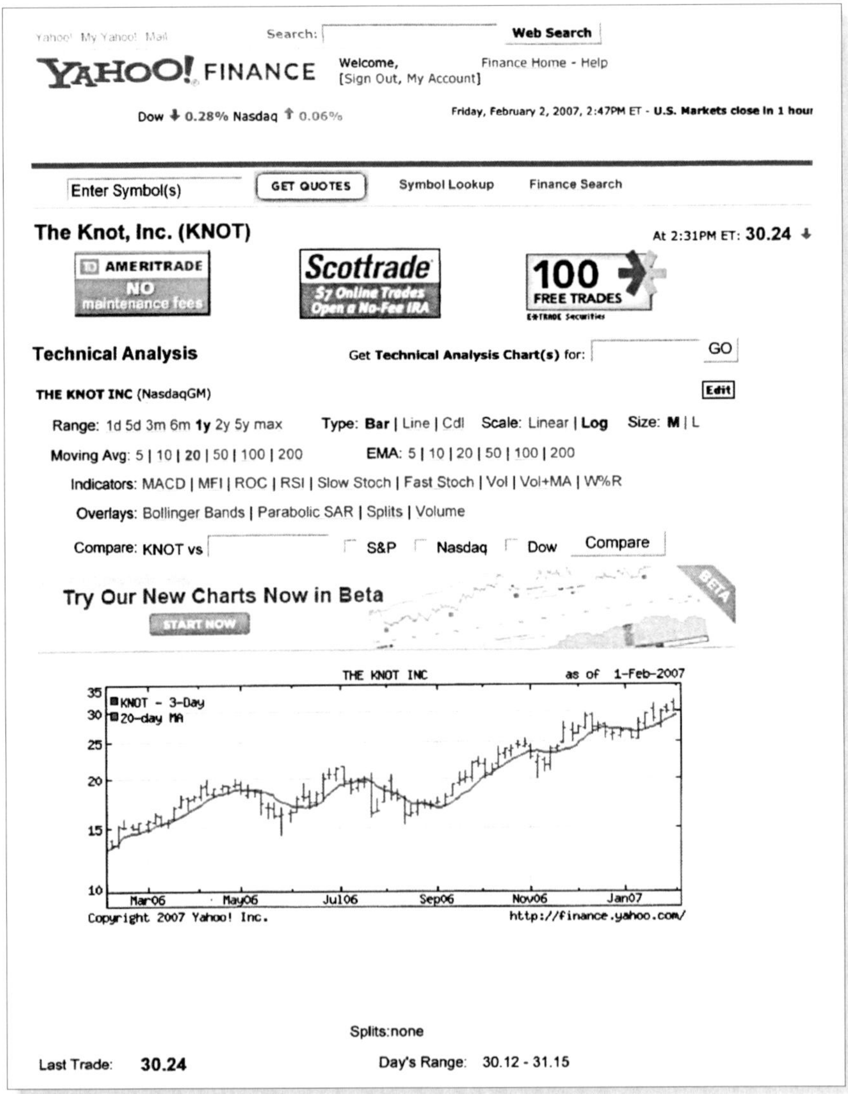

---

13   Yahoo Finance, http://finance.yahoo.com (February 2007).

Now let's take a look at Figure 15[14] and see how the trends shape up on this chart. Note the four, circled horizontal trading ranges (sideways movement). Uptrends are clear in April through October of 1997, and April through October of 1998. We also have a downtrend from August through October of 1998.

Figure 15

The two most popular types of moving averages are the **SIMPLE MOVING AVERAGE (SMA**) and the **EXPONENTIAL MOVING AVERAGE (EMA).** The SMA is formed by computing the average price (mean) of a security over a specified number of days. Most are created using the closing prices.

Since we will be selling predominantly one month options, we are most interested in the *20 day moving average*. Twenty trading days are approximately four weeks (sometimes holidays change that), which is close to our one month time frame. To calculate a twenty day, simple moving average, we add the closing prices for the last 20 days and divide the total by twenty.

---

14   StockCharts.com, www.stockcharts.com (February 2000).

Figure 14 shows a 20 day simple moving average of the KNOT. Notice that the trend of the SMA is up (favorable) and the price bar is showing closing prices above the SMA (also positive).

All moving averages are **LAGGING INDICATORS** and will always be *behind* the price. If the price of an equity was trending down, the moving average would most likely be above the price. If the price was rising, the SMA would probably be below the stock price. Since moving averages are lagging indicators, they fall into the category of **trend following indicators.**

The *EMA or Exponential Moving Average* is used to reduce the lag in the simple moving averages. They do so by applying more weight to the more recent prices relative to the older prices. For our time frame of 20 days, there will be very little difference between the 20 day SMA and the 20 day EMA (See figure 16, pg. 59)[15]. The critical point to remember is that the EMA puts more weight on the more recent prices. Therefore, it will react quicker to a recent price change than the SMA.

Which moving average should we use? This depends on the type of trading you are doing. The SMA has a lag but the EMA may be prone to quicker breaks. Some traders prefer the EMA for shorter time periods (that's us!) to capture changes quicker. Some investors prefer the SMA for longer time frames to identify long-term trend changes. For our purposes of selling one month options, the difference is almost indistinguishable with a slight edge going to the EMA.

Moving averages will not predict a change in trend since they are lagging indicators. They are best suited for trend identification and trend following purposes, *not for prediction*. In general, an uptrending, moving average will be below the current price, and a downtrending moving average will be above the current price. I call this being *behind the price*.

---

15   Yahoo Finance, http://finance.yahoo.com (February 2007).

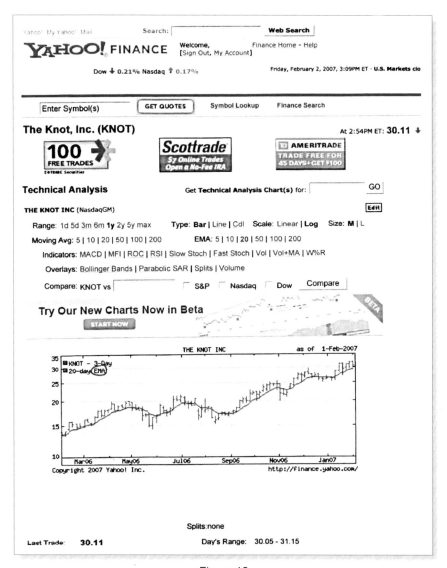

Figure 16

Since moving averages are ineffective when a security moves in a **trading range** (sideways movement) we must visually assess a price chart to determine the worth of utilizing a moving average. In other words, when you see a chart in a trading range you are less likely to use this indicator in your buy/sell decisions.

In its simplest form, a stock's price can be doing one of three things: trending up, trending down, or trading in a range.

An uptrend is established when a security forms a series of *higher highs and higher lows*. A downtrend is established when a security forms a series of *lower lows and lower highs*. A trading range is established if a security cannot establish an uptrend or a downtrend. If in a trading range, a security can start an uptrend by breaking through the upper end of the trading range, and a downtrend begins when the lower boundary is broken. As we touched on above, Figure 15 is a great example of a stock exhibiting uptrends, downtrends and trading ranges. Notice that the moving average worked well in times of trends, but faired poorly in times of trading ranges (circled areas). Note also that the moving average lags behind the trend: It's always under the price in an uptrend and above the price during a downtrend.

Which moving average *settings* should we use? Once we have determined that a stock is showing the characteristics of trading in a trend, we will need to select the number of moving average periods and the type of moving average. Short term traders, like us, may look for evidence of 2-3 week trends with a 20-day moving average. Longer term investors may look for 3-4 month trends with a 40-week moving average. Exponential moving averages are usually best for short term situations like selling one month call options. Simple moving averages work well for longer-term situations that do not require a lot of sensitivity. Therefore, **a *20 day exponential moving average* will be our default of choice** although a 20 day SMA will work almost as well.

Three basic uses of moving averages:

1. Trend identification/Confirmation
If the moving average is rising, the trend is considered up. If the moving average is declining, the trend is considered down. We do not look at every subtle change, but rather look at the general directional movement and changes. In figure 17[16] on the following page, a chart of Walt Disney Company, we see a series of turning points that are easily discernible visually, indicated by the circles.

---

16   StockCharts.com, www.stockcharts.com (March 2000).

Figure 17

The second technique for trend identification is *price location relative to the moving average*. If the price is above the moving average, the trend is considered up. If the price is below the moving average, the trend is considered down. In figure 18[17], we see a chart of Cisco which shows an upward trend through about June of 2000, then a reversal (see arrow) and a subsequent down trend.

Figure 18

The third technique for trend identification is based on the relationship between the shorter and longer term moving averages. If the shorter is above the longer average the trend is considered up. If the longer term MA is above the shorter term MA, the trend is considered down. In figure 19[18] below, a chart for Value Click, we see a definite trend reversal in August, 2006

Figure 19

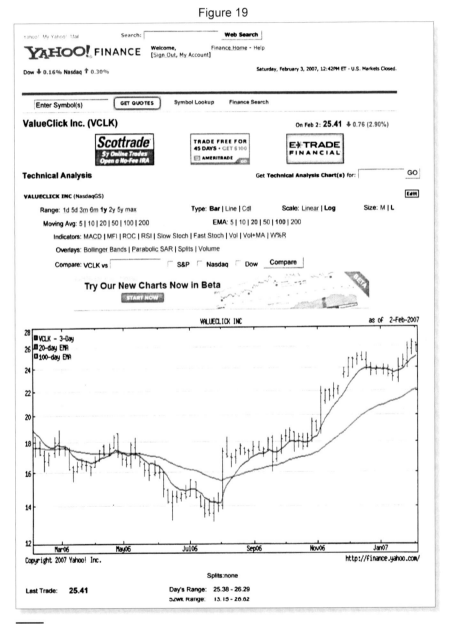

18   Yahoo Finance, http://finance.yahoo.com (February 2007).

from a downtrend to an uptrend. At this point, the 20 day EMA crossed above the 100 day EMA, and since then the stock has gone up in value 50% in three months.

2. Support and Resistance Levels

Another use of moving averages is the identification of support and resistance levels. This is usually accomplished with one moving average and is based on historical precedent. As with trend identification, this works best in trending markets. In figure 20[19], after breaking out of a trading range (known as breaking through resistance), Sun Microsystems declined in price and bounced back up off of its moving average in late July and early August. This *trading range* is demonstrated in the months leading up to June, which show an attempt by the stock to break through a resistance to upward movement until it finally reached $18 a share in mid-June. So, what Figure 20 shows is that an uptrending moving average acts as support for the price movement of a stock.

Figure 20

Thus, the moving average acted as confirmation of **resistance-turned-support.** After this first test, the 50-day moving average went on to four more successful support tests over the next several months. A break of support of the moving average would serve as a warning of a possible trend reversal or of an ensuing trading range.

3. Trading Systems

Moving averages can be effective tools to identify and confirm trend, identify support and resistance levels and help determine which stocks you are going to purchase in a specific month to then sell options on. I like to see these stocks trading above their 20-day EMA while in an uptrend. If they drop below, I would prefer to move on to another equity (especially if confirmed by other indicators), although I may keep that stock on my watch list for a bit longer. The advantages of moving averages must be weighed against their disadvantages....we must know their limitations. These MAs are lagging indicators that are always behind. But, since *the trend is your friend*, you want to trade in the direction of the trend. Once in a trading range, the moving averages are less effective. However, once in a trend, they will keep you in, but also give you late signals. For our purposes, we want that trend to last at least one month. We will not use moving averages alone, but in conjunction with other tools that compliment them. Using moving averages along with other indicators and analysis will greatly enhance your profit potential and minimize your risks.

MOVING AVERAGE CONVERGENCE / DIVERGENCE

(MACD)

Moving average convergence / divergence (MACD) is one of the simplest and most reliable indicators available. It tends to be the *shortest term indicator* on the chart. You can use MACD as an *early warning indicator*, which alerts you as to which stocks to watch closely in the days to come for potential buy or sell signals. View the MACD as a warning to the coming of a valid buy or sell alert, and start watching the stock more closely for that sign. MACD uses moving averages, which are lagging indicators, to include some trend-following characteristics. These lagging indicators are turned into a **momentum oscillator** (I love that phrase) by subtracting the longer term moving average from the shorter term moving average. The resulting plot forms a line that oscillates above and below zero, without any upper or lower limits.

If the shorter term moving average is above the longer term moving average the *MACD will be above zero*, thereby giving a bullish buy signal. This would be one reason to consider purchasing this stock. This may seem complicated at times, and maybe it is, but all you really need to remember is…

Above zero good. Below zero bad.

The most popular formula for MACD is the difference between a security's 26-day and 12-day exponential moving averages. Usually, a 9-day EMA of MACD is plotted along side to act as a *trigger line*. A bullish crossover occurs when MACD moves above its 9-day EMA (trigger signal) and a bearish crossover occurs when MACD moves below its 9-day EMA.

MACD measures the difference between two moving averages. A positive MACD indicates that the 12-day EMA is trading above the 26-day EMA. A negative MACD indicates that the 12-day EMA is trading below the 26-day EMA. If MACD is positive and rising, then the gap between the 12-day and the 26-day is widening. This indicates that the rate of change of the faster moving average is higher than the rate of change of the slower moving average. Positive momentum is increasing and this would be considered *bullish*. If MACD is negative and declining further, then the negative gap between the faster moving average and the slower moving average is widening. Downward momentum is accelerating and this would be considered *bearish*. MACD centerline crossovers (moving above or below zero) occur when the faster moving average crosses the slower moving average. In the Merrill Lynch chart in figure 21[20] below, MACD is represented by the thicker black line and its 9-day EMA as the thin blue line. The gray, bar chart histogram (discussed later in this chapter) in the background is positive when the MACD is above its 9-day EMA and negative when MACD is below its 9-day EMA.

Remember…
Above zero good.   Below zero bad.

Figure 21

---

20   StockCharts.com, www.stockcharts.com (November 1999).

Bullish Signals to look for:

1- Bullish Moving Average Crossover- occurs when the MACD moves above its 9-day EMA or trigger line. In figure 21, this occurs when the thick black line crosses above the thin blue line (check the middle of August, for example).

2- Bullish Centerline Crossover- occurs when the MACD moves above the zero line into positive territory (check the beginning of November, for example). This is a clear signal that the momentum has changed from negative to positive.

Bearish Signals to look for:

1- Bearish Moving Average Crossover- occurs when the MACD moves below its 9-day EMA (check the beginning of September, for example). Crossovers should always be confirmed with other technical indicators.

2- Bearish Centerline Crossover- occurs when MACD moves below zero and into negative territory. This is a clear indication that momentum has changed from positive to negative or from bullish to bearish. This signal can be used as an independent indicator or to confirm a bearish moving average crossover. As with bullish MACD signals, bearish signals can be combined to create more robust indicators.

MACD BENEFITS:

One of the primary benefits of MACD is that it incorporates aspects of both momentum and trend in one indicator. As a trend-following indicator, it will not be wrong for very long. The use of moving averages ensures that the indicator will eventually follow the movements of the underlying security. By using exponential moving averages, as opposed to simple moving averages, some of the lag has been taken out. As a momentum indicator, MACD has the ability to foreshadow moves in the underlying security.

MACD DRAWBACKS:

Even though MACD represents the difference between two moving averages, there can still be some lag time in the indicator itself. This is less likely to occur with the daily charts that we use rather than the longer term weekly charts. This problem can be solved by using the *MACD histogram* (bar chart in background of figure 21). MACD is not particularly good for identifying overbought or oversold levels. That is because there are no upper or lower limits to bind its movement.

Overall, MACD remains *one of the most reliable indicators around*. However, since it is not infallible, it should be used in conjunction with other technical analysis tools.

MACD HISTOGRAM

(Refer to Figure 22[21])
The MACD-Histogram represents the difference between the MACD and the 9-day EMA of MACD, which is also referred to as the trigger or signal line. The plot of this difference is presented as a histogram, making the centerline crossovers and divergences easy to visualize. A centerline crossover for the MACD-Histogram is the same as a moving average crossover for MACD (MACD moves above or below the signal line).

If the value of MACD is larger than the value of its 9-day EMA, then the value of the histogram is positive.

---

21   StockCharts.com, www.stockcharts.com (October 1997).

Conversely, if the value of MACD is less than its 9-day EMA, then the value of the MACD-Histogram will be negative.

Figure 22

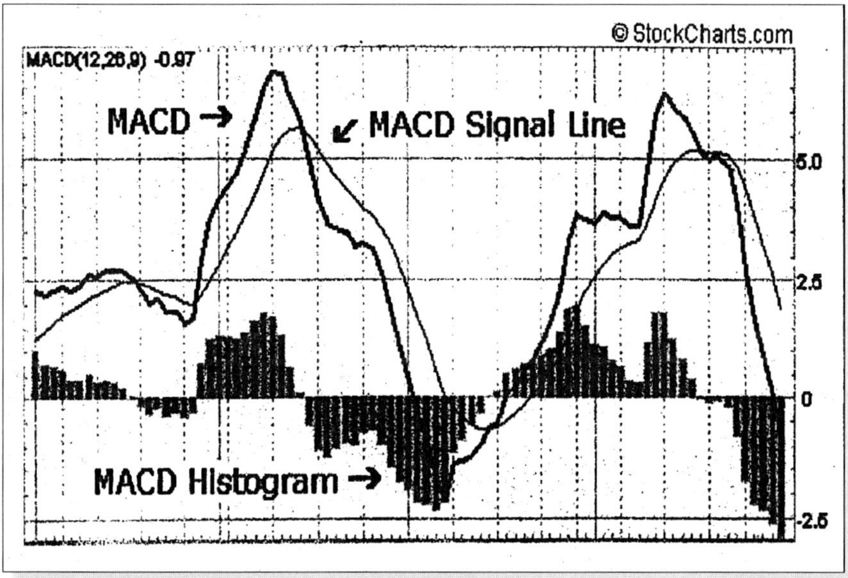

Sharp increases in the MACD-Histogram indicate that the MACD is rising faster than its 9-day EMA, and *bullish momentum* is strengthening. Sharp declines in the MACD-Histogram indicate that the MACD is falling faster than its 9-day EMA, and *bearish momentum* is increasing. **MACD-Histogram movements are relatively independent of the actual MACD.** This is important to you because the histogram will give you an early buy/sell signal, and therefore increase your chances of a successful investment.

Remember…
Above zero good.   Below zero bad.

USAGE:

MACD-Histogram is used as a tool to anticipate a moving average crossover in MACD. A positive divergence in the MACD-Histogram indicates that MACD is strengthening and could be on the verge of a bullish move. A negative divergence in the MACD-Histogram indicates that the MACD is weakening, and can act to foreshadow a bearish move. **Usually a change in the MACD-Histogram will precede any changes in MACD.**

SIGNALS:

A bullish signal develops when there is a bullish centerline crossover (see circle on Figure 22a[22]). A bearish signal is generated when there is a bearish centerline crossover (see lower right arrow on Figure 22a). A centerline crossover for MACD-Histogram represents a moving average crossover for MACD.

Figure 22a

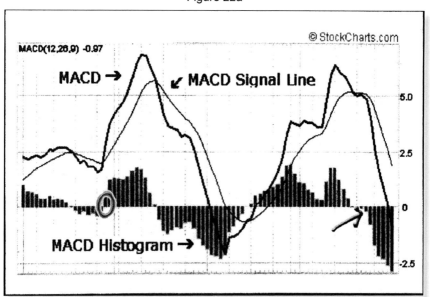

The main benefit of the MACD-Histogram is its ability to anticipate MACD signals.

In summary, regarding MACD, we would like to see the MACD above its trigger and zero line and/or the MACD-Histogram showing a bullish centerline crossover. With the proper charts, these can be visually spotted in a matter of seconds.

STOCHASTICS

Stochastics is a widely used indicator that measures who is winning the daily battle between the bears (who are selling and driving the prices down) and the bulls (who are buying and driving the prices up). It generally uses crossover lines of 20% and 80% to determine when the stock is overbought or oversold. The stochastic oscillator is a momentum indicator that shows the location of the current price relative to the high/low range over a set number of periods (oftentimes, 14 days). Closing levels that are consistently near the top of the range indicate **accumulation (buying pressure**) and those near the bottom of the range indicate **distribution (selling pressure).**

For example, let's say you are interested in going to the World Series. Ticket prices are driven up by the tremendous demand. On the other hand, if your team has a losing record, ticket prices during the regular season will be lower. Ask your local scalper.

In figure 23[23] on the next page, the stochastics oscillator is represented in the bottom portion of the chart. The blue %K tells us what percentile (0 through 100) of the high/low range the closing price was that particular day.

The red %D is a 3-day *SMA* of the %K which acts as a signal or trigger line.

---

23   Yahoo Finance, http://finance.yahoo.com (February 2007).

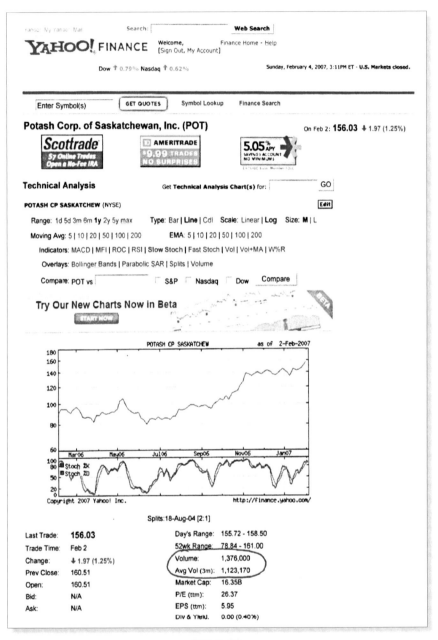

Figure 23

If given a choice of using a fast or slow stochastic oscillator, I find the slow version produces a smoother, easier to read chart.

The stock is **overbought** when the indicator crosses above the 80% line. Just because a stock is overbought does not mean that there are no more buyers. It just means that the buyers are in control of the stock, dictating the action of how the stock is trading. Stocks in strong uptrends can stay overbought for months. DO NOT SELL simply because a stock becomes overbought. Once the oscillator reaches the overbought levels, wait for a negative divergence to develop and then a cross below 80. This usually requires a *double dip* below 80 and the second dip results in the **sell signal** (see figure 24 below, line markings at January)[24]

Figure 24

StockCharts.com, www.stockcharts.com (March 2000).

Another example of a negative divergence occurs in figure 25[25]. Check the stochastics oscillator in late November to early December, and then again in mid to late February.

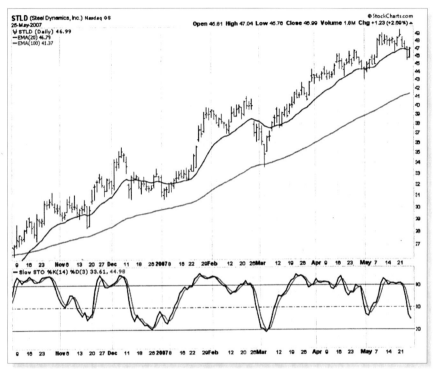

Figure 25

The stock is **oversold** when the indicator drops below the 20% line. Just because the stock is oversold does not mean there are no more sellers. All it means is that the sellers are in control of the stock, dictating the action of how the stock is trading. Stocks in strong downtrends can stay oversold for months. DO NOT BUY simply because a stock becomes oversold. For a **buy signal**, wait for a positive divergence to develop after the oscillator drops below 20. After the positive divergence forms, the second break above 20 confirms the divergence and a buy signal is given (see figure 24, line markings at October/November).

As always, it is prudent to use the stochastic oscillator in conjunction with your other technical tools.

25   StockCharts.com, www.stockcharts.com (May 2007).

VOLUME

The bars at the bottom of the chart of Potash in figure 26[26] below, are a visual representation of how many shares trade each day. Taller bars represent spikes in the volume, where activity significantly increased for that day. This *surge* in activity is

Figure 26

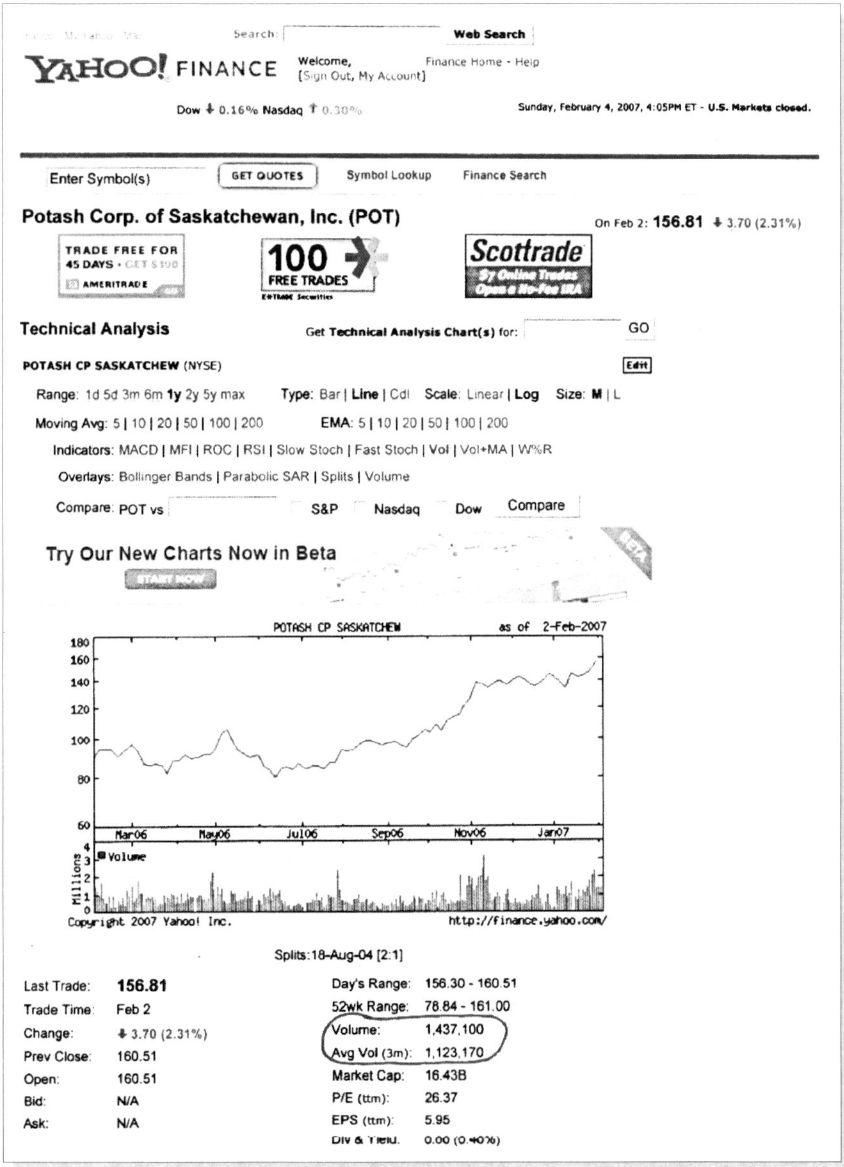

26 Yahoo Finance, http://finance.yahoo.com (February 2007).

usually a sign that institutional money (mutual funds, hedge funds, banks, etc.) is heavily entering or exiting that stock. Volume spikes usually mark the beginning of significant trends. Such a spike can be seen in figure 26 at the beginning of November which preceded the stock trading from the high 130's to the high 150's in about 2 ½ months.

A **volume surge** is considered to be 1.5 times the average volume. The Yahoo Finance example I provided in figure 26, gives you the volume for that day and the average 3 month volume (see circled area). Other charting services may give other time frames for computing average volume. However, just viewing the chart and looking for large spikes makes it easy to spot a significant buy or sell signal.

When positive technical indicators are corroborated with high volume spikes, you are greatly enhancing your chances for successful utilization of these indicators. The volume surge shows the institutions' clear commitment to the stock; as they are buying a lot of it....and institutions rarely buy an entire position in one day. They will normally buy incrementally over a period of time attempting to avoid pushing the price of the stock up too high, too quickly. We, on the other hand, have the ability to take our position early on, before the dramatic price increase, since we are buying shares in small quantities.

Volume surges are particularly important when a stock has been moving sideways. To break through resistance and start an up trend, stocks usually need a volume surge. Just like if you were sitting near a hill with a bicycle, you would have to put a little more energy to get the bicycle to move up the hill. Similarly, stocks need that extra push (volume surge) to get going up the *up trend hill*.

In general, you'll want to avoid buying stocks with very low average volume. These stocks are prone to manipulation and have a higher failure rate on buy signals. **Look for average volume to be above 250,000 shares before entering a stock on buy signals.** Referring again to Figure 26, you can see the share volume is 1,437,100 – clearly above the needed 250,000.

If you do enter a stock on buy signals with lower average volume, be more conservative in your position size to compensate for the potential risks that come along with these types of equities. It is more difficult to get in and out of low-volume stocks at a fair price.

In summary, we use volume to corroborate buy/sell signals. A positive or negative signal on high volume is much more significant than one on low volume. Volume surges (1.5 x normal volume) are especially important.

If you are still awake, you now have my sincere congratulations. You're now well on your way to becoming CEO of your own money. Having the ability to analyze these charts will allow you to determine when to buy and when to sell a stock. You can now fire your stock broker, your financial planner, but never EVER throw away this book!

Technical Analysis Summary

Concluding our Technical Analysis chapter, I will outline below the key settings and indicators we have discussed. In addition, I will highlight some of the important concepts you should be aware of.

Chart Settings:

1. Moving Average: 20-day EMA; 100-day EMA.

2. Prefer a *bar* to a *line* chart – OHLC Bar.

3. MACD: most charts will default to a 26 and 12-day EMA with a 9-day EMA of the MACD as a trigger line. A histogram will give an earlier signal.

4. Stochastics: default to the *slow* stochastics oscillator if available.

5. Daily volume bars at the bottom of the chart, with availability of average daily volume for comparison purposes.

Bullish Technical Signals:

1. Up trending 20-day EMA.

2. Price location above 20-day EMA, with the 20-day EMA serving as support.

3. 20-day EMA above 100-day EMA.

4. A stock in a trading range breaks through resistance on a volume surge.

5. MACD moves above its 9-day EMA (trigger signal).

6. MACD moves above the zero line into positive territory.

7. Positive divergence of MACD-Histogram centerline crossover into positive territory.

8. Positive divergence of stochastic oscillator above the 20% line, confirmed by a second break above the 20% line.

9. All buy signals are more significant if confirmed by other buy signals.

10. All buy signals are more significant if confirmed by a volume surge.

11. A volume surge is particularly important when a stock is coming out of a trading range.

Bearish Technical Signals:

1. 20-day EMA starts trending down.

2. Stock price drops below the 20-day EMA.

3. 100-day EMA moves above the 20-day EMA.

4. A stock in a trading range breaks through support (lower end of trading range) on a volume surge.

5. MACD moves below its 9-day EMA (trigger signal).

6. MACD moves below the zero line into negative territory.

7. Negative divergence of MACD Histogram - centerline crossover into negative territory.

8. Negative divergence of the stochastic oscillator below the 80% line, confirmed by a second dip below the 80%.

9. All sell signals are more significant if confirmed by other sell signals.

10. All sell signals are more significant if confirmed by a volume surge.

11. A volume surge is especially significant if a stock is breaking below a trading range.

On first glance, all these technical indicators appear to be extremely time intense. However, with practice, one can visualize these indicators in a matter of seconds and come to an instantaneous decision as to whether a stock is *in or out.*

It is important to have access to charts where all indicators are on one page. (See figure 27[29] on next page). Yahoo Finance is a free site for such charts. *Investools* is an excellent software program (although a little pricey) that gives a tremendous amount of information on a single screen.

---

29   Yahoo Finance, http://finance.yahoo.com (March 2007).

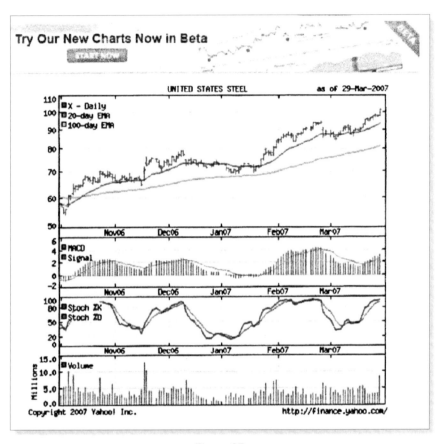

Figure 27

Another great site for charts is:
www.StockCharts.com

Figure 28, on the next page, walks you through the process of setting up the chart on this site. Figure 29[30], on the page following thereafter, shows what such a chart will look like after setting the parameters, typing in a ticker symbol, and hitting *update*. I, personally, prefer this site over the yahoo site since it incorporates the *MACD histogram* which you cannot view on the yahoo site.

---

30   StockCharts.com, www.stockcharts.com (May 2007).

Oftentimes, our technical indicators will give *mixed signals*. I give greatest weight to an uptrending chart wherein the price bars are trading at or above the 20-d EMA and the 20-d EMA is serving as support.

When the moving average is in a trading range we need to turn to the other indicators for buy/sell decisions.

When we get mixed signals, I am more likely to sell **in-the-money** options (for the downside protection) whereas when all indicators are positive, I am more inclined to sell **out-of-the-money** strikes.

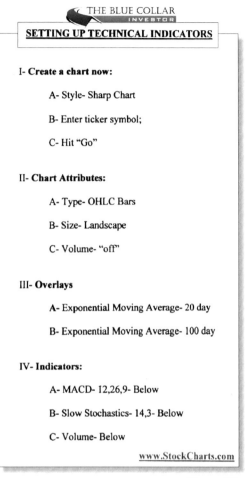

THE BLUE COLLAR INVESTOR

SETTING UP TECHNICAL INDICATORS

I- **Create a chart now:**

 A- Style- Sharp Chart

 B- Enter ticker symbol;

 C- Hit "Go"

II- **Chart Attributes:**

 A- Type- OHLC Bars

 B- Size- Landscape

 C- Volume- "off"

III- **Overlays**

 A- Exponential Moving Average- 20 day

 B- Exponential Moving Average- 100 day

IV- **Indicators:**

 A- MACD- 12,26,9- Below

 B- Slow Stochastics- 14,3- Below

 C- Volume- Below

www.StockCharts.com

Figure 28

Thus far we have screened our stocks fundamentally by locating them from the IBD 100 list, screening the stock and its sector through the IBD website, and then doing a risk/reward screen through the Money Central Scouter Rating screen.

Then we have taken the *surviving stocks* and evaluated them via technical analysis. Please bear in mind that technical analysis is as much an *art* as it is a *science*. It paints a picture, and after viewing hundreds of charts you will become very much the *art connoisseur*. Mastering technical analysis will

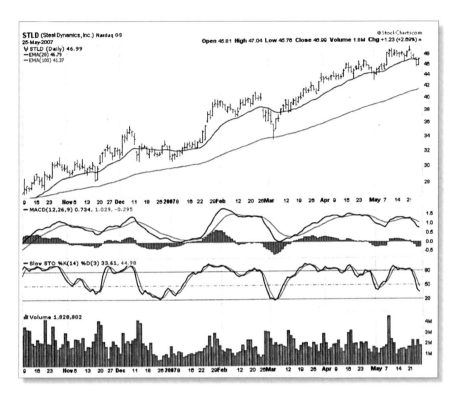

Figure 29

empower you to make your buy/sell decisions confidently and meaningfully.

This process does NOT take a lot of time once you have mastered the system!

Each step of this system decreases the risk of your investment and enhances the potential profit you will earn.

Now that we have our watch list of some of the greatest performing stocks in the stock universe, it's time to start generating cash into our accounts. One of the critical determining factors that will help us decide which stocks to own (and sell options on) in any particular month is the calculation of our premium returns, and for that we will need to access the Option Chain.

Chapter 9

Calculating Option Returns

Let us take a deep breath and review in our minds what we are doing: First some of the greatest performing optionable stocks in the stock universe are purchased. These are stocks we would like to own separate and apart from the option, income-producing aspect. We are then selling call options on these stocks....we are giving some unknown option buyer the right, but not the obligation, to purchase our shares (in 100 share increments) at a certain price (which we determine), by a certain date (which we determine), at a certain premium (which the market determines). We are receiving this premium for undertaking the aforementioned obligation.

Notice that I have developed this watch list without ever looking at the potential returns that would be realized from selling the options. This is because minimizing risk is more important to me than maximizing rewards. We will be rewarded handsomely if we follow the rules of the system.

The Option Chain:

We start our calculations by accessing the *Option Chain*. This is a list that quotes options prices for a given security. For each underlying security, the option chain lists the various strike prices, expiration dates and whether it is a call or put option.

These option chains can be found at various free web sites like Yahoo Finance (www.finance.yahoo.com), and CNBC (www. cnbc.com), or through the online broker you are using for your accounts. See figure 30[29] below for a typical option chain.

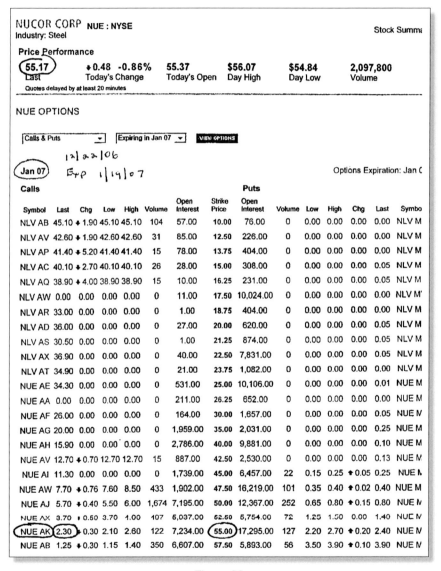

Figure 30

The underlying security is Nucor Corp. Here is the *critical information you are looking for:*

1. Current stock price is $55.17.

2. The next month option expires on January 19, 2007. It is currently December 22, 2006.

3. The strike price closest to the stock price is 55.00 (circled).

4. The premium we receive for selling this option is $2.30 per share, or $230 per contract.

5. The option ticker symbol is NUE AK.

This is all the information we need to do our calculations. I will simplify the numbers by leaving out commissions which are negligible since we are using an online discount broker (I currently pay $5.95 per trade through USAA Brokerage[30]).

The Calculations:

1. Our *COST BASIS* for 100 shares (one contract) of NUE is $5517 ($55.17 x 100).

2. Our profit is $230 for the month.

3. Our one month return on investment is 230 / 5517 = 4.2%.

4. The annualized return is 4.2 x 12 = 50%.

5. Since this strike price is *In-The-Money* (below the current market value of the stock), there will be a $17

    loss if called out (paid 55.17, sold for 55.00 creating a loss of .17 x 100 = $17).

6.   Our profit would then be reduced to 213 for the month. This represents a one month return of 3.9%, or 46% annualized....Not bad! This return is referred to in my system as **ROO**, or **return on option.**

With an In-The-Money strike price, as in this case, there is no *upside potential*. No matter how high the price of the stock goes, our profit is limited to the 3.9% one month return. There is .17 of *downside protection*. This means that if the stock drops from 55.17 down to 55.00 we still earn our 3.9%. Once it drops below 55, we start losing money on the value of the stock (on paper). We don't actually start losing money on the investment as a whole until the stock price drops below 52.87 (55 minus 2.13).

Bookkeeping For In-The-Money Strike Prices:

When I sell an In-The-Money option such as above, here is how I do my *bookkeeping*:

1.   My original cost basis is 5517 for 100 shares.

2.   My premium for the option sale is $230, $17 of which is *in-the-money* or *intrinsic value*.

3.   I break my 230 premium down into $213 and $17 (the intrinsic value).

4.   I take the $17 to *buy down the price of my stock* from 55.17 to 55.00

5.   Now my calculations look as follows: I have purchased 100 shares @ 55 and sold the 55 call for 2.13, yielding a 3.9% one month return.

6. If called out of the stock, my return of 3.9% remains accurate.

7. If the stock drops below 55 and I am not called out, the 55 cost basis is accurate because the extra $17 was never factored into my monthly profit. I used it to *buy down* the price of the stock. This is just a matter of accounting to simplify calculations down the road. Buying down the price of a stock only applies to In-The-Money strike prices.

Only In- The-Money Strike Prices offer downside protection of your premium profit.

I am not suggesting you use this accounting method for tax purposes, but solely for assisting you in making the best informed decisions possible regarding your option trades.

Bookkeeping For Out-Of-The-Money Strike Prices:

Let's look at an example of an *Out-Of- The Money Strike Price*. Figure 31[31] on the next page shows the option chain for NYSE Group Inc (ticker symbol, NYX). We will first evaluate the nearest *Out-Of-The-Money Strike Price*:

1. Our Cost Basis is 9701 for one contract (97.01 x 100).

2. Our initial profit is 285 (2.85 x 100) for the sale of the 100 call option (circled).

3. This represents a one month return of 2.9% (285 / 9701) which annualizes to 35%.

---

31   CNBC.com, www.cnbc.com (December, 2006).

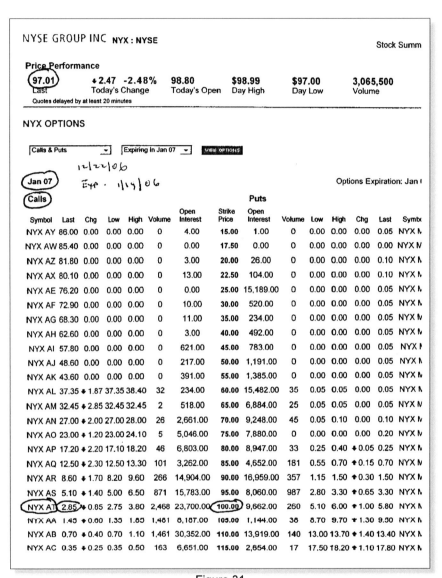

Figure 31

4. If the stock price goes above 100 and we are called out, we make an additional 299 on the sale of the stock (sell for 100, purchased for 97.01 or 299 for 100 shares). This *upside potential* is calculated as follows:

$$299 / 9701 = 3.1\%$$

5. Total profit in this scenario is 299, plus 285; or 584 for the month.

6. Our one month return would be 584 / 9701, or 6%; 72% annualized.

Only Out –Of- The-Money strike prices offer UPSIDE POTENTIAL.

At The Money Strike Prices

offer neither downside protection
(of the option premium)

nor upside potential
(of the stock appreciation),

but oftentimes generate
the most significant premium returns.

ALL OPTIONS OFFER DOWNSIDE PROTECTION
OF YOUR STOCK PURCHASE.

(This is equal to the option premium you generated.)

Another In-The-Money Example:

Let's stay with figure 31 (NYX example) and calculate our returns if we sold the nearest *In-The -Money strike price* of 95 (just above the circled strike of 100):

1. Our cost basis is still 9701.

2. Our profit is 510, but we are 201 In–The-Money ($97.01 - 95 = 2.01$ x $100 = 201$).

3. We will take the premium of 510 and break it down to 309 and 201 (equals 510, 201 of which is intrinsic value).

4. We will use the 2.01 to buy down the price of the stock from 97.01 to 95.

5. Now our total, one month profit is 309 ($510 - 201$), and our cost basis is 9500 ($97.01 - 2.01$).

6. Our one month return is now 309 / 9500 or 3.25%, which annualizes to 39%.

7. There is no upside potential here… no matter how high the stock price goes. We do, however, have 201 in downside protection. If the stock declines from 97.01 to 95.00 we still will have earned our 3.25% for the month. Should the price dip below 95, and we are not called out, our cost basis for future option sales remains at 95.

For an In-The-Money Strike Price, if we take the dollar amount of downside protection and divide by our cost basis we can get a percentage figure. In the above example, selling the 95 call gives us *downside protection* of 201:

$$201 / 9701 = 2.1\%$$
(one month downside protection)

Here's the good news:

**All these calculations are done automatically
by the ESOC (Ellman System Option Calculator) !**

When making your monthly decisions as to which stocks to
buy and sell options on, it is important to get the FULL AND
COMPLETE picture. I have developed a form to use so that
at a glance, I can make my determinations.

In figure 32 below, I have listed the complete option picture
for the sale of the 95 and 100 call option strike prices for the
above NYX example. We see the one month return on the
option sales is 2.9% for the 100 call, and 3.25% for the 95
call. The 100 call also offers great upside potential (3.1%)
while the 95 call offers significant downside protection (2.1%).
Depending on your risk tolerance (if low, go for the 95 call) and
how you feel about the one month outlook for that particular
equity, you will make a determination as to which strike price
to choose. Either way, it's a nice decision to be making! I
make my strike price selections based on technical analysis
and current market conditions.

STOCK	PRICE	ROO	UPSIDE POTENTIAL		DOWNSIDE PROTECTION	
NYX	97.01	2.90%	3.10%		0%	
NYX	97.01	3.25%	0%		2.10%	

Figure 32

This form has been dramatically upgraded. I used to do all
these calculations and forms by hand! However, I had the good
fortune of having a computer savvy, Excel guru participate
in one of my seminars. His name is Owen Sargent. Owen
also happens to be an attorney and an accountant. One
day Owen sent me an email describing this Excel calculator

he developed based specifically on my system. With the information obtained from the above-mentioned option chain, the ROO, upside potential, and downside protection will be calculated for you. Simply plug in the numbers and letters in the *blue areas* and all calculations will appear in the *white areas*.

The **ELLMAN SYSTEM OPTION CALCULATOR (ESOC)** includes the following tabs:

1. **Introduction-** This page explains the different scenarios the calculator is capable of computing.

2. **Single tab-** This page shows the various options sale calculations for a single stock.

3. **Multiple tab-** This page compares returns for a multiplicity of options on different equities so they can be compared. This will help us determine the best ones to sell. It includes upside potential, downside protection, and return on option (ROO). See figure 32a on the right, which is the multiple tab on the calculator that can be used in addition to the single tab page of figure 32.

4. **What Now tab-** This page gives returns for exit strategies. It calculates the returns for buying back and reselling other options. It allows you to compare the different, possible exit strategies to help you make the best investment decisions. Owen's creativity has saved us all a lot of time and energy in addition to helping us maximize profits.

RETURN ON OPTION (ROO) CALCULATOR - MULTIPLE STOCKS

Stock Name or Symbol	Stock $ / sh	Option $ / sh	Strike $	Expires	Intrinsic	Upside	ROO	Up Potential	Down Potntial

See **Appendix V: FORMS**, for landscape version.   Figure 32a

At this point, we have collected a tremendous amount of citical information. It is important to have this data organized in an efficient and easily accessible system. Our next chapter, *Portfolio Management*, will describe how to accomplish this.

Chapter **10**

Portfolio Management

We have thus far worked in an organized, systematic manner, to gather a significant amount of critical information. We have established a watch list of some of the greatest performing stocks available. We also have knowledge of the option returns these equities can provide for us.

It is imperative to continue in the path of being organized by placing this information in a portfolio whereby it can be accessed and acted upon in a timely manner.

Our portfolio must allow us to track the stocks we own, the options we sold, and the stocks we may want to own in the near future.

With the power and resources of the internet, we can more successfully manage our investments in an efficient manner. We can control our investments through the use of Internet tracking devices. Once we create a new portfolio, these tools allow us to organize the information we must have available in order to minimize our risk and maximize our profits.

Such information can include the security symbol, number of shares, purchase price, last price, average volume, current volume, and price change to mention a few (see figure 33[32] on next page).

32   USAA.com, www.USAA.com (February, 2007).

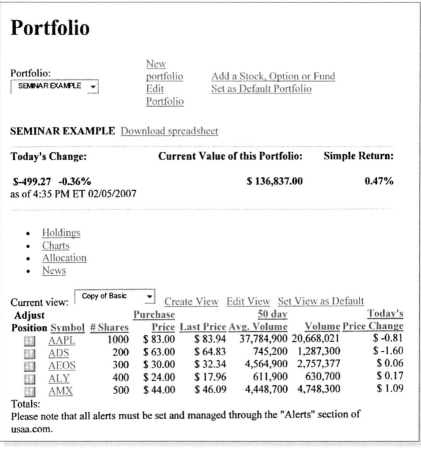

Figure 33

Another example of a stock watch list in my portfolio is seen in my *Invstools Software Program* (figure 33a[33], opposite page).

There are a myriad of software programs & web sites that allow you to set up such portfolio managers. I will use as an example the portfolio manager from my USAA Brokerage Account (www. USAA.com). Once logged onto the USAA website, hit the *Investments* tab. This will take you to a page which has several links on the left side, one of which says *Portfolio Manager*. Hitting this link will take you to your default portfolio, which, in the case of figure 34[34] (next page) is a portfolio called

33   Investools, www.Investools.com (February, 2007).
34   USAA.com, www.USAA.com (February, 2007).

Figure 33a

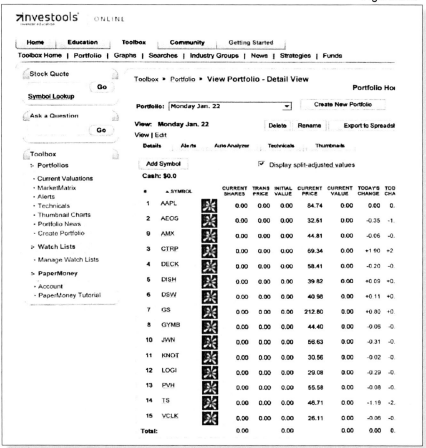

Figure 34

Portfolio

Enter Symbols:

| Quote ▾ |
| Find Symbol |

Portfolio:
| Options ▾ |

New portfolio
Edit Portfolio

Add a Stock, Option or Fund
Set as Default Portfolio

- Place a Trade
- Markets
- Portfolio
    View
    Default
    Portfolio
    View All
    Portfolios
- Alerts
- News
- Equity Center
- Fund Center
- Fixed Income Center
- ETF Center
- Preferences

Options Download spreadsheet

Today's Change:	Current Value of this Portfolio:	Simple Return:
+$0.79 10.18%	$ 8.55	-82.33%
as of 4:01 PM ET 02/05/2007		

	FLK=AO	$ 0.75
	UPU=AP	$ 1.75
	DVN=AN	$ 0.05
	NYX=AA	$ 0.05
	ULP=AC	$ 0.03

Totals:
Please note that all alerts must be set and managed through the "Alerts" section of usaa.com.

options. If you have no portfolios set up, hit the *create a portfolio tab.* On this particular default option page you see merely the option symbol and the current value. Another example of an options watch list in my portfolio is found in my *Investools Software Program* (figure 34a[35]).

Figure 34a

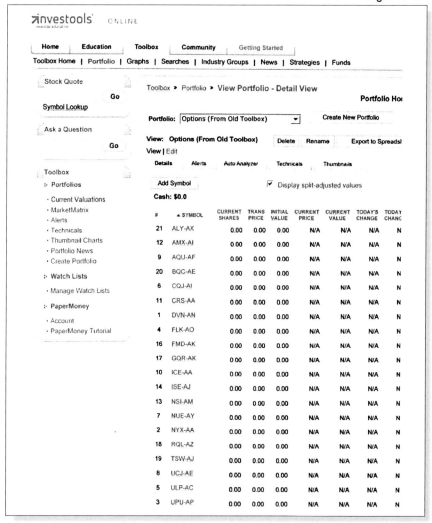

At the top of figure 34a (above), there are options to create a new portfolio or edit the existing one. Let's take a look back, now, at figure 33. In the middle of the page you will see the term, *Edit View.* By clicking on it you can alter the parameters of the current portfolio. For example, in figure 35[36] below, under fundamentals, we can add a column for 52-Week High, 52-Week Low, P/E ratio, and many other bits of information; once selected, will appear in the right hand column and can be organized in any order you choose.

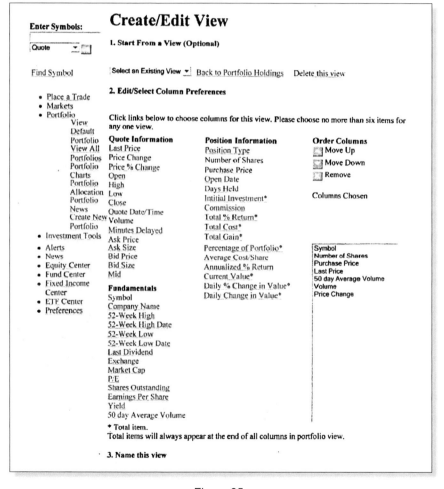

Figure 35

36   USAA.com, www.USAA.com (February, 2007).

Now that we've set up this list, by clicking on any ticker we will be linked to the *Quote Page* (see figure 36[37] below). Here we can access the basic chart and a series of links on the left panel, including the option chain. In a matter of seconds you can access any bit of information about any particular equity or option. Once you decide on a particular portfolio manager, the set-up, and access to information will become second nature.

Figure 36

Finally, on an Excel spreadsheet, I enter the options I've sold that month. For example (see figure 37), in November of

---

37   USAA.com, www.USAA.com (February, 2007).

2006, I sold $8869 worth of options based on $250,000 of underlying stock for a 3.5%, one month return. This includes an initial round of selling options, and then purchasing additional stock with those profits, and now selling options on the newly acquired equities. As we mentioned in Chapter 1, one of the reasons for selling options is that you can *compound your money in minutes!*

DATE	BTC ?	# contracts Premium/ option ticker, Account		month/strike price	Profit
20-Oct	-48	sell (4) GLW KX @ 1.60	45	NOV 22.50	254
24-Oct		sell (1) DVN KN @ 2.75	45	Nov-70	266
2-Nov		sell (4) glw kd @ .70	45	Nov.-20	266
20-Oct	-46	sell (2) AAO KU @ 2.10	500	NOV-37.50	
20-Oct		sell (2) AAO KH @ 1.00	500	Nov-40	431
24-Oct		sell (1) UCJ KF @ 1.35	500	30-Nov	127
24-Oct		sell (2) NUE KL @ 3.20	500	Nov-60	629
30-Oct		sell (2) ADS KL @ 1.90	500	Nov-60	369
30-Oct		sell (2) FLK KM @ 2.50 (FFIV)	500	Nov-65	489
30-Oct		sell (2) QAA KP @ 2.25 (AAPL)	500	Nov-80	439
31-Oct		sell (1) UW 45 (UARM) (	500	NOV_ 45	110
10-Nov		sell (3) ULP KI @ 1.23 (EZPW)	500	Nov-45	468
20-Oct		sell (3) KUO KE @ 1.55 (BEBE)	950	25-Nov	385
20-Oct		sell (2) DQI KJ @ 4.90 (DRIV)	950	Nov-50	348
27-Oct		sell (1) CRS KA @ 4.80	950	11/105	471
30-Oct		sell (1) RUP KD @ 3.30 (RIMM)	950	11/120	321
30-Oct		sell (2) ISE KK @ 1.05	950	Nov-55	199
30-Oct		sell (2) NSI KM @ 2.90 (NTRI)	950	Nov-65	569
30-Oct		sell (4) DSW KG @ 1.05	950	Nov-35	389
30-Oct		sell (6) QPM KW @ 1.01 (SMSI)	950	11/17.50	590
30-Oct		sell (2) AUE KH @ 1.40 (CRDN)	950	Nov-40	209
30-Oct		sell (1) SWF KJ @ 1.40 (SNDK)	950	Nov-50	132
30-Oct		sell (RQL KL @ 2.90 (STLD)	950	Nov-60	459
30-Oct		sell (2) ROG KN @ 1.70	950	Nov-70	329
31-Oct		sell (2) TNL KE @ 1.10	950	25-Nov	209
1-Nov		sell (2) GQR KI @ 1.60 (GRMN)	950	Nov-45	309
10-Nov		sell (2) ISE KJ @ .55	950	Nov-50	102

8869

OPTION LOG NOVEMBER, 2006

Figure 37

Now let's take a quick look back at everything we've covered:

SUMMARY

Our portfolio manager should consist of the following:

1. Watch List of the greatest performing stocks.

2. List of stocks currently owned.

3. List of options sold in the current contract period.

4. Excel spreadsheet (or format of your choice) of options sold showing profits earned.

By having the watch list, we can efficiently locate new stocks to purchase if instituting an exit strategy or if new equities are needed the following contract period.

By including a list of options sold and their current value we can, in a matter of seconds, determine if an exit strategy is indicated (value dips at or below .20).

The option log allows us to keep track of monthly earnings and percent profit earned thereby allowing us to evaluate our success on a monthly basis.

The list of stocks owned (that particular month) is a second method of watching for a possible exit strategy tactic. If the price of the stock is dropping we may want to act to decrease loses or turn losses into gains.

By being organized we will not only become time efficient, but also, dramatically increase our chances of achieving the very highest of returns.

Here are a few brokerage company websites recommended to me by students who have previously attended my seminars:

- o   www.ThinkorSwim.com

- o   www.TDAmeritrade.com

- o   www.optionsXpress.com

- o   www.Scottrade.com

- o   www.USAA.com   (the brokerage firm I use)

It is important to do your own research, making sure you are paying the lowest possible commissions, while receiving stellar online service.

In the next chapter we will see how our portfolio manager will help support our critical exit strategies, thereby enhancing our returns and minimizing potential loses.

Chapter 11

Exit Strategies

Actions Prior To, and During, Expiration Friday

An *exit strategy* is a plan by which an investor intends to get out of an investment he or she has made in the past. It is a decision as to how, and when, a trade will be closed out.

When a call option is sold you are said to be in an *open* position (sell to open).

Closing An Options Position Without Any Action On Your Part:

There are times when your position will be closed without any action on your part:

1. Since these are *American style options* (as opposed to *European style options*) they can be *exercised* by the option buyer any time after the sale, and prior to expiration. It is quite rare that this will occur prior to expiration Friday, but it is possible. This is called *assignment*. If this occurs, you are required to meet the obligations of the contract and sell the underlying equities. Your position is now closed and the cash from

the sale of your stock at the prescribed strike price is sent to your account. This scenario occurs *without any action on your part*. Some brokerage firms will notify you regarding early assignment by phone or e-mail. You can also access the information by hitting the *activity* link of your online brokerage account.

2. The option can expire worthless. If, by expiration Friday, the price of the stock has NOT exceeded the strike price of the call option you sold, the option will not be exercised. Let's say you sold the $50 call option and the current market value of the stock has only reached $48. Why would anyone want to purchase your shares for $50 when they can be purchased at market for $48? The option will expire *unexercised,* thereby closing the position.

Closing An Options Position By Taking Action:

Both of the above situations depict examples wherein your open option position is closed without any action on your part. There are times, however, when you would like to close your option position for purposes of enhancing returns or minimizing risk or loses. This is where *we need to take action*. We do so by *buying back the option*. When this occurs, our option position is closed and we no longer have an obligation to sell our equities at a particular strike price by a specific date. We still own the stock (called *being long the stock*). At this point we are free to take action via selling different options (called *being short the option*) or selling the stock itself. It is as if we never sold the first option to begin with. Such exit strategies can be instituted either prior to or on expiration Friday.

Exit Strategies Prior to Expiration Friday:

You may want to institute an exit strategy if a stock you own is unexpectedly declining in price, or breaking down fundamentally or technically. There is no need to wait for expiration Friday to take action. By acting in a timely manner, we can frequently minimize loses, prevent loses, or even salvage some profit.

POSSIBLE EXIT STRATEGIES

1. Rolling Down- We replace one call option with another that has a lower strike price.

Here are two real life examples of Rolling Down after having purchased stock, and sold its corresponding option.

EXAMPLE #1:   Steel Dynamics (STLD)
                   (see figure 38[38], next page)

     a)   Purchase 100 shares of STLD @ $35 creating a cost basis of $3500

     b)   Sell the 1-month, $40 call option @ $1.50 creating an initial return of 4.3%

     c)   Two weeks later, the stock price has dropped to $31.95

     d)   The value of the call option has dropped to .10

Here we buy back the option for .10 or $10 for the contract. We now sell the same month, $35 call option for .45 or $45 per contract. This will create an additional 1% profit for the two weeks remaining until expiration for the option. This small 1% per 2 week profit adds up over time and only takes a few clicks on your computer.

---

38   CNBC.com, www.cnbc.com (December, 2006).

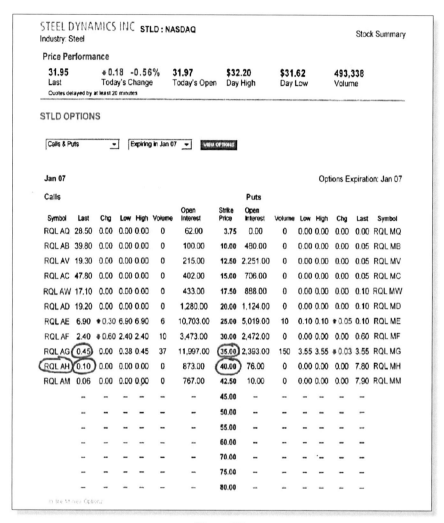

Figure 38

EXAMPLE #2: Altria (MO) (See figure 39[39] on the right)

a) Purchase 100 shares of MO @ 80.14 creating a cost basis of $8014

b) Sell the 1-month, $85 call option @ $1.05 creating an initial return of 1.3%

---

c) Shortly thereafter, the stock price dropped to $78.24

d) The value of the call option has dropped to .20

Here we buy back the option for .20 or $20 for the contract. We now sell the same month, $80 call option for 1.30 or $130 per contract. This will create an additional 1.3% profit for the nearly three weeks remaining until expiration for the Option.

Figure 39

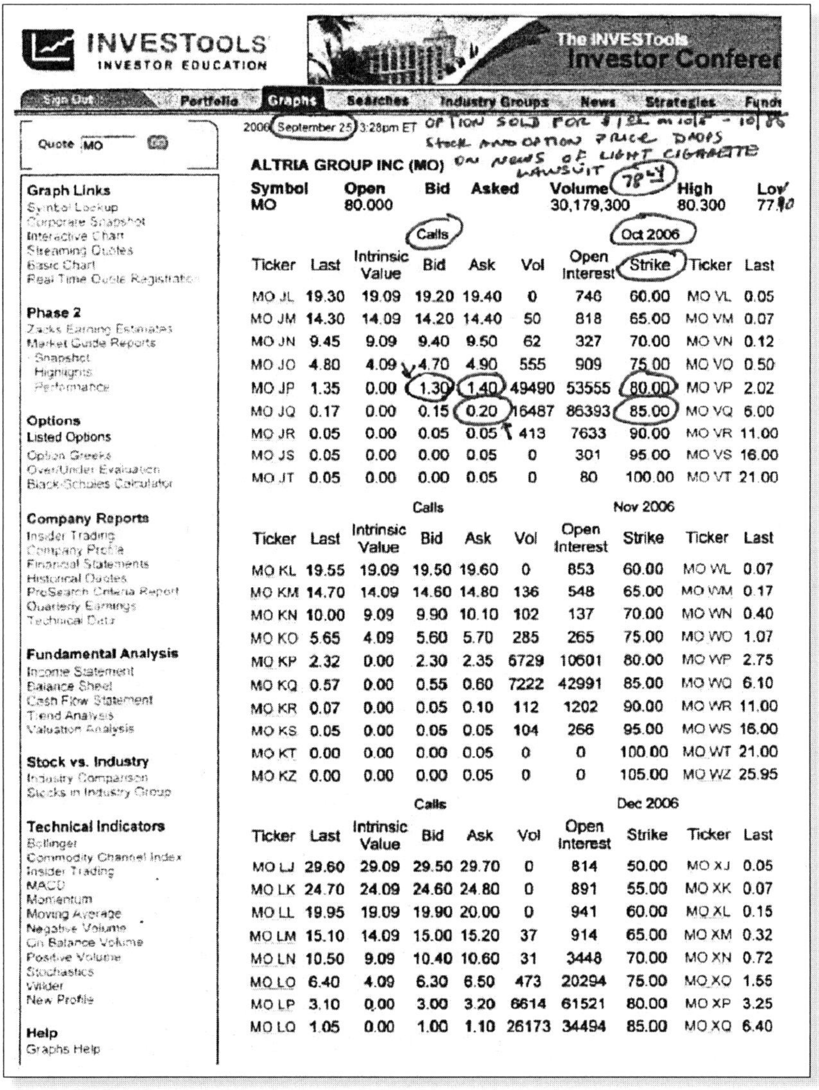

2006 September 25 3:28pm ET

ALTRIA GROUP INC (MO)

Symbol	Open	Bid	Asked	Volume	High	Low
MO	80.000			30,179,300	80.300	77.?0

Calls — Oct 2006

Ticker	Last	Intrinsic Value	Bid	Ask	Vol	Open Interest	Strike	Ticker	Last
MO JL	19.30	19.09	19.20	19.40	0	746	60.00	MO VL	0.05
MO JM	14.30	14.09	14.20	14.40	50	818	65.00	MO VM	0.07
MO JN	9.45	9.09	9.40	9.50	62	327	70.00	MO VN	0.12
MO JO	4.80	4.09	4.70	4.90	555	909	75.00	MO VO	0.50
MO JP	1.35	0.00	1.30	1.40	49490	53555	80.00	MO VP	2.02
MO JQ	0.17	0.00	0.15	0.20	16487	86393	85.00	MO VQ	6.00
MO JR	0.05	0.00	0.05	0.05	413	7633	90.00	MO VR	11.00
MO JS	0.05	0.00	0.00	0.05	0	301	95.00	MO VS	16.00
MO JT	0.05	0.00	0.00	0.05	0	80	100.00	MO VT	21.00

Calls — Nov 2006

Ticker	Last	Intrinsic Value	Bid	Ask	Vol	Open Interest	Strike	Ticker	Last
MO KL	19.55	19.09	19.50	19.60	0	853	60.00	MO WL	0.07
MO KM	14.70	14.09	14.60	14.80	136	548	65.00	MO WM	0.17
MO KN	10.00	9.09	9.90	10.10	102	137	70.00	MO WN	0.40
MO KO	5.65	4.09	5.60	5.70	285	265	75.00	MO WO	1.07
MO KP	2.32	0.00	2.30	2.35	6729	10601	80.00	MO WP	2.75
MO KQ	0.57	0.00	0.55	0.60	7222	42991	85.00	MO WQ	6.10
MO KR	0.07	0.00	0.05	0.10	112	1202	90.00	MO WR	11.00
MO KS	0.05	0.00	0.05	0.05	104	266	95.00	MO WS	16.00
MO KT	0.00	0.00	0.00	0.05	0	0	100.00	MO WT	21.00
MO KZ	0.00	0.00	0.00	0.05	0	0	105.00	MO WZ	25.95

Calls — Dec 2006

Ticker	Last	Intrinsic Value	Bid	Ask	Vol	Open Interest	Strike	Ticker	Last
MO LJ	29.60	29.09	29.50	29.70	0	814	50.00	MO XJ	0.05
MO LK	24.70	24.09	24.60	24.80	0	891	55.00	MO XK	0.07
MO LL	19.95	19.09	19.90	20.00	0	941	60.00	MO XL	0.15
MO LM	15.10	14.09	15.00	15.20	37	914	65.00	MO XM	0.32
MO LN	10.50	9.09	10.40	10.60	31	3448	70.00	MO XN	0.72
MO LO	6.40	4.09	6.30	6.50	473	20294	75.00	MO XO	1.55
MO LP	3.10	0.00	3.00	3.20	6614	61521	80.00	MO XP	3.25
MO LQ	1.05	0.00	1.00	1.10	26173	34494	85.00	MO XQ	6.40

(It is interesting to note that the reason why this stock priced dropped was due to an unexpected *light cigarette* lawsuit.)

2. Do Not Take Any Immediate Action- We buy back the option and do not immediately resell another one. Our hope is the stock will appreciate in value, thereby driving the option premium higher. Perhaps the stock dropped in price, but appears to be bouncing off its moving average support. Maybe the institutional investors are taking profits and you expect the price to turn around quickly. These are some of the scenarios we may find. When the price goes back up, we can then sell the exact same option we bought back, just at a higher price.

I once sold an option, bought it back, resold the same option, bought it back again and then resold the exact option all in one month. I hit a triple!

3. Convert Dead $ to Cash Profits- We buy back the option and sell the underlying equity.

Here is a real life example of Converting Dead $ to Cash Profits.

EXAMPLE: Qualcom (QCOM) / EZCORP Inc. (EZPW) (See figure 40[40] on the right)

I owned 400 shares of Qualcom at an average cost of $36.10 per share. After having gone up to near $38, it declined and appeared to show no signs of recovery. There was one week left for options to expire. I had sold 2 contracts of the Nov. 37.50 and two of the Nov. 40.

---

40   USAA.com, www.USAA.com (November, 2006).

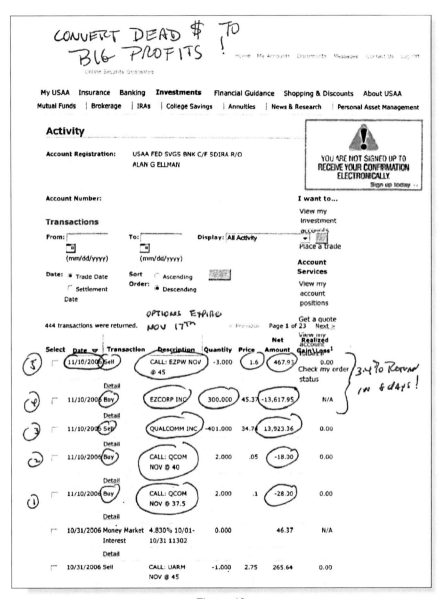

Figure 40

They could be bought back for .10 and .05 per contract respectively. I looked to see if I could turn these loses into gains. I bought back the QCOM options and sold the *dead stock*. Then 300 shares of EZPW were purchased with the cash from the QCOM sale. I immediately sold the

Nov. 45 calls and generated $467 into my account which represented a 3.4% return for 1 week! Even if called out, and the sale of the stock caused a small loss, my 1 week return was still 2.7%. Now that's creating big profits from dead money!

You must keep a list of the options you sell in your portfolio manager. This way you can view their values on one screen. When you see an option value decline to the .20 value or lower, it may be time to implement an exit strategy. Sometimes I will pay a little more to buy back an option if it is earlier on in the contract period (first 7 to 10 days).The reason for this is that there hasn't been significant *time decay* of these options. The bulk of this time decay occurs in the last two weeks prior to option expiration Friday.

One of the beautiful aspects of this system is the control you have. Not every stock you select will be a winner. It is unreasonable to expect such success. However, if you have a lot more winners than losers and if you initiate your appropriate exit strategies, in a timely manner, you are reducing your risk and increasing your chances for greater profits.

You must remain proactive. <u>Don't fall in love with a particular stock</u>. A security is merely a vehicle you are sending out into the financial battlefield and asking it to return with *friends*. If that vehicle becomes incapable of fulfilling its mission, it's time to scrap that model and replace it with a better, more vibrant, more capable courier. In the case of selling stock options the phrase, *what have you done for me lately* rings true.

Many times I will keep these sold stocks on my watch list and come back to them when they are in better health. If I notice that they are not making any kind of comeback, I bump them from my watch list. Now they will have to earn their way back on.

Be as demanding with your stock selection as you are with your children's babysitter or teacher; or your family doctor or dentist. Just as you want your family to eat the healthiest foods, so too, do you want your hard earned money to be managed by the world's greatest performing stocks. Accept nothing less.

Exit Strategies on Expiration Friday:

On or just prior to expiration Friday we must assess our option portfolio. We need to determine if our option strike prices are now in-the money, at-the-money, or out-of-the-money. We should also evaluate our underlying securities to see if they are holding up fundamentally and technically. Remember, also, to make sure that the earnings report is not being made public during the upcoming contract period (see Chapter 12). If so, we avoid selling options on these stocks until after the ER is made public. Finally, calculations for potential next month option returns need to be determined.

Out-Of-The-Money strike prices:

When the strike price is higher than the current market value of the security, there is no need to buy back the option. We simply let the option expire. During the following day or days, we determine if we will resell the next months option for that same equity or sell the stock and exchange the cash for another equity.

The same system criteria to make this decision are used as we did originally: Is the stock fundamentally and technically sound? Is the option return acceptable? If the answer is *no* to either one of these questions, we move on to another stock. To me, <u>it doesn't matter what we paid for that stock</u>. The past is the past. We can't change that. We now have a certain amount of cash sitting in an equity. That security has a name, let's call it company XYZ. We ask ourselves, "Is company XYZ the appropriate vehicle to carry this cash?" The answer to that question is determined by our system. Fundamentals, technicals and option returns will give us the answer.

Look at it as if you're sending these stocks out into the financial battlegrounds and asking them to return WITH FRIENDS. If they are no longer capable of fulfilling their mission, it's time to replace them with stronger gladiators. Don't fall in love with a particular company; fall in love with the deal. Your money must be functioning on all cylinders at all times. Remember how we converted dead money to big profits prior to expiration Friday (The Qualcom / Ezcorp deal above)? The same holds true post-expiration Friday. If a particular stock will not generate significant income for us, we simply sell it and purchase a different stock that will.

If, however, that same stock we owned the previous month, is still sound fundamentally and technically, and gives us great option returns, we simply sell the next months option. Money begets money. The *velocity of money* is the rate at which money changes hands. The more frequently this occurs, the more our chances are of making substantial profits. A stock or the underlying cash value, sitting around, not generating more cash, slows the *velocity of money*. As a result our returns are diminished. Don't let this happen! Be proactive and put your money to work for you AT ALL TIMES.

Strike Price is At-the-Money or In-the-Money:

The concern in this scenario is that we will get called out (assignment) and the shares of the underlying equity will be sold. This may not be the worst possible outcome, but we may want to avoid it. In order to prevent assignment, we will need to buy back the option previously sold. This is called closing a *short position*. Now we are free to sell another option on the same underlying equity. After buying back the option, here are a few follow-up maneuvers:

> **Rolling Out or Forward:** The replacement of one call option with another call that has the same strike price but a later expiration date. In our system, it is usually the next month's call option.

> **Rolling Out and Up:** The replacement of one call with another that has a higher strike price *and* a later date.

I have found that it is rarely financially feasible to **Roll Out and Down** from an in-the-money strike price.

There are many times that the buy back of the option and the subsequent sale of the next month's option does not create an acceptable percentage return. If this is the case, we simply let the option get exercised and the stock sold. We will then take the cash from the sale of the stock to purchase another equity that will give us great returns. It is critical that our money be working for us at all times whether it's in the form of the old stock or a new one.

Remember to always have some cash in your account to buy back options so as to initiate an appropriate exit strategy.

Preventing Assignment:

Here is an example of a situation where a few days before expiration Friday, we became concerned about being called out of Apple Computer: (see figure 41[41] on the following page)

---

41   Investools, www.Investools.com (September, 2006)

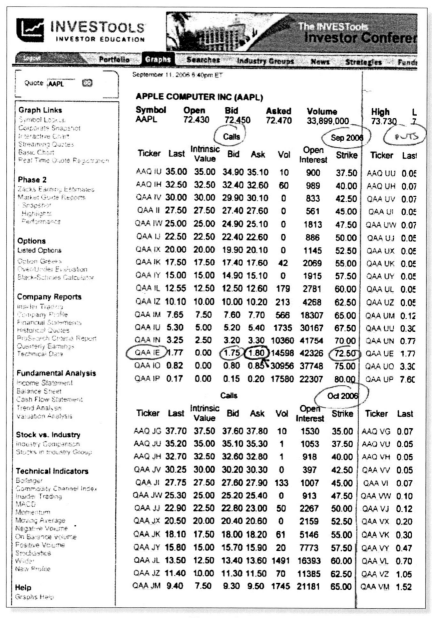

Figure 41

1. Purchased Apple Computer in August of 2006 for $68.27 per share.

2. Sold the September $72.50 calls for $3.50.

3. This created a 5.1% 1-month return or 61% annualized.

4. Do we initiate an exit strategy of buying back the option and reselling the next month option?

5. First we made sure that the stock was still technically and fundamentally sound, and it was.

6. Next we computed the returns for *rolling out*:

   a) In figure 41, we see that to buy back the Sept. 72.50 call option would cost $1.80 per share or $180 per contract.

   b) In figure 42[42] on the next page, we see that to roll out (later date, same strike price) we would get a return of $4.40 per share or $440 per contract.

   c) Subtracting $180 from $440 gives us a per contract return of $260.

   d) This represents a return of 3.6% for 1 month (260/7247) or 44% annualized. What a deal!

7. Next we computed the returns for *rolling out and up*:

   a) We close our option position with the same $180 as above.

   b) We sell the Oct. $75 call option for $3.30 per share or $330 per contract (figure 42).

Investools, www.Investools.com (September, 2006)

c)   Our return drops to 2.1% for 1 month ($330 - $180 = $150) and $150/$7247 = 2.1% or 25% annualized. This is certainly not terrible.

d)   We now have the possibility of appreciation to $75 per share or another $2.53 per share or $253 per contract.

e)   If this occurs, our profit for rolling out and up with appreciation to the higher strike price of $75 per share would be $150 plus $253 or $403.

f)   This now represents a return of 5.6% for one month ($403/ $7247) or 68% annualized.

It is obvious from the option returns above that we will initiate an exit strategy. Our decision is whether to roll out or to roll out and up. This will depend on how we feel about the stock at the time. If our prediction is for continued appreciation, we will roll out and up. A more conservative approach would be to simply roll out and be quite happy with a one month return of 3.6%. We factor in general market conditions (inflation, interest rates, liquidity etc.) and technical analysis of the stock to decide on which strike price to utilize.

The deeper the strike price is *in-the-money* near expiration Friday, the less likely it will be that initiating an exit strategy will pay off financially. All you need to do is run the numbers and see if you are happy with the returns.

If you roll out and up, and your stock is trading higher than the original option strike price, rolling out and up will *increase the value of your stock,* and this fact should be calculated into your decision.

CALLS

		BID	ASK			OCT		
QAA JU	7.55	5.00	7.50	7.60	415	11177	67.50	QAA VU	2.20
QAA JN	5.95	2.50	5.90	6.00	2431	42989	70.00	QAA VN	3.05
QAA JE	4.50	0.00	4.40	4.60	8173	35515	72.50	QAA VE	4.15
QAA JO	3.35	0.00	3.30	3.40	8796	27310	75.00	QAA VO	5.50
QAA JP	1.72	0.00	1.70	1.75	5779	29099	80.00	QAA VP	8.85
QAA JQ	0.82	0.00	0.80	0.85	2419	13924	85.00	QAA VQ	13.00
QAA JR	0.37	0.00	0.35	0.40	931	14327	90.00	QAA VR	17.60
QAA JS	0.17	0.00	0.15	0.20	77	2891	95.00	QAA VS	22.50
QAA JT	0.07	0.00	0.05	0.10	130	3432	100.00	QAA VT	27.50
QAA JA	0.07	0.00	0.05	0.10	30	560	105.00	QAA VA	32.50
QAA JB	0.07	0.00	0.00	0.05	0	2327	110.00	QAA VB	37.50

			Calls				Jan 2007		
Ticker	Last	Intrinsic Value	Bid	Ask	Vol	Open Interest	Strike	Ticker	Last
AAQ AB	62.60	62.50	62.50	62.70	1	4103	10.00	AAQ MB	0.00
AAQ AP	60.20	60.00	60.10	60.30	10	2977	12.50	AAQ MP	0.00
AAQ AC	57.70	57.50	57.60	57.80	0	2418	15.00	AAQ MC	0.05
AAQ AS	55.30	55.00	55.20	55.40	2	11747	17.50	AAQ MS	0.07
AAQ AD	52.85	52.50	52.80	52.90	10	3116	20.00	AAQ MD	0.05
AAQ AT	50.40	50.00	50.30	50.50	0	1019	22.50	AAQ MT	0.07
AAQ AE	48.00	47.50	47.90	48.10	0	3707	25.00	AAQ ME	0.07
AAQ AY	45.55	45.00	45.50	45.60	64	3457	27.50	AAQ MY	0.07
AAQ AF	43.10	42.50	43.00	43.20	0	3596	30.00	AAQ MF	0.07
AAQ AZ	40.70	40.00	40.60	40.80	0	1874	32.50	AAQ MZ	0.10
AAQ AG	38.30	37.50	38.20	38.40	0	6014	35.00	AAQ MG	0.12
AAQ AU	35.85	35.00	35.70	36.00	0	12214	37.50	AAQ MU	0.20
AAQ AH	33.50	32.50	33.40	33.60	6	9356	40.00	AAQ MH	0.25
QAA AV	31.10	30.00	31.00	31.20	0	6087	42.50	QAA MV	0.35
QAA AI	28.80	27.50	28.70	28.90	1	5082	45.00	QAA MI	0.45
QAA AW	26.50	25.00	26.40	26.60	0	5032	47.50	QAA MW	0.62
QAA AJ	24.20	22.50	24.10	24.30	115	17868	50.00	QAA MJ	0.77
QAA AX	22.00	20.00	21.90	22.10	1	5706	52.50	QAA MX	1.05
QAA AK	19.80	17.50	19.70	19.90	44	19930	55.00	QAA MK	1.32
OBR AY	15.65	15.00	0.00	0.00	0	0	57.50	OBR MY	3.45
QAA AY	17.75	15.00	17.70	17.80	184	9999	57.50	QAA MY	1.72
OBR AL	14.05	12.50	0.00	0.00	0	0	60.00	OBR ML	4.30
QAA AL	15.80	12.50	15.70	15.90	81	21568	60.00	QAA ML	2.20
OBR AZ	12.50	10.00	0.00	0.00	0	0	62.50	OBR MZ	5.25
QAA AZ	13.90	10.00	13.80	14.00	17	7245	62.50	QAA MZ	2.80
OBR AM	11.20	7.50	0.00	0.00	0	0	65.00	OBR MM	6.30
QAA AM	12.20	7.50	12.10	12.30	410	25453	65.00	QAA MM	3.55
OBR AU	9.90	5.00	0.00	0.00	0	0	67.50	OBR MU	7.50
QAA AU	10.55	5.00	10.50	10.60	268	20763	67.50	QAA MU	4.40
OBR AN	8.80	2.50	0.00	0.00	0	0	70.00	OBR MN	8.90
QAA AN	9.10	2.50	9.00	9.20	563	33743	70.00	QAA MN	5.40

Figure 42

For example, if you sold an $80 call on a stock you paid $78 but the stock is trading at $83 near expiration Friday, factor in the following:

- Your stock will be sold @ $80 due to your contract obligation if you don't buy back the option.

- If you roll out and up to the $85 strike price, your stock is now worth $3 more or $83 since you are no longer obligated to sell it at $80.

If the buy back returns of rolling out or rolling out and up do not meet with your satisfaction, accept getting called out of your stock and move on to a more suitable courier for your money.

The Ellman System Option Calculator (ESOC) will be extremely helpful in making these determinations.

As with buying stock and selling the corresponding option, it is always best to close your option position and open a new one in the same time frame. If you buy back an option and wait to resell the new one, you may not get a favorable price and your returns will suffer. *Buy back and sell immediately.* The exception to this rule is when you buy back an option in the *early* part of a contract period and feel that there is a good chance that the underlying stock will go back up in a short period of time (remember when I hit that triple?). In this case, it is appropriate to wait a few days or a week before taking other action.

It should also be apparent why we need to *have extra cash in our brokerage account* so that we have the flexibility to buy back these options. Without this ability, our returns will also be hindered. Remember… the first step in any and all exit strategies is to buy back the original option.

Chapter 12

Earnings Reports

How They Effect Our Investment Decisions

From exit strategies to earnings reports, our investment objectives are to first minimize risk and to then maximize profits. If we knew in advance that an event was to take place that could dramatically have a negative impact on our financial assets we would avoid that situation. This is keeping with the spirit of our system's declared goals.

News items can emerge at any time that may negatively impact our investment, such as loss of a significant account, negative earnings guidance for an upcoming quarter, corporate fraud, loss of key personnel, negative economic indicators, and on and on. When this occurs, we put into play one of our exit strategies. The situation is unavoidable.

However, there are times that we can predict the possibility of such an event and take action *before the fact.*

Earnings Reports are the most common and important of these situations. These reports are quarterly filings made by public companies to report their performance and financial well-being. Included in these reports are items such as net income, earnings per share, earnings from continuing operations, and net sales. They are reported at the end of each quarter. Most companies file in January, April, July and October.

In essence, an earnings report is a *report card* for public companies. It is through these reports that companies let its shareholders know how well they have performed over the last period of time. Most often, the key indicators, net income and EPS (earnings-per-share), are measured against the previous years' numbers. By analyzing this comparison, investors can begin to gauge the financial health of the company, and whether or not it deserves their investment consideration.

The securities markets are regulated by the **Securities and Exchange Commission (SEC)**, which is a government commission created to protect investors. It also monitors the corporate takeovers in the U.S. The SEC is composed of five commissions appointed by the U.S. President and approved by the Senate. The statutes administered by the SEC are designed to promote full public disclosure and to protect the investing public against fraudulent and manipulative practices in the securities markets. Generally, most issues of securities offered in interstate commerce, through the mail or on the internet, must be registered with the SEC.

In 2002, Congress passed the **Sarbanes-Oxley Act** which provided stricter supplementation to the existing legislation. This legislation was motivated by the corporate scandals involving Enron, Tyco, Worldcom and others. It established a Public Accounting Oversight Board which inspects and disciplines accounting firms that audit public companies. This represents one of the most important changes to U.S. security laws since the New Deal of the 1930's. As a result of this law, the information gleaned from earnings reports is more reliable.

In addition to these reports being made public, analysts who follow these companies provide us with **earnings estimates.**

These are the analysts' prediction of the company's future quarterly or annual earnings. They use forecasting models, management guidance, and fundamental information on the company in order to arrive at the estimate.

Market Consensus or Street Expectation is a figure based on the combined estimates of the analysts covering a public company. Generally, analysts give a consensus for a company's future earnings per share, and revenue; these figures are made for the quarter, fiscal year, and next fiscal year. The size of the company and the number of analysts covering it will dictate the size of the pool from which the estimate is derived.

When you hear that a company has *missed estimates* or *beaten estimates*, these are references to *consensus estimates*. Based on projections, models, sentiments and research, analysts strive to come up with an estimate of what the company will do in the future. Consensus estimates are not an exact science. This leads some market pundits to believe that the market is not as efficient as often purported, and that the efficiency is driven by estimates about a myriad of future events that may not be accurate. This explains why a company's stock price quickly adjusts to new information provided by quarterly earnings and revenue numbers when these figures differ from the consensus estimate.

First Call is a company that gathers research notes and earnings estimates from brokerage analysts. The estimate is compared to the actual reported earnings, and then the difference between the two is called the **earnings surprise**. First Call is often quoted in the financial media. The other main player in this *estimates game* is **Zacks.**

This now brings us to the infamous **whisper number,** a number that just drives me crazy! It is the unofficial and unpublished earnings per share forecast that circulates among professionals on Wall Street. In this context, whisper numbers are generally reserved for the wealthy clients of a brokerage firm. Whisper numbers are especially useful when they differ from the consensus estimate. They can be used as a tool to spot or avoid an earnings surprise. This is only relevant if they are more accurate than the consensus estimate, and that depends on your source. With increased regulatory scrutiny placed on the brokerage industry, it is more difficult to get a whisper number as an individual investor. For example, the aforementioned Sarbanes-Oxley Act provides for stricter rules on how companies disclose financial data. Employees, financial professionals and brokerages face significant penalties if they provide insider earnings data to a select group of people. It is highly unlikely to get a whisper number as a small investor. However, I think that it is important for you to know that this number exists. For example, if your company beats consensus estimates, but goes down in price, it may not have beaten the whisper number.....very frustrating!

Most of these earnings reports will also include **earnings guidance**. This is information that a company provides as an indication or estimate of future earnings. These guidance reports have some influence over analysts' stock ratings and investor decisions to buy, hold, or sell the equity.

When an earnings report is made public it will either miss, meet, or beat the market consensus and/or the whisper number. Along with the guidance reports, the price of the stock can change dramatically. In my system of selling options, this is a risk that I am NOT willing to take.

When we sell covered call options, we are limiting our upside potential. When an earnings report comes out, there is a greater possibility of a significant price movement up or down. My philosophy on this issue is the following:

Never sell options on equities whose earnings reports are coming out during that option period.

The risk of a large decrease in price is not consistent with the risk protection requirement of my system. Well, you might ask:

What if I like the prospects of this stock and want to own it through the earnings report?

This is a great question which I have asked myself many times. If this is the case, my response is… own the stock long through earnings but *do not sell the option.* This way you can get full benefit of a positive ER and not cap it by selling the call. Once you have your full appreciation from the great ER (we hope!) we can now sell the option and get the best of both worlds.

A free web site to get earnings report data is through Yahoo Finance at the following address:

http://biz.yahoo.com/research/earncal/today.html

(See figure 43[43], on next page, for a typical example of the info you receive.)

Simply by typing in the ticker symbol of your stock, you will get the date of the next announced ER. If that date has not yet been made public, you will get the date of the last ER, and can estimate the upcoming report to be about three months later. Also available, in many cases, is the approximate time of the announcement; before market opens, after market closes, or time not supplied. Another feature of this site is the ability to

---

43   Yahoo Finance, http://finance.yahoo.com (February 2007).

listen to some of the conference calls management makes in association with these reports.

Figure 43

Another great site for obtaining ER information is:

www.earningswhispers.com/calendar.asp

(See figure 43a[44] for a typical example of the information you receive.)

I circled the area where the ticker is typed in, and underlined the release date information.

Figure 43a

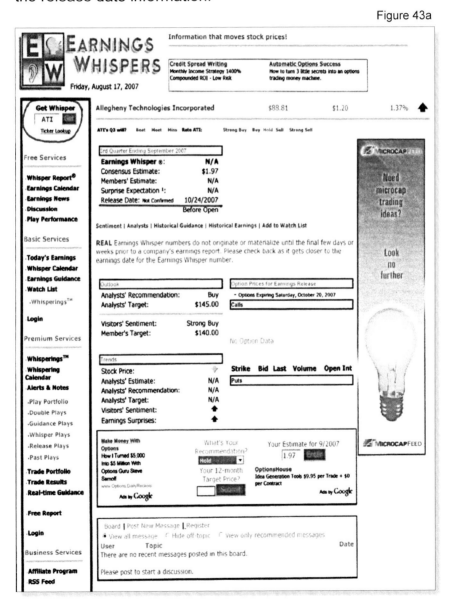

You should be aware of the fact that certain foreign companies trading on the U.S. exchanges (American Depository Receipts or ADR's) may not report with the same three-month regularity as U.S. based companies.

Figure 44

#	SYMBOL	CURRENT SHARES	TRANS PRICE	INITIAL VALUE	CURRENT PRICE	CURRENT VALUE	TODAY'S CHANGE	TODAY'S CHANGE%	PROFIT LOSS	PROFIT LOSS%	TRANS TYPE	ALERT	NOTES
10	AAPL	0.00	0.00	0.00	84.83	0.00	-0.38	-0.45%	0.00	0.00%	Long	N	
51	ACLI	0.00	0.00	0.00	74.25	0.00	+0.12	+0.16%	0.00	0.00%	Long	N	
15	ADS	0.00	0.00	0.00	62.82	0.00	-0.20	-0.32%	0.00	0.00%	Long	N	
13	AEOS	0.00	0.00	0.00	31.63	0.00	-0.48	-1.49%	0.00	0.00%	Long	N	
54	ALB	0.00	0.00	0.00	83.38	0.00	+0.40	+0.48%	0.00	0.00%	Long	N	
7	AMX	0.00	0.00	0.00	48.23	0.00	-0.23	-0.47%	0.00	0.00%	Long	N	
47	ANF	0.00	0.00	0.00	82.87	0.00	+0.26	+0.32%	0.00	0.00%	Long	N	
57	ATI	0.00	0.00	0.00	102.59	0.00	+0.23	+0.22%	0.00	0.00%	Long	N	
38	BAB	0.00	0.00	0.00	112.65	0.00	+0.02	+0.02%	0.00	0.00%	Long	N	
46	BDC	0.00	0.00	0.00	47.82	0.00	+0.63	+1.34%	0.00	0.00%	Long	N	
30	BLUD	0.00	0.00	0.00	31.85	0.00	+0.11	+0.35%	0.00	0.00%	Long	N	
20	BMC	0.00	0.00	0.00	31.76	0.00	-0.10	-0.31%	0.00	0.00%	Long	N	
40	CBG	0.00	0.00	0.00	37.00	0.00	-0.25	-0.67%	0.00	0.00%	Long	N	
	COH	0.00	0.00	0.00	49.98	0.00	+0.69	+1.40%	0.00	0.00%	Long	N	
3	CROX	0.00	0.00	0.00	55.17	0.00	+2.32	+4.39%	0.00	0.00%	Long	N	
2	CRS	0.00	0.00	0.00	120.57	0.00	+0.50	+0.42%	0.00	0.00%	Long	N	
33	CSCO	0.00	0.00	0.00	27.52	0.00	-0.04	-0.15%	0.00	0.00%	Long	N	
24	CTRP	0.00	0.00	0.00	61.74	0.00	+0.49	+0.80%	0.00	0.00%	Long	N	
11	CTSH	0.00	0.00	0.00	93.68	0.00	-0.80	-0.85%	0.00	0.00%	Long	N	
18	DECK	0.00	0.00	0.00	64.32	0.00	+0.96	+1.52%	0.00	0.00%	Long	N	
41	DIGE	0.00	0.00	0.00	47.31	0.00	-0.55	-1.15%	0.00	0.00%	Long	N	
37	DISH	0.00	0.00	0.00	42.53	0.00	+0.53	+1.26%	0.00	0.00%	Long	N	
8	DSW	0.00	0.00	0.00	42.26	0.00	+0.47	+1.12%	0.00	0.00%	Long	N	
17	FFIV	0.00	0.00	0.00	73.59	0.00	-0.62	-0.84%	0.00	0.00%	Long	N	
19	FMD	0.00	0.00	0.00	48.59	0.00	-0.70	-1.42%	0.00	0.00%	Long	N	
59	GES	0.00	0.00	0.00	84.86	0.00	+1.23	+1.47%	0.00	0.00%	Long	N	
32	GS	0.00	0.00	0.00	216.92	0.00	+0.10	+0.05%	0.00	0.00%	Long	N	
36	GYMB	0.00	0.00	0.00	39.06	0.00	-0.71	-1.79%	0.00	0.00%	Long	N	
34	PHPQ	0.00	0.00	0.00	42.77	0.00	+0.09	+0.21%	0.00	0.00%	Long	N	
29	HXM	0.00	0.00	0.00	83.84	0.00	+0.60	+0.95%	0.00	0.00%	Long	N	
12	ICE	0.00	0.00	0.00	158.32	0.00	+3.24	+2.09%	0.00	0.00%	Long	N	
1	INFY	0.00	0.00	0.00	59.84	0.00	+0.23	+0.39%	0.00	0.00%	Long	N	
21	JWN	0.00	0.00	0.00	58.46	0.00	-0.26	-0.44%	0.00	0.00%	Long	N	
25	KNOT	0.00	0.00	0.00	25.05	0.00	-1.15	-4.39%	0.00	0.00%	Long	N	
42	LOGI	0.00	0.00	0.00	29.13	0.00	+0.01	+0.03%	0.00	0.00%	Long	N	
26	LVS	0.00	0.00	0.00	91.95	0.00	+0.08	+0.09%	0.00	0.00%	Long	N	
56	LVS	0.00	0.00	0.00	91.95	0.00	+0.08	+0.09%	0.00	0.00%	Long	N	

I always include earnings report dates on my watch list. (See figure 44[45] on opposite page for a partial summary of the watch list stocks in my portfolio manager.) The dates of the upcoming or previous earnings reports are noted adjacent to the stock ticker symbols. Highlighted in *yellow* are the stocks whose earnings reports WILL NOT be made public during the next option period and therefore are eligible for purchase and option sale. Highlighted in *blue* are stocks whose earnings will be reported during the first week of the next option period, and therefore will be eligible once the report has been announced.

You will find that the premiums you can hypothetically receive on equities about to report earnings are generally much greater than at other times. This is due to the increased volatility potential. As a result, it will be more tempting to buy that stock and to sell that option.

It is this very same volatility that we want to avoid. Don't make the same mistake I made many times in the past before inserting this rule into my system. I would rather invest in a *safer* 2.5%, one month return, than a possible 5%, one month return with serious downside risk. Put differently....**DON'T GET GREEDY!**

SAME STORE RETAIL SALES STATISTICS

Some companies report these same store sales figures on a monthly basis, thereby creating the same risk and volatility as the earning reports. The rule is the same:

Never sell options on stocks that report monthly, same store sales statistics.

---

45   Investools, www.Investools.com (July 2007).

Here is a list of many of the ticker symbols of these equities that are *banned* from our watch lists as of the writing of this book for the above reason:

AEO	CLE	HOTT	ROST
ANF	COST	JCP	SHRP
ANN	CVS	JOSB	SKS
ARO	DBRN	JWN	SMRT
BEBE	DDS	KSS	SSI
BJ	DG	LDG	TGT
BONT	FD	LTD	TJX
BONT	FDO	NWY	WAG
CACH	FRED	PLCE	WMT
CBK	GPS	PSUN	ZUMZ
CHS	GYMB	RAD	

Some of these equities could very well be great stocks to own, but none of them are appropriate for our system of selling covered calls.

Be alert for other companies that may choose to start reporting monthly same store sales or those that decide to no longer report these figures on a regular basis. In other words, this list can change.

In summary, it is critical to be aware of the earnings and same store sales statistics reports so as to avoid the volatility that our system refuses to endure.

Settle for safe and reject the risky.

.

Chapter 13

Mathematics of Covered Calls

Thus far we have gone through a meticulous process of fundamental and technical analysis to locate the greatest performing, optionable securities in the stock universe. We have placed them in our portfolio manager in the form of a watch list so we can easily monitor our choices.

In Chapter 9, we calculated in-the-money, at-the-money, and out-of-the-money option returns utilizing information we gathered from the option chains.

Let's now get to some real life situations where we have determined which stocks to include in our watch list, but want to *figure out the appropriate stocks to select from our list; how many shares to buy, and how many option contracts to sell.* We also need to be organized, using the appropriate forms to expedite the process, and help limit potential errors.

Example 1: We have $100,000 available and 8 stocks we like:

1.   In figure 45, on the following page, we have selected 8 equities using the same form we used in Chapter 9. The best way to set this up is using the multiple tab page of the *ESOC.*

$100,000$ AVAILABLE

	STOCK	PRICE	ROO RETURN ON OPTION	UPSIDE POTENTIAL	PROTECTION
3|105	ATi	102⁵⁹	2.9%	2.3%	—
3|50	COH	49⁹⁵	2.8%	—	—
3|65⁰⁰	CTSH	93⁶⁸	2%	1.4%	—
3|70	MGM	68⁹⁷	3.1%	1.5%	—
3|35	NOTY	36¹⁹	4%	—	3.4%
3|95	PCP	94⁷ˣ	2.67%	—	—
3|70	PCW	68⁰²	2.4%	2.9%	—
3|45	PENN	45²³	3.4%	—	—

Figure 45

2. We have $100,000 cash available in our account.

3. We divide $100,000 by 8 and get $12,500, the average amount we will spend on each stock.

4. We now divide $12,500 by the price per share of each stock, and round off to the nearest increment

of 100. This will correlate to the number of option contracts we will sell.

5. Figure 46 below demonstrates the final breakdown of the number of shares of each stock that we will purchase. Our total expenditure is about $96,000, leaving $4000 in our cash account to utilize for any potential exit strategies. *Remember not to spend down all your cash.* You want to have the flexibility to buy back the option to close your position.

8 STOCKS/ $100,000/ AVERAGES TO $12,500 PER STOCK		
ATI	$102.59/share	100 shares
COH	$49.98 per share	300 shares
CTSH	$93.68 per share	100 shares
MGM	$68.97 per share	200 shares
NCTY	$36.19 per share	300 shares
PCP	$94.74 per share	100 shares
PCU	$68.02 per share	200 shares
PENN	$45.23 per share	300 shares

Figure 46

Example 2: We have $65,000 available and want to limit our purchases to 5 stocks:

1. We have the same 8 stocks in our watch list.

2.   We have $65,000 to spend, and therefore want to limit our purchases to about 5 stocks. Remember that five stocks in different industries is a good minimal guideline for being adequately diversified.

3.   We evaluate the chart in figure 45 by factoring in Return On Option (ROO), upside potential, and downside protection.

4.   Notice that ATI and COH have similar ROO, but ATI also offers 2.3% downside protection, which COH doesn't.

5.   Notice that PCP offers a slightly higher ROO (2.6%) than does PCU (2.4%)   but PCU offers 2.9% upside potential which we don't get from PCP. By having this form in front of you, you can make better investment decisions.

See form 47 to see what such a chart looks like when using the multiple tab of the option calculator (ESOC). Please note that I used different stocks for this example.

RETURN ON OPTION (ROO) CALCULATOR - MULTIPLE STOCKS

Stock Name or Symbol	Stock $/sh	Option $/sh	Strike $	Expires	Intrisic	Upside	ROO	Up Potential	Prtection
aapl	$ 123.00	$ 7.00	$ 120.00	07/20/07	$ 3.00	$ -	3.3%	0.0%	2.4%
aapl	$ 123.00	$ 4.40	$ 125.00	07/20/07	$ -	$ 2.00	3.6%	1.6%	0.0%
deck	$ 93.91	$ 2.50	$ 95.00	07/20/07	$ -	$ 1.09	2.7%	1.2%	0.0%
mt	$ 64.41	$ 1.90	$ 65.00	07/20/07	$ -	$ 0.59	2.9%	0.9%	0.0%
nile	$ 58.40	$ 1.55	$ 60.00	07/20/07	$ -	$ 1.60	2.7%	2.7%	0.0%
nov	$ 108.93	$ 6.20	$ 105.00	07/20/07	$ 3.93	$ -	2.2%	0.0%	3.6%
nov	$ 108.93	$ 3.50	$ 110.00	07/20/07	$ -	$ 1.07	3.2%	1.0%	0.0%
pcln	$ 64.85	$ 2.10	$ 65.00	07/20/07	$ -	$ 0.15	3.2%	0.2%	0.0%
pot	$ 77.00	$ 3.40	$ 76.62	07/20/07	$ 0.38	$ -	3.9%	0.0%	0.5%
pot	$ 77.00	$ 1.95	$ 80.00	07/20/07	$ -	$ 3.00	2.5%	3.9%	0.0%
vip	$ 104.65	$ 3.50	$ 105.00	07/20/07	$ -	$ 0.35	3.3%	0.3%	0.0%

Figure 47

For a review of the terms, ROO, upside potential, and downside protection see figures 48.

RETURN ON OPTIONS (ROO)

Buy stock @ $48/ share. Cost basis per share is now **$48.**
Sell the $50 call for **$2.00**.

ROO = 2/ 48 = 4.2%

UPSIDE POTENTIAL-SAME EXAMPLE AS ABOVE

Applies ONLY to Out of The Money (OTM) strike prices.

If stock goes above $50, we will capture an additional $2/share in stock appreciation over and above what we got paid for selling the call.

Upside Potential = $2/ 48 (what the stock actually cost us) = 4.2%

At The Money (ATM) strike prices offer <u>NEITHER</u> *Upside Potential nor Downside Protection* * BUT usually provide the GREATEST ROO.

These are terms I made up – You will NOT find them in any books (except mine!).

DOWNSIDE PROTECTION/BUYING DOWN STOCK PRICE
Only Applies to IN-THE MONEY (ITM) Strike Prices

Illustration:

-Buy stock XYZ for $52.00/ share
-Sell to Open (STO) $50 Call for $3.50
   Intrinsic Value = Stock Cost (52) – Strike Price (50) = $2.00
   Extrinsic (Time) Value = Call Bid (3.50) – Intrinsic Value (2.00) = $1.50

If we get "Assigned" the stock will automatically be sold for the strike price of our short option which is $50.00. We paid 52, so there is a reduction of $2.00. We received $3.50 when we sold the call, so we still have the difference (3.50-2.00=**1.50**). That 1.50 is our per share profit.

Accounting Solution:

Start with the 3.50 premium we received for selling the call and divide it into its two parts, the <u>Intrinsic Value which is 2.00</u> and the <u>Extrinsic Value (the remainder) which is 1.50.</u> This Extrinsic Value is your guaranteed profit (3.50 Cost – 2.00 Intrinsic Value . .that part of the option price to you which includes the amount between the Strike Price and the Price of the Option.

Calculations:

ROO = 1.5 (Extrinsic Value)/ 50 (Strike Price) = 3%
   We used the $2.00 intrinsic value in our calculations to "Buy Down" the price of the stock from 52 to 50 ("Buy Down" is my term).

DOWNSIDE PROTECTION
   Intrinsic Value/ Original Cost Basis = 2/52 = 3.8%
   This means we will make our 3% ROO even if the stock drops $2.00 from 52 to 50

Figure 48

6.   The form I take to my computer is demonstrated in figure 49 below. It shows the 5 stocks that I have selected from form 45. If I had previously owned any of these equities, it would be noted in the column marked *own*. I indicated this for MGM and NCTY to demonstrate this point. I am now prepared to buy my stocks and sell the corresponding options.

Figure 49

$65,000 AVAILABLE

FORM TO TAKE TO COMPUTER WHEN READY TO BUY OR SELL

TICKER	PRICE	BUY	OWN	OPTION TICKER	NUMBER OF CONTRACTS	OPTION PREMIUM
ATI	102⁵⁴	100		ATI-CA	1	·300
MGM	68 ⁹²		200	MGM-CN	2	645
NCTY	36 ¹²		300	NGT-CG	3	780 - 357 = 423
PCU	68⁰²	200		PCW-CN	2	320
PENN	45 ·³	300		UQN-CI	3	525

7.   In the example shown in figure 49, $62,083 is spent on the 5 equities. This will leave us about $2900 to initiate exit strategies, if necessary.

8.   We collect $2213 in option premiums. This represents a one month return of 3.56% or 43% annualized. Our efforts have been rewarded!

9.   We enter this information in our portfolio manager option log (see Ch 10, *Portfolio Management*, pg. 107).

Once you have mastered the process of stock selection, organized the information in your portfolio manager, and have access to the appropriate calculation forms, you are well on your way to successful option selling.

I always advise those just starting out to *paper trade* for a few months before investing your hard earned money. Some will catch on quicker than others, but I have learned that there is a huge difference between reading something in a book (even this one!) and actually trading in the real world. Practice first, and then reel in the cash rewards.

In fact, to those of you new to stock investing and option selling, here is a list of three critical points to remember:

1   Paper trade before risking your hard-earned money.

2.   Then paper trade some more.

3   When you think you're ready, paper trade a little longer.

C O N G R A T U L A T I O N S !

Now you're ready to start *cashing in on covered calls.*

Many investors new to stock investing may not have enough cash in their brokerage account to properly diversify. The next chapter addresses a course of action to deal with this situation.

Chapter 14

Diversification and Dollar Cost Averaging

Diversification

Diversification is a risk management technique that mixes a wide variety of investments within a portfolio. In a stock portfolio it means selecting equities from different industry of our economy. The rationale behind this technique contends that a portfolio of different types of stocks, will, on average, yield higher returns and represent a lower risk than any single investment found in the portfolio. Risk reduction, as I've referenced throughout this book, is the primary objective of this system.

In my view, your portfolio should have a minimum of five stocks from different industries. Therefore, only 20% of your stock portfolio will be negatively impacted if one particular industry takes a dramatic downturn. It would be even better if you can include closer to ten stocks in your portfolio.

Determining which industry a stock is in can be gleaned from the IBD web site. From the IBD homepage click on the link that reads: *Get IBD Stock Checkup*. The industry group will appear on this checkup page just below the heading that reads: *Performance within industry.*

When selling options, you must own at least 100 shares of that particular equity. This is because an option contract (almost always) consists of 100 shares of the underlying equity. Thus, all stocks are purchased in increments of 100 shares. Now we are faced with two types of *balance objectives*:

1. **Group Balance -** where we own equities in at least five different industries so that no one industry represents more than 20% of our portfolio.

2. **Investment Dollar Balance -** where the amount of money we have invested in each equity should not supersede 20% of our total portfolio value. For example, one hundred shares of an $80 stock is an eight thousand dollar investment. The same 100 shares of a $20 stock is only a two thousand dollar investment. If we own five stocks in five different groups, worth $20,000, each equity *does* meet our criteria of 20% of group diversification. However, the $80 stock represents 40% of our total investment, twice as much as we would prefer to allow. Meeting both criteria requires a certain amount of capital. If this is not an issue we proceed to balance our portfolio with some of the greatest performing stocks in the stock universe. Remember, five stocks at a minimum. Ten are better. If you are well organized and have mastered the system, you can have 20-25 stocks. There is no magic number that is right for each and every investor. The only rule I have is a five stock minimum, with a financially balanced portfolio. I leave it up to you to determine your comfort level as to how many stocks you can manage.

Exchange Traded Funds (ETFs)

What do we do if we do not have the financial resources to balance our portfolio with the two criteria we have set forth?

That's when we turn to *Exchange Traded Funds or ETFs*, which combine the features of a mutual fund with those of a stock. Like mutual funds, ETFs track either a broad index of the stock or bond market, stock industry sector, or international stock. ETFs move up or down as the stocks or bonds they are tracking move. However, these funds trade like stocks insofar as you can buy and sell throughout the trading day, which you cannot do with mutual funds.

When you buy an ETF, you are NOT buying shares of a stock or shares of a mutual fund. You are purchasing units of ownership in a trust that holds shares of the stocks or bonds tracked by a particular index, such as the S&P 500. The percentage of stocks owned is in almost exact proportion to the weighting of the stocks in that index. In effect, an ETF is like an index fund, since you are buying the composition of the entire index. Therefore, an ETF offers a level of diversification that would be difficult to achieve on your own or through outright ownership of individual stocks, yet it trades and behaves like an individual stock. You can buy and sell your shares during the course of the trading day and there is no minimum investment amount that there is with many mutual funds. We are, however, obligated to purchase 100 shares minimum for purposes of selling options. Each option contract you sell, with an ETF as the underlying asset, represents 100 shares of that ETF, similar to individual stocks. The key point to be made is that because an ETF consists of a basket of stocks being tracked, there is **automatic diversification.** One share of an ETF tracking the S&P 500 is diversified into 500 equities! For the *best diversification,* consider the funds that track the broader market indices like the aforementioned S&P 500 or the Wilshire 5000.

On the next page I've listed the most popular Exchange Traded Funds available at the time of this writing that you can sell options on

Most Popular Exchange Traded Funds
(you can sell options on)

- ✓ QQQQ Nasdaq-100 Trust 1
- ✓ SPY SPDR Trust; 1
- ✓ IWM iShares; Russ 2000 Idx
- ✓ EWJ iShares; Japan
- ✓ XLE Sel Sector; Energy SPDR
- ✓ SMH Semiconductor HOLDRS
- ✓ OIH Oil Service HOLDRS
- ✓ XLF Sel Sector; Finl S SPDR
- ✓ DIA DIAMONDS Trust 1
- ✓ EEM iShares; MSCI emerging Market
- ✓ EFA iShares; MSCI EAFE Idx
- ✓ EWZ iShares; Brazil
- ✓ MDY MidCap SPDR Trust; 1
- ✓ XHB Streettracks Ser Tr
- ✓ RTH Retail HOLDRS
- ✓ EWT iShares; Taiwan
- ✓ XLU Sel Sector; Util SPDR
- ✓ IYR iShares; Dow US Rl Est
- ✓ XLB Sel Sector; Matris SPDR
- ✓ FXI iShares; FTSE/Xinhua
- ✓ TLT iShares; Lehm 20+ Trs

For me personally, I prefer the QQQQs (the Qs) because the options produce respectable returns and I simply have a preference for the *Nasdaq 100 tracking stocks.* For years, I have been generating hundreds of dollars of income into my (now 83 year old) mother's brokerage account selling options on the Qs . At least once a month, I call my Mom and tell her how much money she can withdraw from her account as a result of selling options on the Qs. *This has made a difference in her life.*

I must tell you that I get more satisfaction with the hundreds of dollars a month I generate for my mother each month, than the thousands I make for myself. Now, I am in the process of teaching this system to my sons who are finally ready to listen to *investment talk* after many years of their education. As I write this book, Jared is a psychiatrist, Craig is an attorney, and David is a recent college graduate. All will earn good incomes in their respective professions. However, I am confident that selling options will become part of their portfolio strategy and will make a positive impact on the quality of their lives. Why not do the same for your family?

Dollar Cost Averaging Into The Exchange Traded Funds:

As we are accumulating capital and equities (stocks and ETFs) to lay the foundation for our covered call selling, our system requires us to keep within the spirit of risk reduction. That is why I recommend using a technique called *dollar cost averaging* to get started. This is a technique of buying a fixed dollar amount of a particular investment (like an ETF) on a regular schedule, regardless of the share price. More shares are purchased when the prices are low, and fewer shares are bought when the prices are elevated. This is also referred to as a *constant dollar plan*. Eventually, the average cost per share will become smaller and smaller. Dollar cost averaging lessens the risk of investing a large amount in a single investment at the wrong time.

Dollar Cost Averaging Example:

For example, let's refer to figure 50[46] on the opposite page. Assume you have $12,000 to invest and you are interested in a stock or ETF currently valued at $10 per share. That would allow us to purchase 1200 shares. What if, over the course of the next year, the price of the investment share dropped to $5 per share? Obviously, we would lose half of our investment or $6000. Dollar cost averaging allows us to hedge against such risk.

Instead of initially investing the entire $12,000, we decide to invest $1000 per month for 12 months. Should the price of the stock drop from $10 to $5 per share, as in our hypothetical, we would end up owning many more shares after one year, thereby decreasing our loses. As the price of the equity drops, our $1000 monthly investment will result in the purchase more shares. In the example in Figure 50, you can see the price of the stock and the corresponding number of shares $1000 will purchase. In this example, after one year, you will have purchased 1717 shares as opposed to the 1200 shares if bought initially in one lump sum. This will result in a loss of $3415 as opposed to $6000 thanks to the utilization of dollar cost averaging.

Of course, if the price of our ETF had gone up, we would have less total value because we would own more shares at the higher prices. In this system, risk reduction supersedes profit potential. Therefore,...

we use dollar cost averaging as our means of accumulating ETFs to get started in covered call selling.

---

46   Suze Orman, *The Road To Wealth : A Comprehensive Guide to Your Money (*New York: Penguin Group, 2003), p. 400

400   S T O C K S

DOLLAR COST AVERAGING: AN EXAMPLE		
Month	Price	Shares Bought
1	$10	100
2	$9	111
3	$8	125
4	$7	143
5	$8	125
6	$9	111
7	$6	167
8	$8	125
9	$7	143
10	$6	167
11	$5	200
12	$5	200
TOTAL: $12,000 invested; 1,717 shares bought		

share, and you now have a paper loss of $6,000 on your 1,200 shares.

Dollar Cost Averaging

If you had taken that same $12,000 and invested it using dollar cost averaging, you would have divided up your lump sum and invested the same percentage of it, or the same sum of money, month in, month out, regardless of what the market was doing—in this example, $1,000 per month. And here is how you would have come out in the same scenario. (See the chart above.)

As you can see, by using dollar cost averaging, you are able to buy *more shares* of stock when the price is low, and therefore more shares overall. After one year, instead of having 1,200 shares you have 1,717 shares, and even though the price per share is still down, at $5 per share your holdings are worth $8,585 instead of $6,000 and

your loss on paper is only $3,415, or about $2,585 less than if you had purchased the stock outright.

Comparison:
$3,415 loss with dollar cost averaging
$6,000 loss with outright purchase

But there is continuing good news when you use dollar cost averaging instead of making an outright purchase.

Let's say that after a year, you decide you don't want to invest any more money in your stock but just want to wait and see what happens to it. So you leave your $12,000 invested and become an observer.

Eighteen months later, the market starts to go back up, and slowly but surely the price of the stock you purchased inches back up to $10 a

Figure 50

Once you have accumulated a few hundred shares (I will use 300 or more as a guide), you can start selling options on these ETFs. During this period of building a foundation of equities for option selling, you can practice the system with individual stocks. Set up fictitious accounts and *paper trade,* buying stocks and selling options. Use all the exit strategies as if this were for real. This way, by the time you have built a foundation of capital large enough to diversify into individual stocks, you will be fundamentally and practically prepared to begin trading options. You can also start to familiarize yourself with individual stocks and learn their behavior. This system is mostly *science* but there is a little *art* to it as well. That aspect, where you get a certain *feel* for a specific situation, only comes with experience. Why not start getting that valuable experience during these early stages of your option career?

As an example of this *art and feel* reference, I would like to tell you about my handling of the stock, Apple Computer, in June and July of 2007:

I had been selling options on this equity for years and generating substantial returns. Apple's iPhone was about to be released in June and its earnings report was coming out on July 25th. Because of my familiarity with this equity, I decided to own this stock and not sell options until after the earnings report. This may potentially give me a greater return than the option sale if the result of the report is favorable. Only experience and time will allow you to confidently make such decisions. In the meantime, follow the parameters of the system and you should do quite well. By the way, Apple did have a great earnings report and I generated thousands of dollars into my account that month.

Once you have reached the point where you can purchase at least five individual stocks in five different industries, balanced relatively equally in terms of dollar investment, you can move from ETFs to individual equities. This, in turn, will allow you to move from good returns to great returns!

Thus far, a majority of this book has been spent analyzing fundamental and technical analysis, as well as stock and option calculations. There are, however, other factors that will influence our investment results. Many of these conditions are discussed in the next chapter.

Chapter 15

Other Factors Effecting Stock Performance

Now that we have screened our stocks fundamentally and evaluated them technically, a neophyte investor might believe that these equities can only perform in a positive manner. Although we have increased the odds in our favor of this occurring, it is not necessarily true.

There are other factors which we cannot quantify in our system that influence the price performance of our watch list stocks. These conditions can be broken down into **four main categories**:

1. Changing Information on the Publicly Traded Company

2. Market Psychology

3. Key Economic Indicators

4. Globalization

Changing Information on the Publicly Traded Company

Our system prohibits us from going through an earnings report after having sold an option. It does allow us to own a stock *long* through that report if we feel extremely positive about the company. The fundamentals and technicals can change dramatically as a result of an earnings report. This is a risk we must avoid as an options seller.

This does not preclude the possibility of information surfacing between earnings reports that can reflect negatively on a company's outlook, and therefore, its stock price. Such events as loss of important contracts, key members of the board of directors resigning, corporate fraud (see Enron, Tyco, Worldcom and the like), questionable backdating of stock options, and analysts downgrades are just some of the events that can adversely effect the stock price. We must come to an understanding that no system is perfect and there are many occurrences that cannot be factored into the equation. *There is always some risk in the stock market. Our system merely reduces that risk. It does not eliminate it.* In the long run, we will be handsomely rewarded for assuming this risk!

Market Psychology

This is the overall sentiment or feeling that the market is experiencing at any particular time. Greed, fear, expectations, and circumstances are all factors that contribute to the group's overall investing mentality.

While conventional financial theory describes situations in which all investors in the market behave rationally, not taking into consideration the emotional aspect of the market can sometimes lead to unexpected outcomes that can't be predicted by simply looking at the fundamentals.

Technical analysis uses trends, patterns, and other indicators to assess the market's current psychological state, and will help us to *some* extent predict whether the market is heading in an upward or downward direction. The difficulty is how to quantify and / or predict the effects of human emotions, such as greed and fear, on the performance of our equities.

So often, investors get caught up in **greed.** After all, most of us have a strong desire to acquire as much wealth as possible in the shortest amount of time. The Internet boom of the late 1990's is a perfect example. It seemed that any stock with a ".com" at the end of it was purchased indiscriminately. Buying activity in internet-related companies, many of which were just start-ups, reached a fever pitch. This occurred despite the fact that none of these companies showed a positive earnings report! Investors got greedy, fueling further greed and leading to securities being grossly overpriced. This created a *bubble* which burst in mid-2000 and kept the leading indexes depressed through 2001.

The get-rich mentality makes it difficult to maintain gains and keep to a strict investment plan over the long term, especially amid such frenzy. Former Federal Reserve Chairman, Alan Greenspan, referred to this as the "irrational exuberance"[47] of the overall market. It is crucial, especially in times like these, to stick to our system of fundamental screening and technical analysis. These internet-related stocks NEVER would have made it past our initial fundamental screens since they were all losing money!

Just as the market can become overwhelmed with greed, the same can occur with **fear.** When stocks suffer large losses for a sustained period of time, the overall market can become more fearful of sustaining further losses. Being too fearful can be just as costly as being too greedy.

Just as greed dominated the market during the dot-com explosion, the same can be said of the prevalence of fear following its bust. In their attempts to stem the losses, investors

---

47   Greenspan, Alan. *The Challenge of Central Banking in a Democratic Socity.* Speech presented at Annual Dinner of The American Enterprise Institute for Public Policy Research, Washington, D.C., Dec. 5, 1996.

quickly moved out of the stock market in search of less risky investments. Money poured into money-market securities, stable value funds, and principal-protected funds - all low risk and low return securities. According to the financial media, in 2002, $40 billion dollars left the stock market, and a record $140 billion flowed into the bond market!

This mass exodus out of the stock market shows a total disregard for the long-term historical performance of the equity markets. Remember the long term chart of the S&P 500? It goes up on average 11% per year. The bond market appreciates, on average, 5-6% per year. Why ignore these facts? Granted, losing a large portion of your portfolio is a difficult pill to swallow, but even harder to digest is the thought that the new vehicles that initially received the inflows have very little chance of ever rebuilding that wealth. Let me take you back to one of our three golden rules I presented in Chapter 2: *You must be able to tolerate risk.*

All of this talk of fear and greed relates to the volatility inherent in the stock market. When investors lose their comfort level due to losses or market instability, they become vulnerable to these emotions, often resulting in very costly mistakes.

Avoid getting swept up in the prevailing market sentiment of the day, which can be driven by a mentality of fear and/or greed, and stick to our system of fundamental and technical analysis. Let the numbers and the charts guide us *to* intelligent investment decisions and *away* from emotionally driven mistakes**.**

It is also important to choose a suitable asset allocation mix. For example, if you are an extremely risk-averse person, you are likely to be more susceptible to being overrun by the fear dominating the market, and therefore your exposure to equity securities should not be as great as those who can tolerate more risk. Warren Buffet, one of the most successful investors of our time, was once quoted as saying, "Unless you can watch your stock holding decline by 50% without becoming panic-stricken, you should not be in the stock market."

Market psychology, in particular, greed and fear, are factors that will influence the price of our equities. Technical analysis will give us clues to the market direction these factors are influencing. As long as we are not, ourselves, victims of greed and fear decisions, we can oftentimes utilize the emotions of others to our benefit. Finding a system of investing we are confident in, and adhering to its principals without emotion, is a long term recipe for success.

Key Economic Indicators

These are statistics used to measure current economic conditions as well as to forecast trends. They are used to predict the future profitability potential of public companies. Our economy is quite complex and there are a myriad of these statistics available. During the course of a typical trading week, the market reacts favorably or unfavorably as these pieces of the economic puzzle become available.

Here is a list of SOME of the economic statistics that will affect the market and its equities:

- Inflation Data
- Interest Rates
- Bond Yields
- Employment/Unemployment Statistics
- Income Statistics
- Gross Domestic Product
- Consumer Price Index
- Producer Price Index
- Housing Starts/ Building Permits
- Same Store Sales – Retail / Food Services
- Transportation Economic Indexes
- And many more!

In my view the main concept to take away from these statistics is that they are all part of our American economy. Some will please the market, others will not. One day the market will move up as a result of positive surprise, and the next it could move down on news of a negative report. This is just the nature of a marketplace and one should not make dramatic investment decisions every time there is a market reaction to these numbers.

Just be aware that economic reports can move the market, and our reactions should be tempered by the fact one individual report should not change our investment philosophy.

Should we consistently get negative reports over a period of time (a rare occurrence) in a diverse cross section of these indicators, it may be time to consider safer investment vehicles like *treasuries or money market securities*. Our economy would have to be in lot of trouble for this to occur!

One of the economic factors of concern at the time of the writing of this book is the possible slow motion collapse of the 1.3 trillion dollar, sub-prime mortgage industry and the effect it may have on the rest of the economy. Many believe that it could contribute to widespread credit losses among companies that provide short-term funding to the sub prime lenders. Also of concern are the pension funds, insurance companies, and hedge funds that hold the securities backed by the growing pile of bad loans. These losses could lead to tighter lending standards which will make capital more scarce and contribute to a credit crunch which could stagnate economic growth.

However, at the same time, inflation numbers look good, unemployment statistics are positive, and corporate earnings appear solid. As a result, at this time, I am fully invested in the stock portion of my portfolio.

Globalization

This is the tendency of investment funds and businesses to move beyond domestic and national markets to other markets around the globe, thereby increasing the interrelatedness of different markets. Globalization has had the effect of markedly increasing not only international trade, but also cultural exchange.

The advantages and disadvantages of globalization have been heavily scrutinized and debated in recent years. Proponents say that it helps developing nations *catch up* to industrialized nations much faster through increased employment and technological advances. Critics of globalization say that it weakens national sovereignty and allows rich nations to ship domestic jobs overseas where labor is much cheaper. Whichever side of the debate you fall on, it appears that globalization is here to stay and must be factored into our investment decisions.

One prominent example of how globalization can affect our economy, and therefore our investment decisions, is the **currency carry trade.** This is a strategy in which an investor sells a certain currency with a relatively low interest rate and uses the funds to purchase a different currency yielding a higher interest rate. A trader using this strategy attempts to capture the difference between the rates - which can often be substantial depending on the amount of leverage the investor chooses to use.

Here is an example of a **yen carry trade:**

A trader borrows 1,000 yen from a Japanese bank, converts the funds into U.S. dollars (USD), and buys a bond for the equivalent amount. If the bond pays 4.5% and the Japanese interest rate is set at 0%, the trader stands to make a profit of 4.5% if the exchange rate between the two countries does not change. The big risk is the uncertainty of the exchange rate. In the above example, if the U.S. dollar were to fall in value relative to the Japanese yen, then the trader would run the risk of losing money. If heavily leveraged, huge risks could occur.

In March of 2007, this very issue was dominating the financial news. The Japanese economy has been strengthening, leading to conjecture that their policy of 0% interest rates could be coming to an end. This policy has lasted for more than ten years and is the first source of potential liquidity bubbles here in the U.S.

There are literally trillions of USD of yen carry trade positions scattered amongst hedge funds, insurance companies, and mutual funds. The concern is that if the Yen Carry Trade is *unwound*, US treasuries will become less desirable. Other markets in this country, and worldwide, could be adversely affected. There could be a massive liquidity reduction, thereby driving down the prices of US securities and those of other markets around the world.

Our already elaborate and complex economy is now further complicated (exponentially) by the fact that globalization has to be factored in. This should not frighten us from investing in our great economy. It should just require us to be aware of the factors that will effect our investments so we have an understanding as to why our equities are performing the way they do. Remember, we are investing in the greatest economy in the world. From that pool, we are accepting only the greatest performing stocks. The odds are with us!

Although the amount of information necessary to make your investment decisions has increased dramatically over the years, there are many factors that are quite favorable for the average investor. For example, information can be gathered in a matter of seconds via the internet. Software programs can filter through the information and allow you to come to instantaneous conclusions. Also, US security laws have made disclosure so transparent that the blue collar investor nearly stands on equal ground with many Wall Street *big shots*. Furthermore, the commissions for online trading are so low that it has become a *non-event*.

All in all, for the average blue collar investor like you and me, the world of trading US securities has become a beautiful place to call home!

Earlier in this book, we started our search for the *greatest performing stocks* by checking the IBD 100 list in the Monday edition of the *Investor's Business Daily*. However, over the years, I have found other sources of locating cash-generating securities. These will be discussed in the following chapter.

Chapter 16

Additional Sources for Locating the Greatest Performing Stocks

The IBD 100 is not the only source I use for locating the greatest current day performing stocks. It is my main source for locating equities to sell options on, and, in reality, other sources aren't necessary. But why shut doors when there may be gems hiding behind them?

Stocks Increasing in Price on High Volume

Another place I look is on the IBD Home Page (www.investors.com) under the section entitled *Stocks On the Move.* Here we have a daily list of stocks that have gone up in price on a high increase in volume %, or in the number of shares traded. This normally is indicative of buying pressure from the institutional players. Oftentimes, this is a train we want to be on. I run these stocks through all the screens we previously discussed. Each week, I locate a few gems from this source that will be added to my watch list.

Stocks Hitting New 52-Week Highs

Another area I check periodically is the **MSN Money Central** site for **Stock Power** searches:

http://moneycentral.msn.com/investor/finder/
deluxestockscreen.aspx?query=New+52-Week+Highs

I particularly like the search for stocks with new *52 week highs*. These are equities trading at the highest price they have achieved in the last year. We check to see which of these stocks are optionable, and then run them through the system screens. I will often uncover some gems from this source, as well. Generally, I will look at those screened stocks whose price is $20 or more. I value this particular screen because it shows price momentum, institutional support, and no selling pressure from those who purchased the stock at a higher price and are looking to *get their money back.*

Stocks With Superior Analyst Support

Another stock screener I have utilized is at the **Yahoo's Finance site:**

http://screen.yahoo.com/ca?gr=175%2F&grfy=175%2F
&ar=1%2F2&pr=5%2F&b=1&z=grfy&db=stocks&vw=1

This screen is especially useful for those who value analyst opinions. It gives us the following information:

Strong Forecasted Growth

This screen displays companies with solid growth forecasts, and that averages a *buy rating* or better from Wall Street analysts. The screen also filters stocks out with share prices less than $5 in order to separate more speculative investments on the *OTC Bulletin Board.* These stocks are also projected to have a 1-year and a 5-year earnings growth of 25% or better. For those of you who value the opinion of professional analysts, this site is for you. Make sure you run the screened stocks through our system, and again look only at stocks valued at $20 or more.

Jim Cramer's *Mad Money* Television Program

This is one of the most, if not the most, entertaining program on the tube. That is amazing since the content is based on the financial markets, a subject that does not normally create a lot of excitement.

Jim Cramer is a former hedge fund manager who has helped millionaires make millions more. Now he is focused on making money for the middle class, for the blue collar investor, like you and me.

His genius is evident in his knowledge of nearly every stock he is questioned about. It is even more apparent in his quick wit and humor. Mr. Cramer (whoops, that's his father).... Jim readily admits that he can't be correct with every call he makes, and therefore tells his viewers: "Do your homework." **Great Advice!** He means run it through our system!

I have found his assessments of many of the equities he discusses make a lot of sense. Does that mean we should go out and purchase every equity that he mentions? *Absolutely not*. However, let's take those stocks that he mentions and that catch our attention, and evaluate them fundamentally and technically. If they meet our criteria that means that the equity has passed two tests, ours and that of Jim Cramer. Now we've got something to give serious consideration to. Each week, I find a few stocks that I add to my watch list as a result of watching this entertaining and energetic program. *I highly recommend it.*

Keeping your eyes and ears open:

Here are more avenues to consider in locating the greatest performing stocks in the stock universe.

- o   One day, in my dental practice, I had a young woman in my chair who was talking about her upcoming wedding. She was telling me that she located a band, a caterer, a source for invitations, a flower specialist, and many other related businesses, all from one single web site called *The Knot.* She was bestowing accolade upon accolade on this site. It made her life cost effective, simpler, and took all the stress out of making wedding plans. I was so impressed with everything she had to say about this site that I decided to check it out when I got home. First and foremost, I had to determine if it was a publicly traded company. I went to a financial site and typed in "KNOT". Sure enough it WAS a publicly traded company! I ran it through *the system* and it passed with flying colors. Selling options on the KNOT proceeded to generate over $1000 for me over the next three months, until an earnings report sent it south, temporarily.

- o   My wife went shopping with a friend. When she returned, I was told of this wonderful experience she had having lunch at a restaurant called the *Cheesecake Factory.* I checked it out.

- o   *Borders Bookstore* and *Staples* are two of my favorite places to shop.   These are both publicly traded companies I have run through my system.

What are yours favorite web sites, businesses, restaurants, and places to shop? Why not check them out? You can become part owner of the very store you are browsing in. How about at work? *Who do you do business with?* As a dentist,

I checked out *Henry Schein* Dental Supply, and others. Who can you check out?

Running these companies through our system only takes a minute or two. Every so often you will find gold, and it will pay dividends many times over. Just by keeping your eyes and ears open you can create additional streams of income.

Stock Splits

I will also check companies announcing stock splits as a possible source for watch list candidates. Checking these, along with the other situations mentioned above, is going to make you an elite, successful, and wealthy investor. See the following chapter on stock splits for more information on this subject.

Chapter 17

Stock Splits

A stock split refers to a corporate action that increases the number of shares in a public company. The price of the shares are adjusted such that the *before and after* market capitalization (number of outstanding shares times the stock price) of the company remains the same and *dilution* (reduction in the earnings per share due to an increase in the number of shares) does not occur. Options are included.

Market Capitalization Example - using small numbers for demonstration purposes:

A company has 100 shares of stock outstanding, each with a price of $50. The market capitalization is 100 x $50 = $5000. The company splits its stock "2-for-1." There are now 200 shares of stock and each shareholder holds twice as many shares. The price of each share has been adjusted to $25. The market capitalization is 200 x $25 = $5000, the same as before the split.

Ratios of 2-for-1, 3-for-1, and 3-for-2 splits are the most common, but any ratio is possible. The biggest I've seen was a 10-for-1 split approximately 4 years ago

It is often claimed that stock splits, in and of themselves, lead to higher stock prices. Research, however, does not bear this out. What is true is that stock splits are usually initiated after a large run up in share price. Momentum investing would suggest that such a trend would continue regardless of the stock split. The fact that a stock has run up and split makes it an interesting equity to look at, and one to run through our system.

Other effects of a split could be psychological. If many investors think that a stock split will result in an increase in price, and therefore, they purchase the stock, the share price will tend to increase. Others contend that the management of a company, by initiating a stock split, is implicitly conveying its confidence in the future prospects of the company.

If you have sold options that expire after the stock split has occurred, the option series will need to be adjusted. The expiration date will remain the same. What is altered is the number of contracts sold, the strike price, and the contract ticker symbol.

In **FIGURE 51** below, I show you a *real life example*:

REAL LIFE EXAMPLE

- Buy 100 shares of POT @ $205
- Sell 1 contract of the June /210 @ $530
- ROO = 2.6% (1 month) = 31% annualized.
- Upside potential = 2.4%
- Stock splits 3-for-1 before expiration

Figure 51

1. I purchased 100 shares of POT @ $205 per share.

2. Then, 1 contract of the June/$210 was sold @ $530. This gave me a 2.6%-1-month return, with upside potential of 2.4% if the stock reached $210 by expiration Friday.

3. The stock splits 3-for-1 prior to expiration.

4. Note *the pre and post split comparison (Figure 51a)*:

   a. Initial profit from the option sale and expiration date remains the same.

   b. The number of shares triples.

   c. The cost basis is cut in thirds.

   d. Market capitalization does not change.

   e. The number of contracts sold triples.

   f. The contract ticker symbol changes.

Pre and Post Split Comparison

- $530 initial profit

- Expires June 15th

- Own 100 shares

- Cost basis is $205

- Sold (1) June/210

- Ticker is PVZ FB

- $530 initial profit

- Expires June 15th

- Own 300 shares

- Cost basis is 68.33

- Sold (3) June/70

- Ticker is PVZ FN

Figure 51a

By the way, POT did surpass the strike price, and my total 1-month return was the initial 2.6% plus the 2.4% upside potential, for a total of a 1-month 5% return!

Mergers and Acquisitions

Another (rarer) occurrence that will effect our option contracts are *Mergers and Acquisitions*. These are also referred to as *M and A's*. A *Merger* is when two companies combine to form a new company. An *Acquisition* is the purchase of one company by another with no new company being formed.

Option contract information on both *stock splits* and *M and A's* can be obtained as follows:

- o   Go to www.cboe.com

- o   Go to *tools.*

- o   Type in ticker to access information.

You can also sign up for a free service for split announcements at:

www.InvestmentHouse.com

Another site to go to for upcoming and recent stock splits is:

http://biz.yahoo.com/c/s.html

Let me emphasize that you should NOT purchase a stock simply because it has announced a split. There are times when a company announces a split (with the approval of the shareholders) simply to attract interest. Do not be fooled. Make sure the chart and fundamentals justify such a split. However, if there is a stock already on your watch list that also announces a split, you may want to give that equity stronger consideration as I did in the case of POT.

Coming up……the big, impressive finish!

Conclusion

YOU **CAN** DO THIS !

My system is based predominantly on common sense. This is not rocket science!

Read The Book.

Watch The DVDs.

Listen To The CDs.

This time investment will pay dividends for years, and decades to come. Pass it on to your children, your parents, and anyone who wants to take control of their financial lives. It took me years to develop this system....It will take you only months to master it!

PUTTING IT IN PERSPECTIVE

I have mentioned that I generate *monthly* returns of 2%-4%. While you are learning the system, the returns will be at the lower end of the range. As you improve your skills, monthly returns of greater than 3% will be quite the routine.

Let's look at the impact of these small, but consistent, monthly returns over the long haul:

We will assume a *conservative,* 1-month option return of 2% in this example:

For this hypothetical, we have $100,000 to invest. I refer you now to the **Rule of 72.** This rule states that if you divide the *annual* rate of return of your investment into the number 72, the resulting figure is the approximate number of years that it will take you to double your money.

If you invest this amount of money in a 6% CD, you will have $200,000 in 12 years (72 divided by 6=12).

Now let's take that same $100,000 investment, and 12 year time frame, and sell options @ 2% per month:

2% per month annualizes to 24% per year. We divide 24 into 72 and get 3. Therefore, every three years we double our money. Here is where the fun begins:

- At the end of year 3 our $100,000 doubles to $200,000.
- At the end of year 6 our $200,000 doubles to $400,000.
- At the end of year 9 our $400,000 doubles to $800,000.
- At the end of year 12 our $800,000 doubles to a staggering **1.6 million dollars!**

Even more breathtaking is a monthly return of 3% which would generate a 12 year return of **6.4 million dollars!**

How's that for cashing in on covered calls?

To recap…

- ❖   Learn the system.

- ❖   Become CEO of your money.

- ❖   Keep hitting those singles and doubles.

- ❖   Become financially independent.

A FAVOR

Please send me emails of your success stories.

At the very least, they will put a smile on my face.

More than likely, though, they will bring a tear to my eye.

Wishing you all the best as you are *cashing in on covered calls,*

Alan G. Ellman

APPENDIX I

Quick Start Form

I. Buy Monday Edition of Investors Business Daily – Section B

- Circle all stocks with an "o" next to the price. These are optionable stocks.

USE STOCK WATCH LIST LOCATOR FORM FOR II, III, and IV

(see Appendix V: FORMS herein)

II Go to www.investors.com

- Type in ticker and hit *get quote.*

- Scroll down under price chart.

- Look for *SmartSelect* rating.

- Accept only stocks with six green circles.

III. Research institutional components

- Mean Analyst Rating (accept 3 or less)

- On Balance Volume (favor "trend up" and "trend steady"

IV. Go to www.stockcharts.com

- Set up chart as per figure 28.

- Accept only those equities with a favorable chart pattern.

V. Place all stocks remaining from screening process onto a **watch list.**

VI. Go to http://biz.yahoo.com/research/earncal/today.html or

www.earningswhispers.com

Access ER dates and avoid those companies reporting during the current contract period.

VII. Use **option calculator (ESOC)** to determine return on option (ROO), upside potential, and downside protection, *when ready to sell options.*

VIII. Select an appropriate number of stock/option combinations based on available cash. Make sure you are well diversified with at least 5 stocks in different industries.

IX. Fill out *Form to Take to Computer* before actually buying stock and selling options.

X. Place all stocks purchased and options sold in your **portfolio manager.**

XI. Keep track of your monthly option profits in your **option log.**

XII. Be alert for possible **exit strategies**, especially if option value drops to .20 or lower.

APPENDIX II

E-mail Alerts
The Evolution of *The Blue Collar* Blog

The Blue Collar Investment seminars were entreed in early 2007. I watched, with excitement, as my students hungered for more. Week after week, their craving for stock option information grew exponentially, and I realized the importance of feeding this growing appetite between meals... I mean workshops. So, I decided to expand the menu.

It was clear that real life samples of trades I'd made, not made, and the reasons why would be the most palatable way to churn education into practical application. I categorized my trades into the principals and concepts I'd presented at my seminars. When needed, I expanded the main course of basic, trading data with delectable details to further the experience.

These recipes described why I bought or sold certain equities or options, and became known as my *E-mail Alerts*, or simply, *E-Alerts*.

The reviews were amazing! I was inundated with critical praise, and thanked for mincing didactic ideas into a user-friendly cuisine of digestible tips and information. This franchise was on the move! I knew, then, it was time to Blog. So I added one to my website, TheBlueCollarInvestor.com. Now I can feed the world!

My goal for you is to invest with the same confidence I enjoy, to dine on the intrinsic value of my early e-alerts that follow, and to feast on the success that awaits just beyond. Go ahead. Turn the page. No reservation necessary.

For desert, visit my Blog at www.thebluecollarinvestor.com/blog.

January 25, 2007

Hi to all,
Here is an example of a stock I recently added to my watch list:
Value Click
Ticker symbol: VCLK

IBD Rating: A plus; left column A or better; group technical B

MSN Rating 7

Stock trading above it's 20 day moving average

Option return (3 weeks to expiration):

> Stock trades @ $25.71 or $2571 for 100 shares= 1 contract
> Feb. $25 call option (In The Money) sells for $1.25 or $125 per contract
> 3 week profit % is 125 divided by 2571= 4.86%
> Since there are 52 weeks per year, this annualizes to 83% per year

If called out you sell at $25 but purchased at $25.71 so you lose $71 on the sale of the stock.

This will bring your 3 week return down to 2.16% which annualizes out to 36%, still not bad. Either you Win or you WIN.

To those of you just starting out, give yourselves a few months to fully grasp all these concepts......that's what it took me.
Best regards.
Alan

January 27, 2007

Hi to All,
Linda spent the morning going through the IBD 100 while I was at work.
She found some GREAT STOCKS that are eligible to be added to my watch list.Below are 5 of those stocks along with 3 that just missed.
See if you can find the 5 winners and the 3 imposters. I will post the answer on Monday:

NYX
BLUD
CBG
VIP
STLD
SYX
DLB
GS

Also those planning to attend the 1st advanced workshop and haven't responded as to your availability please let me know BY SUNDAY:
ARE YOU AVAILABLE FEB. 22nd, MARCH 1st OR BOTH.
Thank you.
Alan

January 29, 2007

Hi to all,

1- OUR CLASS OVERWHELMINGLY VOTED TO CHANGE THE DATE OF OUR NEXT SEMINAR TO MARCH 1st. There were 2 or 3 of you who could only make the 22nd. I will be calling you shortly to make other arrangements since this is a seminar I don't want you to miss and setting the original date during holiday was my oversight. The , now, official date of Advanced Workshop I is March 1st. Thanks for your cooperation.

2- The answer to our Saturday quiz:

the 5 winning stocks eligible to be added to my watchlist are:
NYX, CBG, VIP, STLD, and GS

the 3 imposters were:

BLUD- due to B- attractiveness rating on left column of IBD site
We require a B+ rating or better

DLB- due to the D- Technical group rating on the right column of the IBD site. We require a C or better.

SYX- due to a stock rating of 3 on the money central site.
We require a rating of 5 or better.

3- Due to the incredible number of positive and complimentary emails I have received, I have decided to devote an entire chapter in the book I'm writing to your testimonials.
Prior to publication , I will be contacting some of you to get permission to use your names.

Remember, all novices should only be paper trading at this point. There is a lot more to be told.
Best regards,
Alan

January 31, 2007

Greetings,
Some of you may have noticed that on Tuesday KNOT dropped $1.69.
I checked the news and could find no substantive reason for the drop.
In the last few months this stock has gone from the low 20's to the low 30's.
A drop of this magnitude for no apparent reason often times means profit taking by the "big boys".
I view it as a stock "on sale".
I purchased 400 shares @ 30.44 and sold the Feb. $30 option @ 1.50, kicking $590 into my account. This is a 2 1/2 week return of 5%.
If called out (this is in the money by .44) my 2 1/2 week return would drop to 3.5% or 70% annual.
Getting stocks on sale is another way of enhancing your already significant option returns.
Let me know if you find any such sales.
Al

February 4, 2007

Hi to all,
Yesterday I was bringing in my copy of IBD which had been delivered to my home. As I walked into my house, Linda grabbed the paper from me and started circling stocks. Then she went upstairs to our computer to start running these stocks through our system.
I think I've created a monster!......BEWARE OF OPT-ZILLA!!!!!

As you develop a watch list, you will find that many of the stocks you circle are already on your that list. Simply cross them off and save time in your screening process.

Here are three of the stocks that Linda found that I am adding to my watch list (keeping an eye on them, not necessarily buying them- that depends on option returns and a few other factors that we will get into in upcoming seminars).

POT
PENN
PCAR

Once again, those of you new to option trading should only be paper trading at this point.
Best reagrds,
Alan

February 6, 2007

Last week I heard on CNBC that an analyst had upgraded Abercrombie and Fitch. I normally don't pay much attention to analysts because they're wrong as often as they're right.
In this case it caught my attention because it is a stock I've owned and profited from in the past. Although it is not in the IBD 100, I ran it through my system and now it's on my watch list. Check it out and see what you think. The ticker is ANF.
Keep your eyes and ears open You may shop in a store that really impresses you. Find out if it's a publicly traded company and if so, run it through the system. You may find a gem that will pay for your next cruise!
Alan

February 11, 2007

Hi to all,
A very interesting occurence happened this week with one of my option trades. I'd like you all to follow along because it demonstrates a way to make extremely high returns on your investments:

1- on Jan. 26th I purchased 200 shares of PCU @ $59.69
2- I immediately sold the Feb. $60 (out-of-the-money) for $1.45
3- This represented a 2.4% 1-month return or 29% annualized.
4- Amazingly, I was called out of this stock on Feb. 8th (the option was exercised and my stock was sold at $60 -currently selling at market for $64). This is only the 3rd time in 8 years that I have been called out of a stock before expiration Friday....NO BIG DEAL!
5- Since I bought PCU @ 59.69 and sold for $60, the additional profit brings my 1-month return to 2.9% or 35% annualized.
6- Now I have 12k sitting in the bank (200 shares x $60)....got to put it to work! Normally with only 1 week left to expiration you cannot find a good stock buy/option sale for Feb. and may have to look to the March expirations....BUT I DID!
7- On Feb. 9th, I puchased 100 shares of ICE @ 146.84 (using the 12k plus a little extra cash in the account).
8- I immediately sold the Feb. $145 (in-the-money) calls for $510 giving me an additional return of 3.8% or 42% annualized.
9- Since I am in the money by $184 (146.84 - 145.00) , if called out my return on this investment will drop to $326 (510 - 184).
10- This will give me an additional 1-month return of 2.2% or 27% annualized.
11- AT MINIMUM my 1-month return is as follows (per contract):

    a- $145 for sale of PCU option
    b- $31 for sale of PCU stock
    c- $326 for sale of ICE option (if called out- worst case scenario)
12- This is a total return of $502 on an investment of $5969 (per contract)
13- You have accomplished a 1-month return of 8.4% or 101% annualized!!!!!!!!!!

All of you continuing on with the advanced workshops will continue to receive these email alerts for free throughout the seminar series.
I hope you find them interesting and helpful.
Alan

February 13, 2007

Today was a great example of why you don't want to sell options on stocks when their earnings reports are coming out during that option period.
Such an example was the Knot. The earnings report wasn't bad at all but below what the "market" was expecting. The stock took a $5.99 hit!
My system is all about risk reduction. At a future workshop, I will talk about how to get out of stocks about to report earnings and back in after the report.
As far as this stock is concerned, I would wait for it to get above its moving average and then consider it a "stock on sale".
Congratulations to those of you who have started generating income by selling options.
Beginners should only be paper trading at this point.
To those of you who haven't quite caught on yet, DO NOT WORRY. There is a learning curve. It took me a while also.
My goal is for each and every one of you to become successful at selling options.
Alan

February 17, 2007

Greetings,
On Feb. 11th I sent you an email explaining that I was called out on PCU and used the cash to purchase 100 shares of ICE @ 146.84 per share. I immediately sold the option and made $510 or 3.8% for 1 week.
Yesterday I used one of the exit strategies I will be discussing at the March 1st seminar to avoid getting called out on my stock. ICE closed yesterday @ $158.32 and I sold a deep in-the-money option generating another $370 into my account. That is a 5 week return of $880 or 6% (over 72% annualized).
If called out, I will lose $184 on the sale of the stock, but my 5 week return will still be 4.8% or 48% annualized.
This return is GUARANTEED even if ICE drops $13.32 to $145!
Your average monthly returns will be more in the 2-4% per month range but as you get better at mastering the system, a play like this one will not be uncommon.
I will go over exit strategies using in-the-money strike prices at the next seminar.

By the way, last week I noticed a stock that I never heard of before (NCTY) was trading on high volume (I ask myself what do the big boys know that we don' t? Doesn't matter-we just know they're up to something). This is NOT a stock on the IBD 100 but I checked it out. See what you think and especially look at the March $35 in-the-money option and compute the returns.
For those of you having trouble remember we're in elementary school.....3 more seminars till we graduate college. BE PATIENT and I will get you there.
Best to all.
Alan

February 20, 2007

Hello fellow investors,
I'd like to thank Harvey Krug for emailing me a great question regarding this months option premiums. Harvey astutely recognized the fact that this month's returns are lower than the last 2 months.
Here is why:
1- We are past earnings season. This means a decrease in the volatility of the market and therefore the corresponding options.
2- The main reason is that February is a short month. We also lost a trading day due to President's Day. This seriously erodes the "time value" of our options.

We must keep things in perspective. Some months we will get returns over 3%. Should we have months where our returns are between 2 - 2.5% is that so bad? That annualizes to 24-30%.
During the dotcom explosion of the late 90's 25% returns per year were considered a "bonanza". For me, selling options one month out has worked best. This past weekend I did a few hours of preparation and spent about 2 hours on my computer today selling options.
The results: I kicked over $7000 into my account which represented about a 2.5% return. Beats working!
The icing on the cake: I made $825 for my mother selling options on a small % of her stocks.
As always, it's important to recognize that there is some risk. The risk is in the stock, not in selling the option. As you will see in the upcoming seminars, I have gone to an extreme to minimize risk and maximize returns.
There are a few who we haven't heard from regarding the March 1st seminar. If you intend to participate please advise ASAP as we are making the final seating arrangements with the Plainview Holiday Inn.
Regards.
Alan

ps: Thanks for all the kind emails you have sent. I am saving them to use as testimonmials in the book I am writing.

February 23, 2007

Greetings,

Last week, I was driving to my office listening to the financial news.

I heard a story about Allegheny Technology (ATI) , a manufacturer of titanium products. The story reported a labor settlement with its union workers. Sounds kind of boring, doesn't it?

It would have to me as well except that this was a stock that I once owned and profited by. Then it broke down technically (the chart) and I kicked it off my watch list. It does NOT appear on the IBD 100.

At the next traffic light, I made a note to run it through the system. I did so and found a diamond in th rough!

I purchase 100 shares @ $103.45 and sold the March 105 calls for $3.10, generating an immediate monthly profit of 3% or 36% annualized.

As of this writing the stock is trading @ $108.62. If called out @ $105, my proft will increase another $1.55 per share giving me a one month profit of $465. This represents a one month return of 4.5% or 54% annualized.

One of the beautiful aspects of our system is that you can evaluate equities from all sources. Even if you walk into a store that impresses you, run it throught the system (if it's a publically traded company). You never know. Don't depend on others to tell you what to do. Become CEO of your own money!

I have attached directions to the Plainview Holiday Inn for this Thursdays seminar which starts @ 7PM.

In a few days all those registered will receive a copy of the course outline with definitions so as to help you prepare. We will also review the entire Basic Seminar.

Wishing you successful investing results.

Alan

February 25, 2007

Hi,

It is extremely rewarding for me to see how quickly so many of you are catching on. And we have only just begun!

Well, Linda (aka OPT-ZILLA) was at it again this weekend. She found 3 stocks that weren't previously on our watch list:

TSS
PCAR
MT

You may have noticed that on the MSN Money Central site, there was no rating for MT. That is because it is a foreign company that trades on a US Stock Exchange (American Depository Recept or ADR) and this site does not rate such companies. I have decided NOT to eliminate such stocks from my watch list if all other criteria are met.

All those who have registered for Thursday's seminar will receive a course outline with definitions no later than Tuesday to help you prepare.

I am also creating a form that will guide you through the stock evaluation process. It will simplify things until you get more comfortable with the process. This form will be handed out at Thursdays seminar.

Regards to all.

Alan

March 1, 2007

Hi to all,

Two weeks ago I heard that Goldman Sachs had downgraded American Airlines.
I didn't think much of it but was slightly curious why all of a sudden an analyst would downgrade a stock in an industry that had been suffering for so long.
Last week I heard another story that may or may not be related.
Evidently there are rumors that Goldman Sachs is forming a conglomerate that may try to buy American Airlines!
Is it possible that the downgrade was a precursor to such a deal? Drive the price down before a buyout. Well, probably not but you never know.
The point here is that you should always take an analyst upgrade or downgrade with a bit of skepticism. That is why it is so critical that you are able to make your own decisions.
Gather all the information and come to your own conclusions.
Wishing you all the best.
Alan

March 6, 2007

Greetings,
Today I will walk you through an evaluation of Cabot Oil (COG).
This stock caught my eye because I previously owned it and last week it announced a 2-for-1 stock split.
Here is the breakdown:
1-IBD website:
    Overall Diagnosis- A-
    Technical- A
    Of special note: this stock is rated #1 out of 105 stocks in its industry!
    Fundamental- A-
    Attractiveness- B+
    GROUP TECHNICAL- D- uh oh!.....but let's move on anyway.

2- MSN Money Central Scouter (risk- reward)
    Scouter Rating of 10- highest possible rating

3- Technical Analysis
    Short term moving average (20-d EMA) above long term (100-d EMA)
    Price Bar above 20-d EMA

4- Option Return
    Buy stock @ $65.50
    Sell **APRIL $65** (too close to March expiration) @ $3.40. This is an in-the-money strike price (below $65.50)
    Use .50 of the $3.40 premium to "buy down" the stock price to $65
    Our profit becomes $2.90 (3.40 - .50) divided by our cost basis of $6500 ($65-per share x 100 shares per contract).
    This is a return of 4.5% for 6 weeks or 38% annualized.
    * I know calculations have been a problem for some of you. I will be going through these calculations over and over again the last 2 seminars.

WHAT TO DO?
The Group Technical Rating of D- prohibits us from buying this stock or selling options on it. However, it is an intriguing stock.
I put a "post-it" note near my computer and keep an eye of the Group Technical rating. When the "big boys" start buying energy stocks, I am ready to jump in and enjoy the ride. It will happen, just a matter of time.
Good luck to all.
Alan

March 11, 2007

Greetings fellow investors,

GREAT IDEA- before I get into the "meat and potatoes of this alert, I must tell you about a great idea one of the members of our class thought of (I can't recall who it was). He pays his 7 year old child $2 per week to go through the IBD 100 and circle the optionable stocks. It is not the 10 minutes of time that he saves that makes this brilliant. It is getting your children involved with reading the financial papers and starting to get a basic understanding of investing. This can surely lead to a child going through the IBD and MSN sites as well. It is so easy, a 7 year old can do it. This is a skill you can pass on from generation to generation. Our education system is seriously lacking in this area, but now it's something you can pass on to them. This is such a good idea that I have decided to include it in the book I'm writing (almost done!)
In my home (no kids here anymore!), Linda locates the stocks and I evaluate them for option sales based on premium returns. It is a family affair. Why not make it a family affair in your home as well?

Today I would like to take you through a technical analysis of Astec Industries, Inc. (ASTE), a company I recently added to my watch list.
PLEASE PRINT OUT THE CHART I ATTACHED TO THIS EMAIL AND FOLLOW ALONG.

1- Point 1- we see the short ter^m moving average (red) drops below the long term (green). Also the price bars are below the 20-d EMA (short term-red). This is a double red flag and certainly a point we would sell a stock if we owned it.

2- Point 2- The price bars rise above the short term EMA, a sign of a possible turnaround. However, the 20d EMA is still below the 100-d EMA (red below green). Although we are alerted to a possible turnaround, this is still not a buy point.

3- Point 3- The 20-d EMA crosses above the 100-d EMA confirming the first positive signal we got at point 2. This is our buy point @ about $27/share.

4- Point 3 through point 4- Price bars have remained at or above the 20-d EMA and the 20-d EMA has remained above the 100-d EMA. No reason to sell. The stock has appreciated about 50% to $40/share in 4 1/2 months.

Although we are not privy to all the information the mutual and hedge fund managers evaluate, by looking at the charts we can make educated assessments as to their thinking. We may not know the particulars, but we can determine whether they are buyers or sellers. Once the technicals are in place, we jump aboard and let them take us money-making ride.
We will be adding a few more technical indicators at the last seminar.

All those registered for the March 22nd seminar will receive a course outline with the associated definitions no later tha March 20th. There will be additional handouts at the seminar.

Those in need of "extra help", I will be offering a free 1/2 Q&A session from 6:30-7PM prior to the March 22nd seminar. No need to contact me, just show up.

I want to thank you for your constructive comments and positive feedback. I value your opinions as I am always looking to improve the quality of these seminars.
Best regards.
Alan

E-1   CHART [48] - March 11, 2007

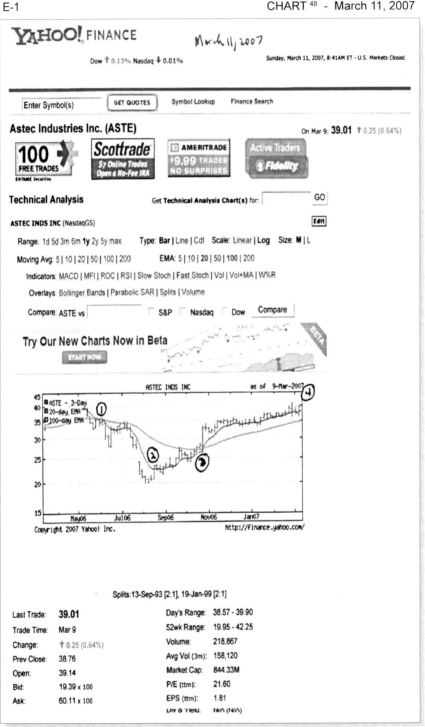

YAHOO! FINANCE   March 11, 2007

Dow ↑ 0.13% Nasdaq ↓ 0.01%   Sunday, March 11, 2007, 8:41AM ET - U.S. Markets Closed.

| Enter Symbol(s) | GET QUOTES | Symbol Lookup | Finance Search |

Astec Industries Inc. (ASTE)   On Mar 9: **39.01** ↑ 0.25 (0.64%)

100 → **Scottrade** | **AMERITRADE** $9.99 TRADES NO SURPRISES | Active Traders Fidelity
FREE TRADES $7 Online Trades Open a No-Fee IRA

Technical Analysis   Get **Technical Analysis Chart(s)** for: [   ]   GO

ASTEC INDS INC (NasdaqGS)   Edit

Range: 1d 5d 3m 6m **1y** 2y 5y max   Type: **Bar** | Line | Cdl   Scale: Linear | **Log**   Size: **M** | L

Moving Avg: 5 | 10 | 20 | 50 | 100 | 200   EMA: 5 | 10 | 20 | 50 | 100 | 200

Indicators: MACD | MFI | ROC | RSI | Slow Stoch | Fast Stoch | Vol | Vol+MA | W%R

Overlays: Bollinger Bands | Parabolic SAR | Splits | Volume

Compare: ASTE vs [   ]   ☐ S&P ☐ Nasdaq ☐ Dow   Compare

Try Our New Charts Now in Beta
START NOW

Copyright 2007 Yahoo! Inc.   http://finance.yahoo.com/

Splits:13-Sep-93 [2:1], 19-Jan-99 [2:1]

Last Trade:	**39.01**	Day's Range:	38.57 - 39.90
Trade Time:	Mar 9	52wk Range:	19.95 - 42.25
Change:	↑ 0.25 (0.64%)	Volume:	218,867
Prev Close:	38.76	Avg Vol (3m):	158,120
Open:	39.14	Market Cap:	844.33M
Bid:	19.39 x 100	P/E (ttm):	21.60
Ask:	60.11 x 100	EPS (ttm):	1.81
		Div & Yield:	N/A (N/A)

March 15, 2007

Fellow Optioneers,
This alert involves one of the exit strategies we discussed at the March 1st seminar.
It also leads into one of topics we will discuss on March 22nd. Finally, it will have a surprise ending!
First, print out the option chain I have attached to this email and follow along:

1- I purchased DSW @ a cost basis of $38.54
2- I sold the March $40 call receiving a 3.5% return
3- As of this writing DSW was trading @ $40.83 creating the likelihood of being called out @ the $40 strike price.
4- Enter the Expiration Friday Exit Strategy: Buy back the option and "roll foward " to the next months option.
5- Remember we buy at the ask (higher price) and sell at the bid (lower).
6- Buy to close DSW-CH @ $1.15
7- Sell to open DSW-DH @ $2.50
8- This creates a profit of $1.35 (2.50 minus 1.15)
9- A profit of $135/contract divided by my cost basis of $3854 gives me a 1 month
   3.5% return or 42% annualized.
10- This is an example of an Expiration Day Exit Strategy that creates a fabulous return on a stock we still like.
11- **THE SURPRISE ENDING**- I will not do this deal! No way! This has to do with the fact that DSW will report it's earnings on March 26th, prior to expiration of the next month's options. This important subject will be discussed in detail at the March 22nd seminar..

I will get the course outlines with definitions out to those registered for this seminar no later than Tuesday.

Congratulations to Bruce Steifman who got his 13 year old daughter involved in the process of stock selection. Nice going Bruce!
Best to all.
Alan

E-2   CHART [49] - March 15, 2007

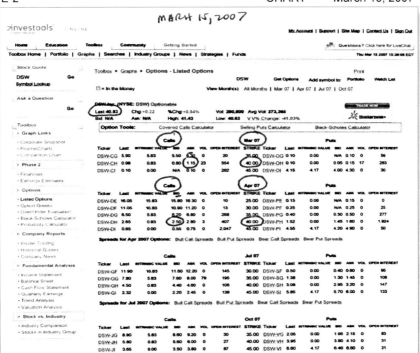

March 19, 2007

Hi to all,

I am writing this email despite the fact that my fingers are sore from selling stock options today (in sports it's called taking one for the team). Between Friday and today I generated $7450 cash into my account and I'm not done yet. This represents about a 1-month 3% return on my stock investment. I am convinced that many of you will be doing the same thing in the not too distant future. I am really impressed with the hard work many of you have put into learning this system. IT WILL PAY DIVIDENDS.

Last Thursday there was news about "metal" prices at a one year high with Copper in particular leading the way. News of China's economy growing faster than anticipated along with declining metal inventories caused copper prices to rise 6% Thursday. Now how can this put cash in our pockets? I immediately reviewed my watch list and found 3 stocks that could be positively influenced by this news:

PCU
X
RTI

I increased my position in PCU on Friday. This is a Phoenix-based copper mining company with mines in Peru and Mexico. It is a company that has made me substantial money in the past. I already had a position with X and initiated a position with RTI today. Be careful not to have too much of a particular industry in your portfolio- we must be well-diversified in case things turn around. **BUYING STOCKS IN A HOT SECTOR IS A WAY OF INCREASING OUR PROFITS EVEN MORE!**

Here are 3 of the stocks I have recently added to my watch list:
BWLD
TPX
TEX

After the 400 point drop in the market a few weeks ago, I have been watching my watch list stocks to see their recovery ability. Several have not responded as well as I would like to earn the "privilege" of being on my list. So several got bumped. Here are a few:
ANF
NYX
INFY
BAB

Finally, I suggest you keep an eye on Caterpillar (CAT). Several months ago it broke down technically but is now coming back. In addition, institutional money is starting to flow back into this company. I would be back in myself if I was convinced that the housing market was about to turn around. I'm not ready to pull the trigger on this one, but I'm close.

Alan

March 25, 2007

YOU GUYS ARE GREAT! You're really catching on. A few more months of practice and the real fun will begin.

Well, Linda found several GREAT stocks yesterday which we've added to our watch list.
Interestly, I noticed that 4 of them were related to the oil production or oil services industries (industry names located on IBD check-up page).
Here are the 4 stocks I am referring to:

NOV
CAM
TSO
HOC

Is this just a coincidence that 4 related stocks are added to my list in the same week? NOPE.
Money is starting to flow into these industries from mutual funds, hedge funds and insurance companies. This will positively affect the IBD screening process especially the institutional sponsorship. **Please see the attachment as to where to locate this.** "A" is the top 20%, "B" the next 20% and so on, in terms of money flowing into these equities. These stocks were D's and E's until this week. More specifically:

NOV and CAM went from the 26th percentile to the 58th percentile
TSO and HOC went from the 15th to the 55th percentile

We must remember that institutions who want to increase a position in a certain industry can't do it all at once. If they did it would force the prices up too rapidly. So they do it gradually.
We, on the other hand, can buy our few hundred shares all at once.
Normally, I wait at least one more week to confirm this inflow of dollars into an industry before I get in. I would definitely keep an eye on these oil-related stocks.
The numbers and the charts are trying to tell us something.

EARNINGS REPORTS:
In a previous email alert, I suggested keeping an eye on CAT. If you run CAT through the ER site I gave you at the last seminar, you will see that it will report on April 20th, the last day of this months options period. I would NOT sell options on CAT if I owned it until after the ER. I would either sell it, or own it "long" without selling options.
Since I don't own it, I will simply continue to watch it throught the ER and make an evaluation at that time.

***One of the members of our class made $4100.00 in option sales this past Monday! **CONGRATULATIONS!** I anticipate many more such emails in the months ahead.
My best to all.
Alan

E-3   CHART [50] - March 25, 2007

B6 MONDAY, MARCH 26, 2007

SMARTSELECT® COMPOSITE RATING

Rank	Company	Price			Rel Str % Chg	Annual EPS Est % Chg	Last Qtr EPS % Chg	Next Qtr EPS % Chg	Last Qtr Sales % Chg	Pretax mrgn	ROE %	Mgmt Own %	Spon- ship Rtg

COMPANIES 81-100

81	**Aeropostale**	40.97 98 93 91	+16	+33	+25	+16	32	11	3			C
	►Banc of America Securities downgrades teen retailer from buy to neutral.											
82	**II–VI**	33.10 93 91 94	+31	+76	+28	+18	17	16	21			C
	►Laser maker meets or beats Wall Street views past 4 qtrs by up to 19%.											
83	**Zumiez Inc**	41.51 98 91 92	+31	+70	+50	+49	25	..	47			C
	►Retailer sees $0.94–$0.96/share profit in '07, Wall SL expected $0.92.											
84	**Hurco Companies**	42.15 95 90 95	+33	+75	+27	+47	23	15	14			B
	►Machine maker's Q1 sales up 47%, but its earning growth has been uneven.											
85	**Almost Family Inc**	26.17 96 86 99	..	+63	..	+36	15	..	38			..
	►Home–health services firm improved margins and ROE past 3 years straight.											
86	**Hologic Inc**	59.14 98 99 82	+46	+85	+50	+86	11	16	4			C
	►Medical imager sped up annual sales growth from 6% to 61% y–o–y past 4 yrs.											
87	**Under Armour Cl A**	51.20 98 98 83	+24	+175	+11	+55	20	13	36			C
	►Number of funds in athletic clothing maker climbs from 34 to 88 over 4 qtrs.											
88	**S W S Group**	25.20 84 97 91	+52	+55	..	+29	9	10	19			B
	►Financial firm raised its qtrly dividend by 9% to $0.08/share, payable 4/2.											
89	**D S W Inc**	44.11 94 97 86	+38	+44	+30	+10	18	6	15			C
	►Earnings out Thurs. Analysts see profit growing 30% to 30 cents a share.											
90	**C T C Media Inc**	26.18 96 95 87	+39	+18	..	+31	35	43	2			B
	►Billionaire Leonard Blavatnik ups stake in Russian media firm to 6.1%.											
91	**Allegiant Travel Co**	32.99 97 95 86	+162	+999	+225	+58	38	..	59			C
	►Vegas–based low–fare airline's planes were 81.9% full in February.											
92	**Natl Oilwell Varco**	77.36 99 95 85	+40	+114	+87	+51	14	15	1			C
	►Oil & gas drilling equipment maker's EPS grew 105%, 89%, 114% past 3 qtrs.											
93	**Cameron Intl Corp**	61.92 99 94 87	+30	+96	+56	+46	20	14	3			C
	►Matrix Research upgraded oil&gas equipment maker to strong buy from buy.											
94	**Icon PLC ADS**	42.89 91 93 92	+18	+75	+30	+46	10	12	..			C
	►Earnings growth has accelerated for five straight quarters.											
95	**Manitowoc**	62.00 98 92 90	+43	+188	+68	+32	26	8	5			C
	►Lifting gear maker adopts poison pill actionable if someone buys 20% stake.											
96	**Legacy Reserves**	26.80 99 92 89	+34	+22	..	+76	53	30	35			..
	►Agreed to buy oil and natural gas properties in Oklahoma for $45 million.											
97	**Las Vegas Sands**	91.20 98 92 88	+16	+12	–16	+27	27	25	61			C
	►Analysts expect gaming firm's earnings growth to slow in the next 2 qtrs.											
98	**Penn VA Gp Hldgs**	25.67 92 91 92	+31	+69	+32	–21	..	6	1			..
	►Manages coal mining and natural gas properties across the U.S.											
99	**Republic Airways**	22.24 97 89 92	+13	+24	+10	+17	19	..	25			C
	►Airline buys 2 million shares from ex–majority holder WexAir at 20.50 each.											
100	**Cutera Inc**	35.55 98 88 92	+34	+34	+123	+27	16	24	12			C
	►Q1 EPS consensus for cosmetic laser firm is for 29 cents/share, up 142%.											

March 28, 2007

Fellow investors,

Calculations seem to be the group "nemesis" based on calls and emails I've received since last Thursday.

DO NOT WORRY! This will come with practice and eventually become second nature.

I've created (**see attachments**) a few hypothetical scenarios to further explain **return on option (ROO), upside potential, and downside protection.**

Save these examples and keep them in front of you when computing your returns and filling out the **option evaluation form**.

First determine if the strike price is IN, AT, or OUT of the money. Then go to the appropriate example and follow the formula.

I plan to do several calculation examples at the April 19th seminar and it should click in by then. For those of you who requested 1-on-1 coaching, I will have information on this at the final seminar.

Keep up the great work.

Alan

E-4   ATTACHMENT - March 28, 2007

RETURN ON OPTIONS (ROO)

Buy stock @ $48/ share. Cost basis per share is now **$48.**
Sell the $50 call for **$2.00.**

ROO = 2/ 48 = 4.2%

UPSIDE POTENTIAL-SAME EXAMPLE AS ABOVE

Applies ONLY to Out of The Money (OTM) strike prices.

If stock goes above $50, we will capture an additional $2/share in stock appreciation over and above what we got paid for selling the call.

Upside Potential = $2/ 48 (what the stock actually cost us) = 4.2%

At The Money (ATM) strike prices offer <u>NEITHER</u> *Upside Potential nor Downside Protection** BUT usually provide the GREATEST ROO.

*These are terms I made up – You will NOT find them in any books (except mine!).

DOWNSIDE PROTECTION/BUYING DOWN STOCK PRICE
Only Applies to IN-THE MONEY (ITM) Strike Prices

Illustration:

-Buy stock XYZ for $52.00/ share
-Sell to Open (STO) $50 Call for $3.50
         Intrinsic Value = Stock Cost (52) – Strike Price (50) = $2.00
         Extrinsic (Time) Value = Call Bid (3.50) – Intrinsic Value (2.00) = $1.50

If we get "Assigned" the stock will automatically be sold for the strike price of our short option which is $50.00. We paid 52, so there is a reduction of $2.00. We received $3.50 when we sold the call, so we still have the difference (3.50-2.00=**1.50**). That 1.50 is our per share profit.

Accounting Solution:

Start with the 3.50 premium we received for selling the call and divide it into its two parts, the <u>Intrinsic Value which is 2.00</u> and the Extrinsic Value (the remainder) which is 1.50. This Extrinsic Value is your guaranteed profit (3.50 Cost – 2.00 Intrinsic Value . .that part of the option price to you which includes the amount between the Strike Price and the Price of the Option.

Calculations:

    ROO = 1.5 (Extrinsic Value)/ 50 (Strike Price) = 3%
       We used the $2.00 intrinsic value in our calculations to "Buy Down" the price of the stock from 52 to 50 ("Buy Down" is my term).

DOWNSIDE PROTECTION
       Intrinsic Value/ Original Cost Basis = 2/52 = 3.8%
       This means we will make our 3% ROO even if the stock drops $2.00 from 52 to 50

March 31, 2007

Greetings:

Question of the day:

HOW CAN A LUNATIC ON THE OTHER SIDE OF THE WORLD MAKE US SOME CA$H?

President Ahmadinejad?#%&*% of Iran (can I please buy a vowel!) is at it again.
He took 15 British sailors as hostages, is totally ignoring UN demands regarding his nuclear program and is threatening the US and its allies with declining oil shipments. All this geopolitical turmoil is NOT good for our economy in general but I say how can this make us some ca$h? Many clouds have silver linings.
Oil prices have been elevating as a result and this has led to increasing interest in **ETHANOL,** a fuel oil alternative. Since ethanol is derived from corn, I looked at the corn producing stocks. Archer Daniels Midland **(ADM)** is one that I am familiar with and have owned in the past. It is definitely a company on the rebound but its technicals are still not proven and institutional sponsorship is in the 29th percentile. It is a stock to keep an eye on.
I would not stop there. I would look at the companies that produce agricultural farming equipment. Three that come to mind are **CAT, IR and DE.** Of the three, CAT has the strongest fundamentals and as I reported in a previous email alert, it is strengthening with more institutional sponsorship and improving technically. I am waiting for the April 20th earning report. If favorable, I will purchase CAT and sell options on the next option period.
Even if the situation in Iran calms, there is a strong likelihood that the "ethanol train" will continue to build up speed and companies like ADM, CAT, DE, and IR will benefit. Because we are "way-above-average" investors, we too will benefit!

Oil stocks update:

On the March 25th email alert I highlighted 4 oil-related stocks; **NOV, CAM, TSO, and HOC.** I noted that in addition to all entering the IBD 100, they were showing growing interest from the institutions. Well, all were up again this month in that regard. All are in the mid-60's percentile. At the end of February all 4 were in the "0" percentile!

Earnings Reports:

At the last seminar I stated that I NEVER sell options if the earnings report is coming out prior to expiration Friday.
Please print out the attached chart and see why:
- At point "1", **MOV** breaks above its 20-d EMA after being in a trading range (sideways)
- At point "2" we see the early March "aberration followed by a nice recovery
- - At point "3" (last Thursday) here comes the earnings report....down over $5/share....YIKES!!!!!!!! I rest my case.

Finally, I added **BWLD** back onto my watch list . It is now technically and fundamentally sound. It closed @ $63.70. If we sell the April $65 (out-of-the-money) @ $1.40 we get a 3-week return on option (ROO) of 2.2% (multiply by 17 to annualize=37%).
We also have upside potential of $1.30 ($63.70 to $65.00) = 2% ≈ 34% annualized.

Thanks for your support.
Alan

YAHOO! FINANCE

Dow ↑ 0.39% Nasdaq ↑ 0.03%   Thursday, March 29, 2007, 9:58PM ET - U.S. Markets Closed.

| Enter Symbol(s) | **GET QUOTES** | Symbol Lookup | Finance Search |

Movado Group Inc. (MOV)
At 4:02PM ET: **28.74** ↓5.84 (16.89%)

Active Traders 🔵 **Fidelity** | Switch to *Scottrade* and get up to $100 back | 🅣 **AMERITRADE** NO maintenance fees | **E✹TRADE** FINANCIAL

Technical Analysis
Get **Technical Analysis Chart(s)** for: [   ] GO

MOVADO GROUP INC (NYSE)   [Edit]

Range: 1d 5d 3m **6m** 1y 2y 5y max   Type: **Bar** | Line | Cdl   Scale: Linear | Log Size: **M** | L

Moving Avg: 5 | 10 | 20 | 50 | 100 | 200   EMA: 5 | 10 | 20 | 50 | 100 | 200

Indicators: MACD | MFI | ROC | RSI | Slow Stoch | Fast Stoch | Vol | Vol+MA | W%R

Overlays: Bollinger Bands | Parabolic SAR | Splits | Volume

Compare: MOV vs [   ] ☐ S&P ☐ Nasdaq ☐ Dow Compare

Try Our New Charts Now in Beta
START NOW   BETA

MOVADO GROUP INC   as of 29-Mar-2007

{ YIKES!!

Copyright 2007 Yahoo! Inc.   http://finance.yahoo.com/

Splits:02-May-97 [5:4], 30-Sep-97 [3:2], 28-Jun-04 [2:1]

Last Trade:	**28.74**	Day's Range:	28.07 - 33.60
Trade Time:	4:02PM ET	52wk Range:	17.91 - 35.40
Change:	↓5.84 (16.89%)	Volume:	1,998,300
		Avg Vol (3m):	250,651
Prev Close:	34.58	Market Cap:	739.62M
Open:	33.46	P/E (ttm):	19.56
Bid:	N/A	EPS (ttm):	1.47
Ask:	N/A	Div & Yield:	0.61 (0.79%)

April 4, 2007

Hi,

On March 19th, I sent an email alert highlighting 3 "metal play" stocks: X, PCU, and RTI. I told you metals were hitting one year highs and this could bode well for these stocks and well it has! X and RTI have since hit 52-week highs and PCU is close. All are up substantially in recent weeks.

One of the reasons I stress the **GROUP** technical ranking of our watch list stocks is because of the momentum caused by money flowing into an industry (or out) and how that can influence the stocks within that industry. Remember we only accept stocks with a **Group Technical Ranking of "C" or better** (found on the IBD stock check-up page).

PLEASE SEE ATTACHMENT: I have attached two industry charts. One is the "steel industry" which has been a thing of beauty since October and the "computer hardware industry" which has been in snoozeland since December.

FROM WHICH INDUSTRY WOULD YOU RATHER OWN A STOCK?

Hint: it starts with "S".

So let's say I bought "X" today (I actually own it @ $89.50!). How would I play it?

First let's assume that the earnings report was not coming out on April 24th.

Here are the #'s as of this writing:

Stock Price: $102.26

May $100 strike price (in-the-money) pays $6.40 or $640 per contract. Since this is an in-the-money option, we deduct the intrinsic value ($2.26) and use it to **"buy down"** the stock price to $100/share.

The difference is the profit ($414).

Our ROO is 4.1% to May expiration which is 6 weeks.($414/$10000)

Our downside protection is ($226/$10226) or 2.2% for 6 week return.

NOT BAD!

What if we opted for the May $105 out-of-the-money?

Our option premium is $390 which gives us a 6-week return of 3.8% (390/10226).

Our upside potential is 2.7% 6-week return (274/10226).

Given that "X" has had such a great run-up in recent weeks, I would tend to be more conservative **(risk reduction is our primary focus)** and go with the May $100 in-the-money. There could be some profit-taking soon.

I will go over MANY of these calculations @ the April 19th meeting.

Two other metal stocks that were already on my watch list that caught my eye recently due to gorgeous chart patterns are **MT and STLD.**

STLD was also recently upgraded by an analyst at UBS. MT , on the other hand, is only followed by 3 brokerage firms and could really take off when word gets around.

Finally, I heard an economist on the radio say that when inflation is between 1-3% as it is presently, the stock market goes up about 13% per year. As an option seller, that is our sweet spot! Although I don't think the market will be up that much this year (company profits are slowing a little), we can make a lot of $ even if the market only rises in single-digits.

Keep working those formulas.

Alan

April 8, 2007

Happy Holidays to all.

I hope you are saving these alerts I am sending out. Refer back to them from time to time. They contain "real life tricks" that I have learned over the years that will help **enhance your profits even more!**

Today I want to highlight two of the stocks that Linda found yesterday that we've added to our watch list:

DRQ
GRP

Both stocks have an overall IBD rating of A+
Both have an MSN Scouter (risk/reward) rating of 9
Both show a positive chart pattern
Both show a recent crossover of the 20-d EMA over the 100-d EMA

Both are great examples of how we can still make BIG PROFITS in a short period of time (only 2 weeks to expiration Friday). This can relate to our exit strategy where we convert "dead money" to big profits. The example I gave at the seminar was selling my Qualcom and buying Ezcorp, then selling the Ezcorp option for an 8-day return of 3.4%. Check out these 2-week returns:

Buy DRQ for $45.02
Sell the April $45 call (DRQ DI) for $1.10)
This represents a 2.4% - 2 week return or a **62% annual return**

Buy GRP for $49.84
Sell the April $50 call (GRP DJ) for $1.35
This represents a 2.7% 2-week return or a 70% annual return

Last week, I noticed that Southeby's (**BID**)was trading up on very high volume. I decided to run it through our system and sure enough I added it to my watch list. When I looked at the chart of BID, I noticed something interesting:
A pattern that keeps repeating itself. It reminded me of a stock I traded years ago, Motorola (MOT). Years ago, I noticed that MOT traded between $50 and $60. I'd buy it at $50 and sell at $60. Then it would go back down to $50 and I'd buy it back and so on. Eventuall;y the pattern stopped but I made a lot of money while it lasted.
Please **print out the (attached) chart** I created for BID and follow along:

The pattern

1-2   Runs up in price (trend)
3   Drops below the moving average
4-5   Price moves sideways (trading range)

Now the pattern repeats:

6-7   Runs up in price
8   Drops below moving average
8-9   Price moves sideways

Pattern repeats again:

10-11   Runs up in price
12   Drops below moving average
12-13   Price moves sideways

Pattern repeats again:

14-15   Runs up in price
16   Drops below moving average
16-17   Price moves sideways

Pattern beginning to repeat

18   Price currently running up in price

As you look at more and more charts, you **WILL** be able to pick up these patterns that can enhance your returns. Use these patterns as one of your tools in making your investment decisions.
Remember, very few investors know how to read a stock chart. That is one of the reasons (as way above average investors) why your returns should beat the "market" year in and year out.

I invite you all to attend a free teleconference I am hosting this Thursday, April 19th from 7:8 PM. Those who have registered for the next seminar series or who are interested in attending will be participating. I am sure they would be interested in hearing your feedback. Here is the conference information:

Dial-In Phone # : 646-519-5800

Pin # : 4122 #

Best regards.
Alan

E-8   CHART [54] - April 8, 2007

YAHOO! FINANCE

Dow ↑ 0.24% Nasdaq ↑ 0.51%   Sunday, April 8, 2007, 12:37PM ET - U.S. Markets Closed.

| Enter Symbol(s) | | GET QUOTES | Symbol Lookup | Finance Search |

Sotheby's (BID)   On Apr 5: **47.20** ↓ 0.12 (0.25%)

AMERITRADE NO maintenance fees | Switch to **Scottrade** and get up to $100 back | **Active Traders** Fidelity | **5.05%** APY SAVINGS ACCOUNT NO MINIMUMS E*TRADE Bank Member FDIC

Technical Analysis   Get **Technical Analysis Chart(s)** for: [   ] GO

SOTHEBYS (NYSE)   [Edit]

Range: 1d 5d 3m 6m **1y** 2y 5y max   Type: **Bar** | Line | Cdl   Scale: Linear | **Log**   Size: **M** | L

Moving Avg: 5 | 10 | 20 | 50 | 100 | 200   EMA: 5 | 10 | 20 | 50 | 100 | 200

Indicators: MACD | MFI | ROC | RSI | Slow Stoch | Fast Stoch | Vol | Vol+MA | W%R

Overlays: Bollinger Bands | Parabolic SAR | Splits | Volume

Compare: BID vs [   ]   ☐ S&P ☐ Nasdaq ☐ Dow Compare

Try Our New Charts Now in Beta
START NOW

SOTHEBYS   as of 5-Apr-2007

Copyright 2007 Yahoo! Inc.   http://finance.yahoo.com/

Splits:none

Last Trade:	**47.20**	Day's Range:	47.06 - 47.72
Trade Time:	Apr 5	52wk Range:	22.78 - 48.07
Change:	↓ 0.12 (0.25%)	Volume:	1,399,200
Prev Close:	47.32	Avg Vol (3m):	1,205,570
Open:	47.50	Market Cap:	3.10B
Bid:	N/A	P/E (ttm):	27.38
Ask:	N/A	EPS (ttm):	1.72
		Div & Yield:	0.40 (0.80%)

April 14, 2007

Fellow optioneers,
Thanks to those of you who listened to the teleseminar I hosted last Thursday. It was very well received. Must sound pretty basic to you at this point!
If you missed it, here is a link to the replay:

http://www.lireia.com/audioclub/ellmancallreplay.html

Well the airline sector is finally starting to rebound. Continental Airlines (CAL) repoprted a 3.4% increase in traffic while the % of seats filled climbed to 82.6%. Southwest Airlines (LUV) and Delta (DALRQ) reported similiar increases.
So I decided to run these 3 airlines through our system to see if they are candidates for our watch list: NOPE, NOPE and NOPE.
So what do we do? Go to the frig for a snack and forget about it? NOPE again.
We are "way above average investors" so we think it through a little more.
With summer right around the corner, what about all these travel web sites that get us all these packages and deals?
First I checked Expedia (EXPE) which is the market leader. It looked pretty good overall but fell short on the fundamentals. Tempting but I passed.
Then I checked Priceline **(PCLN)** and BINGO it hit.
Check out the gorgeous chart pattern (**print out the attachment**) of this stock since August. It's in a gradual uptrend with the price bouncing off the climbing 20-d EMA....beautiful! Lately it has been consolidating (sideways) and may be in for another takeoff soon.
Ironically, I would have added this stock to my portfolio anyway this week as it was one of the stocks Linda found today.
Another stock that we added was **CLB** ranked A+ on the IBD site.

I have been testing the options calculator Owen created for us and it is absolutely fabulous! I sent it to you recently as an email attachment.
Today I am highlighting these aforementioned stocks, PCLN and CLB and the excel calculator:
SEE ATTACHMENTS:
The information circled in blue is what you fill in-simple.
Everything below will come up automatically.
I circled in red : ROO (return on option), downside protection, upside potential and annualized percentages.
I suggest you use this tool and practice with it. Calculations should no longer be an issue.
Thanks again to Owen Sargent for taking the time to create this wonderful tool for us.
I appreciate all the positive feedback you have been sending me and look foward to our final seminar next Thursday....I'm planning a surprise! (No, Imus will not be attending!)
Alan

CHART [55] - April 14, 2007

YAHOO! FINANCE

Dow ⬆ 0.04% Nasdaq ⬆ 0.34%   Tuesday, April 10, 2007, 7:57PM ET - U.S. Markets Closed.

| Enter Symbol(s) | **GET QUOTES** | Symbol Lookup | Finance Search |

Priceline.com Inc. (PCLN)

At 4:00PM ET: **54.89** ⬆ 0.68 (1.25%)

▶ Trade Smarter Fidelity   **100** ✱ FREE TRADES E*TRADE SECURITIES   AMERITRADE ONLINE BROKER ACCORDING TO BARRON'S   Switch to **Scottrade** and get up to $100 back

Technical Analysis

Get **Technical Analysis Chart(s) for:** [   ] GO

PRICELINE.COM INC (NasdaqGS)   Edit

Range: 1d 5d 3m 6m **1y** 2y 5y max   Type: **Bar** | Line | Cdl   Scale: Linear | **Log**   Size: **M** | L

Moving Avg: 5 | 10 | 20 | 50 | 100 | 200   EMA: 5 | 10 | 20 | 50 | 100 | 200

Indicators: MACD | MFI | ROC | RSI | Slow Stoch | Fast Stoch | Vol | Vol+MA | W%R

Overlays: Bollinger Bands | Parabolic SAR | Splits | Volume

Compare: PCLN vs [   ] ☐ S&P ☐ Nasdaq ☐ Dow   Compare

Try Our New Charts Now in Beta

START NOW

PRICELINE.COM INC   as of 9-Apr-2007

■ PCLN - 3-Day
■ 20-day EMA
■ 100-day EMA

Copyright 2007 Yahoo! Inc.   http://finance.yahoo.com/

Splits:16-Jun-03 [1:6]

Last Trade:	**54.89**	Day's Range:	54.09 - 54.98
Trade Time:	4:00PM ET	52wk Range:	23.72 - 56.11
Change:	⬆ 0.68 (1.25%)	Volume:	393,098
Prev Close:	54.21	Avg Vol (3m):	1,056,000
Open:	54.42	Market Cap:	2.06B
Bid:	54.65 x 200	P/E (ttm):	32.63
Ask:	55.85 x 300	EPS (ttm):	1.68
		Div & Yield:	N/A (N/A)

E-10   Attachment #1 - April 14, 2007

RETURN ON OPTION (ROO) CALCULATOR - SINGLE STOCK

Stock name >>
Stock symbol >>   clb   Stock share price >> $ 88.31

	Symbol	Strike Price	Exp Date	Price / share
Option choice #1 >>	clb er	90.00	05/18/07	2.65
Option choice #2 >>				
Option choice #3 >>				
Option choice #4 >>				

Option selected   clb MAY 90.00

Today's date	04/14/07	04/14/07	04/14/07	04/14/07
Days to expiration	34			
Cost for 100 shares of stock	$ 8,831.00	$ 8,831.00	$ 8,831.00	$ 8,831.00
Proceeds from one contract	$ 265.00			

IN / OUT OF THE MONEY	OUT	IN	IN	IN
INTRINSIC VALUE	$ -	$ 88.31	$ 88.31	$ 88.31
UPSIDE AMOUNT	$ 169.00	$ -	$ -	$ -
UPSIDE POTENTIAL	1.9%	0.0%	0.0%	0.0%
DOWNSIDE AMOUNT	$ -	$ 8,831.00	$ 8,831.00	$ 8,831.00
DOWNSIDE PROTECTION	0.0%	100.0%	100.0%	100.0%

RETURN ON VARIOUS OUTCOMES				
Proceeds from option sale	$ 265.00			
Amount of buy-down	$ -	$ 8,831.00	$ 8,831.00	$ 8,831.00
Actual option profit	$ 265.00	#VALUE!	#VALUE!	#VALUE!
Option profit	$ 265.00	#VALUE!	#VALUE!	#VALUE!
Upside profit	$ 169.00	$ -	$ -	$ -
Total profit	$ 434.00	#VALUE!	#VALUE!	#VALUE!
Cost of shares	$ 8,831.00	$ -	$ -	$ -
Return On Option (ROO)	3.0%	#VALUE!	#VALUE!	#VALUE!
Return on Upside	1.9%	#DIV/0!	#DIV/0!	#DIV/0!
Total return	4.9%	#DIV/0!	#DIV/0!	#DIV/0!
Annualized return	52.6%	#VALUE!	#VALUE!	#VALUE!

Run: 4/14/2007 3:06 PM

E-11   Attachment #2 - April 14, 2007

RETURN ON OPTION (ROO) CALCULATOR - SINGLE STOCK

Stock name >>

Stock symbol >> pcln   Stock share price >> $ 55.57

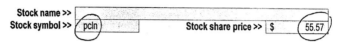

	Symbol	Strike Price	Exp Date	Price / share
Option choice #1 >>	puz ek	55.00	05/18/07	2.90
Option choice #2 >>				
Option choice #3 >>				
Option choice #4 >>				

Option selected   pcln MAY 55.00

Today's date	04/14/07	04/14/07	04/14/07	04/14/07
Days to expiration	34			
Cost for 100 shares of stock	$ 5,557.00	$ 5,557.00	$ 5,557.00	$ 5,557.00
Proceeds from one contract	$ 290.00			

IN / OUT OF THE MONEY	IN	IN	IN	IN
INTRINSIC VALUE	$ 0.57	$ 55.57	$ 55.57	$ 55.57
UPSIDE AMOUNT	$ -	$ -	$ -	$ -
UPSIDE POTENTIAL	0.0%	0.0%	0.0%	0.0%
DOWNSIDE AMOUNT	$ 57.00	$ 5,557.00	$ 5,557.00	$ 5,557.00
DOWNSIDE PROTECTION	1.0%	100.0%	100.0%	100.0%

RETURN ON VARIOUS OUTCOMES

Proceeds from option sale	$ 290.00			
Amount of buy-down	$ 57.00	$ 5,557.00	$ 5,557.00	$ 5,557.00
Actual option profit	$ 233.00	#VALUE!	#VALUE!	#VALUE!
Option profit	$ 233.00	#VALUE!	#VALUE!	#VALUE!
Upside profit	$ -	$ -	$ -	$ -
Total profit	$ 233.00	#VALUE!	#VALUE!	#VALUE!
Cost of shares	$ 5,500.00	$ -	$ -	$ -
Return On Option (**ROO**)	4.2%	#VALUE!	#VALUE!	#VALUE!
Return on Upside	0.0%	#DIV/0!	#DIV/0!	#DIV/0!
Total return	4.2%	#DIV/0!	#DIV/0!	#DIV/0!
Annualized return	45.1%	**#VALUE!**	**#VALUE!**	**#VALUE!**

Run: 4/14/2007 3:04 PM

April 17, 2007

Fellow investors,
On April 8th I mentioned that Southeby"s **(BID)** caught my attention because it had been trading up on high volume. I will be addressing this in more detail at Thursdays seminar. Since then BID has absolutely been on fire!
I plan to purchase BID and sell the May option next week.
Please see attachment as I fed the information into our excel option calculator.
I made the 6 entries (circled in blue) and all other information appeared automatically. I circled in red key information including a 5% return, 58% annualized! NOT BAD!

Those of you following earnings reports will note that many of our watch list stocks will report during the upcoming expiration period. The months of January, April, July and October are considered the height of earnings season. During these months our list of available stocks from our watch list is depleted. As a result, our % return will be slightly less than other months but still substantial compared to most other investments.

Here are 3 stocks in addition to BID that I will strongly consider for purchase next week:
DECK
STLD
VIP

Since we are in earnings season there has been a lot less talk about the sub-prime debacle. We have had 14 straight quarters of double-digit earnings growth. Analysts, however, are predicitng only a 3.8% growth for this 1st quarter of 2007 and 6.7% for the year.
Since this quarter has gotten off to a much better start, the analysts may have to eat their words. And we may be "forced" to pocket more ca$h!

This is the last email alert prior to completion of our 4-seminar series. I hope you've enjoyed them and found them to be useful adjuncts to the learning process.

I look foward to seeing you all this Thursday (still planning a surprise).
Alan

RETURN ON OPTION (ROO) CALCULATOR - SINGLE STOCK

Stock name >>

Stock symbol >> BID   Stock share price >> $ 50.21

	Symbol	Strike Price	Exp Date	Price / share
Option choice #1 >>	BID EJ	50.00	05/18/07	2.70
Option choice #2 >>				
Option choice #3 >>				
Option choice #4 >>				

Option selected   BID MAY 50.00

Today's date		04/17/07		04/17/07		04/17/07		04/17/07
Days to expiration		31						
Cost for 100 shares of stock	$	5,021.00	$	5,021.00	$	5,021.00	$	5,021.00
Proceeds from one contract	$	270.00						

IN / OUT OF THE MONEY		IN		IN		IN		IN
INTRINSIC VALUE	$	0.21	$	50.21	$	50.21	$	50.21
UPSIDE AMOUNT	$	-	$	-	$	-	$	-
UPSIDE POTENTIAL		0.0%		0.0%		0.0%		0.0%
DOWNSIDE AMOUNT	$	21.00	$	5,021.00	$	5,021.00	$	5,021.00
DOWNSIDE PROTECTION		0.4%		100.0%		100.0%		100.0%

RETURN ON VARIOUS OUTCOMES

Proceeds from option sale	$	270.00						
Amount of buy-down	$	21.00	$	5,021.00	$	5,021.00	$	5,021.00
Actual option profit	$	249.00		#VALUE!		#VALUE!		#VALUE!
Option profit	$	249.00		#VALUE!		#VALUE!		#VALUE!
Upside profit	$	-	$	-	$	-	$	-
Total profit	$	249.00		#VALUE!		#VALUE!		#VALUE!
Cost of shares	$	5,000.00	$	-	$	-	$	-
Return On Option (**ROO**)		5.0%		#VALUE!		#VALUE!		#VALUE!
Return on Upside		0.0%		#DIV/0!		#DIV/0!		#DIV/0!
Total return		5.0%		#DIV/0!		#DIV/0!		#DIV/0!
Annualized return		58.9%		#VALUE!		#VALUE!		#VALUE!

Run: 4/17/2007 6:49 PM

April 20, 2007

Thanks for all those wonderful testimonials many of you took the time to write on my behalf.
I look foward to seeing them in print once my book is published.
It's only appropriate that I write one for you:

I couldn't have asked for a finer audience of intelligent, motivated and generous participants than you to launch my "stock option speaking career". Your excitement to learn encouraged me and made the experience so much more meaningful than I ever anticipated.
Your feedback was well thought out and will lead me to improve the quality of my presentations in the future.
I am now in the process of creating a DVD and CD series along with putting the finishing touches on a book I recently wrote. Your support was a major factor in my decision to pursue these goals.
My hope is that the information I shared with you will enhance the quality of your lives just as you have heightened mine.
THANK YOU.

Thanks to Kenneth Teape for locating a free web site that has the MACD histogram as part of its indicators. As I said last night, the Yahoo/Fiance site only has the MACD line chart.
I have attached a sample chart from this site. The only disadvantage is that you will use the yahoo site for options and this new site (if you choose) for technical analysis, instead of yahoo for both.
Here is what you need to do:

1- Go to www.stockcharts.com
2- Hit the "free charts" tab on top.
3- Under "sharp charts" type in the ticker symbol to create a chart
4- Change the settings as follows:
    a- Range; 1 year
    b- Type: OHLC Bars
    c- Size: Landscape
    d- Overlays:
        1- EMA 20
        2- EMA 100
    e- Indicators:
        1- MACD- position- below
        2- Slow Stochastics- below
        3- Volume- below
5- Hit Update
6- The chart will default to these settings until you leave the site.

I find the charts in this site to be clearer than that of Yahoo and have the added benefit of the MACD Histogram.
Thanks, Ken.

Wishing you all the best in investing.
Alan

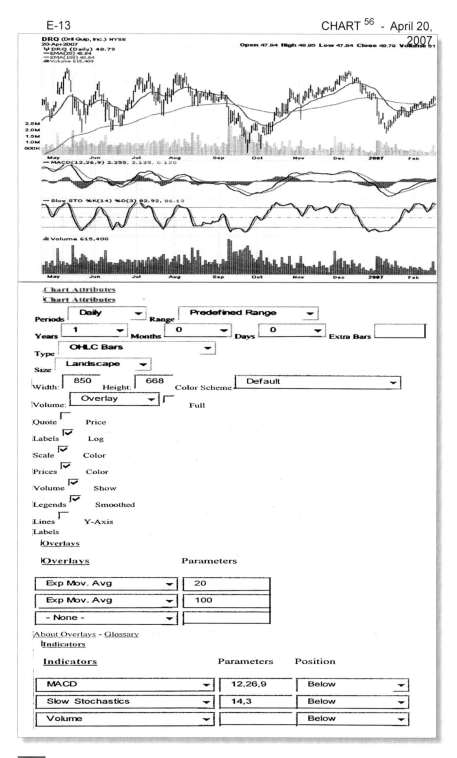

April 29, 2007

Greetings to all,

Thank you for the privilege of speaking before you last Thursday.

I will be sending out 1-2 of these alerts each week for the duration of our seminars. I hope you find that they assist you in the learning process.

Please print out the attached option chains and follow along:

Here are 3 of the stocks that Linda located for us yesterday from the IBD 100 list. They are now part of my watch list of 40-60 stocks:

VSEA
ESRX
PTNR

If you run them through our system criteria you will see that they meet all requirements.

Let's run our calculations. Remember there are 3 weeks to expiration Friday. Since there are 52 weeks in a year, we will multiply our returns by 17 to annualize (17 x 3 = 51 weeks- close enough).

VSEA - $69.99/share- 100 shares = $6999 (our cost basis or investment)

May 70 call option: UES EN @ 2.65
100 shares x $2.65= $265 - our option return or profit
265/6999 = 3.8% 3-week return
3.8% x 17 weeks =65% annualized

PTNR - $16.88/share or $1688 cost basis

May 17.50 call: QPO EW @ .30
Profit is .30 x 100 or $30 per contract (100 shares)
30/1688 = 1.8% 3-week return
1.8% x 17 = 30% annualized

ESRX- $95.57 per share or $9557 investment

May 95 call: XTQ ES @ $2.50
Profit is 2.50 x 100 = 250 per contract
250/9557 = 2.6% 3-week return

However if we are "called out" and our stock is sold @ $95/ share as is our obligation, we will lose .57 per share or $57 per contract. We then deduct the 57 from our 250 initial profit giving a true profit of $193 for the 3-week period.

193/9557 = 2% 3-week return
2% x 17 ≈ 34% annualized

Don't worry if this doesn't make 100% sense to you at this time. It will by the end of the 4th seminar.

Remember, the option excel calculator is on the way!!!!!!!!

pg 2 - April 29, 2007

For now, I want you to understand what I am doing and why. This is going to put you amongst the ELITE stock inverstors- top 5-10% for sure.

On a personal note, I am truly overwhelmed by your response to the Basic Seminar.
Your complimentary emails are very much appreciated. Also, nearly every one of you signed up for the remaining seminars.
There is a lot more to learn but by the time we are done you will know every trick and nuance to this investment strategy (that I know) that will bring your profits to the highest possible level.

PLEASE NOTE:
Remaining 3 seminars will be held in the EXECUTIVE ROOM on the other side of the hotel.
Enter the main (left) entrance of the hotel and take the first left past the front desk.

This Thursdays seminar will be broken down into 3 parts:
1- Full review of the Basic Seminar as this is the foundation of principals that will generate your future stock market fortune
2- New material: Exit Stategies, portfolio management, and additional technical analysis indicators.
3- Interactive session- **feel free to bring ticker symbols for the class to evaluate.**

Linda and I look foward to seeing you on Thursday.
Best regards.
Alan

E-14   CHART #1 [57] - April 29, 2007

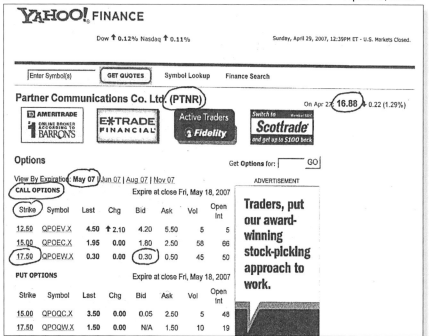

E-15   CHART #2 [58] - April 29, 2007

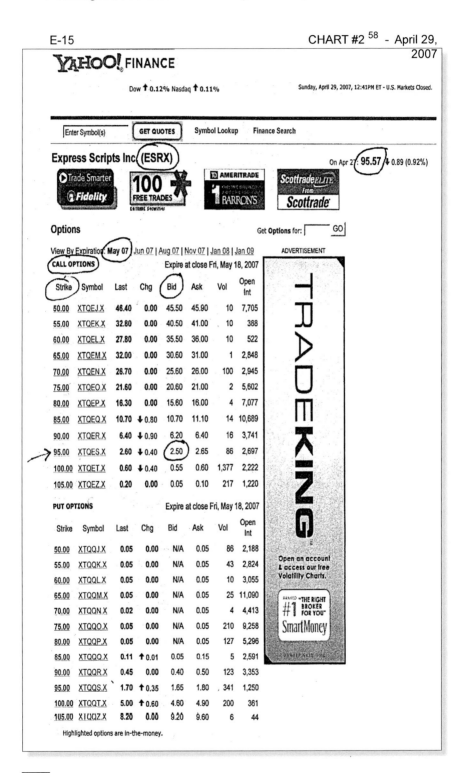

YAHOO! FINANCE

Dow ↑0.12% Nasdaq ↑0.11%   Sunday, April 29, 2007, 12:41PM ET - U.S. Markets Closed.

| Enter Symbol(s) | **GET QUOTES** | Symbol Lookup | Finance Search |

Express Scripts Inc (ESRX)

On Apr 27: **95.57** ↓0.89 (0.92%)

Options   Get **Options** for: [   ] GO

View By Expiration: **May 07** | Jun 07 | Aug 07 | Nov 07 | Jan 08 | Jan 09   ADVERTISEMENT

CALL OPTIONS   Expire at close Fri, May 18, 2007

Strike	Symbol	Last	Chg	Bid	Ask	Vol	Open Int
50.00	XTQEJ.X	46.40	0.00	45.50	45.90	10	7,705
55.00	XTQEK.X	32.80	0.00	40.50	41.00	10	388
60.00	XTQEL.X	27.80	0.00	35.50	36.00	10	522
65.00	XTQEM.X	32.00	0.00	30.60	31.00	1	2,848
70.00	XTQEN.X	26.70	0.00	25.60	26.00	100	2,945
75.00	XTQEO.X	21.60	0.00	20.60	21.00	2	5,602
80.00	XTQEP.X	16.30	0.00	15.60	16.00	4	7,077
85.00	XTQEQ.X	10.70	↓0.80	10.70	11.10	14	10,689
90.00	XTQER.X	6.40	↓0.90	6.20	6.40	16	3,741
95.00	XTQES.X	2.60	↓0.40	2.50	2.65	86	2,697
100.00	XTQET.X	0.60	↓0.40	0.55	0.60	1,377	2,222
105.00	XTQEZ.X	0.20	0.00	0.05	0.10	217	1,220

PUT OPTIONS   Expire at close Fri, May 18, 2007

Strike	Symbol	Last	Chg	Bid	Ask	Vol	Open Int
50.00	XTQQJ.X	0.05	0.00	N/A	0.05	86	2,188
55.00	XTQQK.X	0.05	0.00	N/A	0.05	43	2,824
60.00	XTQQL.X	0.05	0.00	N/A	0.05	10	3,055
65.00	XTQQM.X	0.05	0.00	N/A	0.05	25	11,090
70.00	XTQQN.X	0.02	0.00	N/A	0.05	4	4,413
75.00	XTQQO.X	0.05	0.00	N/A	0.05	210	9,258
80.00	XTQQP.X	0.05	0.00	N/A	0.05	127	5,296
85.00	XTQQQ.X	0.11	↑0.01	0.05	0.15	5	2,591
90.00	XTQQR.X	0.45	0.00	0.40	0.50	123	3,353
95.00	XTQQS.X	1.70	↑0.35	1.65	1.80	341	1,250
100.00	XTQQT.X	5.00	↑0.60	4.60	4.90	200	361
105.00	XTQQZ.X	8.20	0.00	9.20	9.60	6	44

Highlighted options are in-the-money.

E-16

CHART #3 [59] - April 29, 2007

Toolbox » Graphs » Options - Listed Options   Print

VSEA   [Get Options]   Add symbol to: [Portfolio] [Watch List]

☐ = In the Money   View Month(s): All Months | May 07 | Jun 07 | Aug 07 | Nov 07 | Jan 08 | Jan 09

Varian Semiconductor (NASDAQ: VSEA) Optionable

Last 69.99   Chg:+12.99   %Chg:+22.79%   Vol: 7,879,801 Avg Vol: 1,554,013
Bid: 69.80   Ask: 70.00   High: 70.38   Low: 66.01   VV% Change: +407.06%   ✳ thinkorswim

Option Tools: Covered Calls Calculator   Selling Puts Calculator   Black-Scholes Calculator

MAY CALLS

Ticker	Last	INTRINSIC VALUE	BID	ASK	VOL	OPEN INTEREST	STRIKE	Ticker	Last	INTRINSIC VALUE	BID	ASK	VOL	OPEN INTEREST
UES-EC	54.90	54.99	54.70	55.10	0	10	15.00	UES-QC	0.05	0.00	N/A	0.05	0	40
UES-EW	52.45	52.49	52.20	52.70	0	15	17.50	UES-QW	0.05	0.00	N/A	0.05	0	0
UES-ED	49.80	49.99	49.50	50.10	0	3	20.00	UES-QD	0.05	0.00	N/A	0.05	0	0
UES-EX	47.40	47.49	47.10	47.70	0	13	22.50	UES-QX	0.05	0.00	N/A	0.05	0	13
UES-EE	44.60	44.99	44.40	44.80	0	40	25.00	UES-QE	0.05	0.00	N/A	0.05	0	82
UES-EF	39.85	39.99	39.60	40.10	0	87	30.00	UES-QF	0.05	0.00	N/A	0.05	0	207
UES-EG	34.95	34.99	34.70	35.20	0	153	35.00	UES-QG	0.05	0.00	N/A	0.05	0	374
UES-EH	30.00	29.99	29.80	30.20	0	280	40.00	UES-QH	0.10	0.00	N/A	0.10	0	1,749
UES-EI	24.85	24.99	24.70	25.00	0	503	45.00	UES-QI	0.05	0.00	N/A	0.05	0	2,787
UES-EJ	20.15	19.99	20.00	20.30	0	4,339	50.00	UES-QJ	0.05	0.00	N/A	0.05	0	7,521
UES-EK	15.20	14.99	15.00	15.40	0	1,653	55.00	UES-QK	0.08	0.00	0.05	0.10	0	6,813
UES-EL	10.40	9.99	10.30	10.50	0	2,691	60.00	UES-QL	0.30	0.00	0.25	0.35	0	2,684
UES-EM	6.10	4.99	6.00	6.20	0	563	65.00	UES-QM	0.95	0.00	0.90	1.00	0	54
UES-EN	2.75	0.00	2.65	2.85	0	0	70.00	UES-QN	2.58	0.01	2.50	2.65	0	0
UES-EO	0.95	0.00	0.70	1.20	0	0	75.00	UES-QO	6.00	5.01	4.60	7.40	0	0
UES-EP	0.38	0.00	0.10	0.65	0	0	80.00	UES-QP	10.10	10.01	7.70	12.50	0	0

Spreads for May 2007 Options: Bull Call Spreads Bull Put Spreads Bear Call Spreads Bear Put Spreads

Calls							Jun 07			Puts				
Ticker	Last	INTRINSIC VALUE	BID	ASK	VOL	OPEN INTEREST	STRIKE	Ticker	Last	INTRINSIC VALUE	BID	ASK	VOL	OPEN INTEREST
UES-FH	30.10	29.99	29.80	30.40	0	0	40.00	UES-RH	0.05	0.00	N/A	0.05	0	10
UES-FI	25.05	24.99	24.90	25.20	0	12	45.00	UES-RI	0.10	0.00	N/A	0.10	0	135
UES-FJ	20.40	19.99	20.20	20.60	0	6	50.00	UES-RJ	0.12	0.00	0.10	0.15	0	205
UES-FK	15.30	14.99	15.10	15.50	0	196	55.00	UES-RK	0.28	0.00	0.20	0.35	0	615
UES-FL	11.10	9.99	10.90	11.30	0	304	60.00	UES-RL	0.77	0.00	0.70	0.85	0	3,041
UES-FM	7.10	4.99	7.00	7.20	0	153	65.00	UES-RM	1.78	0.00	1.70	1.85	0	11
UES-FN	3.95	0.00	3.90	4.00	0	6	70.00	UES-RN	3.70	0.01	3.60	3.80	0	1
UES-FO	1.98	0.00	1.95	2.00	0	0	75.00	UES-RO	6.65	5.01	5.30	8.00	0	0
UES-FP	0.90	0.00	0.65	1.15	0	0	80.00	UES-RP	10.80	10.01	8.70	12.90	0	0

Spreads for Jun 2007 Options: Bull Call Spreads Bull Put Spreads Bear Call Spreads Bear Put Spreads

Calls							Aug 07			Puts				
Ticker	Last	INTRINSIC VALUE	BID	ASK	VOL	OPEN INTEREST	STRIKE	Ticker	Last	INTRINSIC VALUE	BID	ASK	VOL	OPEN INTEREST
UES-HE	45.20	44.99	44.90	45.50	0	5	25.00	UES-TE	0.10	0.00	N/A	0.10	0	8

May 6, 2007

Hello fellow optioneers,

It's a pleasure addressing such a group of intelligent, highly motivated investors who are putting in so much time and effort.

I predict that most of you will be successful options sellers in the near future.

Last Thursday we spoke about exit strategies. One of the topics was "converting dead money into cash profits". The example I gave was selling Qualcom and buying Ezcorp.

I looked around yesterday to see if I could find some current examples (they are ALWAYS there!). But instead of turning to my watch list I decided to check the financial news. Here's what caught my eye:

1- CROX a stock already on my watch list had a great earnings report and declared a 2-for-1 stock split (a 4th seminar topic). We'll come back to this one.

2- The following stocks (that I have previously owned) were up in **price and volume:**

AH
DXPE
SPWR

Now why would they be up in price and volume?
Either:
1- AnnMarie, Christina, Sharon, Neeraj, Shavana, and one of the camera guys each bought 200 shares of each stock OR
2- The "big boys" decided to take substantial postions in these equities.

HINT: it's not # 1

So I decided to run them through our system. CROX has already passed our screening process. All 3 passed through but I had to eliminate DXPE because it was NOT optionable.

Let's caculate the 2-week return on these remaining 3 stocks and see if we could get rid of a "dog" in our portfolio and generate $$$$$$$$$$$$$$$.

AH sells for $82.15. The May 80 call premium is 3.70. If called out we sell the stock for 80 and lose 2.15. We deduct the 2.15 from the 3.70 profit to get a true profit of 1.55 or 155/contract. Divide by our cost basis: 155/8215=**1.9%** 2-week return. Now multiply by 26 to annualize (26x2=52 weeks)= **49%**

SPWR sells for 58.34. The May 60 call premium is 1.10. 110/5834 = **1.9%** which again annualizes to **49%**

CROX sells for 68.85. The May 70 call premium is 2.15. 215/6885 = **3.1%** which annualized to **81%**

These great returns are all for **2-week obligations.**
I'm sure that if I checked my watch list I could have found a lot more. I just wanted to demonstrate that great investments are right in front of you no matter which direction you are looking. I will give you other places to look at the 4th seminar. Most of my investments are from the IBD 100 but there is money to be made everywhere.

When you go through this weeks IBD, I suggest you do your option calculations for the June expiration since we are 2 weeks from the May expiration. Just multiply by 8.5 to annualize as we did in the last seminar.

Off to the Yankee game(sorry Mets fans)
Alan

May 8, 2007

Hi to all,

First a reminder: No seminar this week. Dates of last 2 seminars are:
May 17th
June 7th

Here are the 4 stocks that Linda found for us (from this weeks IBD) to add to our watch list (there were many others that were already on our list):
ESI
DRC
SCHN
WNR
All with great fundamentals and beautiful chart patterns.

Today I added a 5th stock, thanks to one of the members of our group, **Brice Sheppard, who sent me an email telling me about this equity.** This stock was not in the IBD 100 but meets our system requirements:
TDW
Great work Brice and thanks for sharing that with us.

In March there was news that the "metal" prices had hit a one year high, with copper in particular leading the way. Related to that was news that China's economy was up 11% in the quarter. China and India are two countries whose infrastructure is being built up and this bodes well for the metals. Add to this, the fact that metal inventories are low.
I decided to check my watch list for metal plays and found the following stocks:
PCU
X
RTI
MT
STLD

This train ride has been a lot of fun the last 2 months and demonstrates that when a particular industry is "hot", riding the stocks in that industry will boost our profits even higher.

There are two attachments I've included in this email alert:

1- My response to one of our group members regarding a question about the "buy and hold" philosophy of stock investing.

2- An incredible web page designed by a member of our class, **Jesse Friedman.**
You can use this page for your entire stock analysis and option premium information without having to go from address to address, a great time saver. Many thanks to Jesse for your creativity and your generosity in sharing this with us.

I reviewed the unedited DVDs of the first two seminars. Not only are your questions and comments intelligent and to the point but more importantly you look great!
Linda and I really appreciate your participation in this project.
I'll be in touch prior to the 17th
Best regards
Alan

(2nd e-alert) - May 8, 2007

There are many investors who subscribe to the "buy and hold" philosophy.
I am not one of them.
It implies that no matter what new information surfaces, you will stick with your investment and hope that even newer information turns that around. Enron was once the 7th largest company in the US with tremendous earnings quarter in and quarter out. Should we have bought and held Enron as it went from 80/share to pennies/share?
That being said, if you prefer not to be pro-active in stock selection but want to be in the market, here is what I would do:
Dollar cost average into the S&P 500 or Total Stock Market Index Funds. I would use the Vanguard family of funds since they have the lowest expense ratios.
Here are the fund #'s

0040
0085

As far as buying stocks but not selling options on them:
Use the same system but don't limit them to "optionable " stocks.
Let me know if you need further explanation.
Alan

May 14, 2007

Greetings,

In the last alert I sent, I mentioned the metals industry as one that has made significant profits for me recently.

Another industry that is "smokin' hot" is the **Construction and Agricultural Machinery Industry.** As a whole the industry is up 40% since November.

Here are the top 5 performing stocks within this industry. Four of them meet our system criteria. You may want to add one or more of the these to your watch list:

CNH
BUCY
AG
MTW
DE

Remember, one of these does not meet our requirements.

Here are the 5 stocks that Linda found from this weeks IBD that we have added to our watch list. I also bumped off a few stocks that were below the 20-d EMA for over a week:

WCG
PCR
NILE
CRDN
CENX

Let's take another look at the stock that Brice found for us, **TDW:**

- The Oil Services Industry is ranked in the 82% - excellent.
- Money flow into this industry from the "big boys" is ranked "A" - even better
- If we bought the stock today and sold the 6/65 call, we would receive an annualized return of 30%, about 5 times that of your banks CD.
- The only slightly negative is that the advanced technicals are not ideal. This is a subject we will discuss at tha 4th (June 7th) seminar.
- All in all, a stock worthy of my watch list.

This Thursday's seminar will include the following:

1- Exit Strategies Review
2- New Material
    a- Earnings Reports
    b- Advanced Calculations
    c- Calculating stock and Option positions (how many shares should I buy?)
    d- **Introducing the Options Calculator- Special guest speaker**
3- Interactice Session

Things to bring:
1- all printouts from Advanced Workshop I
2- calculator
3- ticker symbols of stocks you want the class to evaluate.

Thank you very much to those of you who have given or who have scheduled video-testimonials to be included in my DVD series.

Anyone interested in being included in these filmed testimonials please let me know and I'll have a member of our film crew contact you. Or just let them know when you come to the next seminar.

Finally, **thanks to Donna and Mike Pacheco** for converting the Stock Watch List Locator Form into a PDF and Excel File.

Please see attachment to take advantage of their great work.

Looking foward to seeing you this Thursday @ 7 PM. The seminar will be in the Executive Conference Room as was the AW I. Use the main entrance into the hotel.

Alan

May 20, 2007

Fellow Optioneers,
Three seminars down and one to go.
You are making such unbelievable progress!

I want to follow up on a few points that came out at the last seminar:

1- I mentioned **SRCL**, a company I use in my dental practice that announced a 2-for-1 split on Thursday. It made it all the way through our screening process but the option returns were low. This in spite of the favorable position of the price near a strike price. When it is apparent that a great performing stock like Stericycle, does not yield an impressive option return, I do not allow it on my watch list....why waste a spot?

2- The first Friday in June is the 1st, the third or expiration Friday is therefore the 15th, making this next option period a short one. This will effect the "time value" of our options. Therefore you will notice a lower return this next option period than others. No big deal. You will still average between 2 and 3 %, even in shorter periods.

3- I continually stress how important it is to be CEO of your own money and not to listen to any particular expert or analyst. To bring home this point I printed out the analyst opinion sheet for US Steel, one of the meatal plays that hasmade me significant profits the last 4 months. **Please print out the attachment**
-Notice that in the last 4 months there have been 5 upgrades and 5 downgrades.....
Really helpful!
- Now let's look at the analyst opinion list....what a mess of buy and sell opinions. Most are "hold" opinions. I've been in the market for almost 17 years now and I still don't know what that means! **Should I buy it or sell it?** Have some guts...take a stand!
- I'm not saying to ignore what they are saying. I'm simply suggesting you factor in all the information you want to analyze and make your own decision as to what you will do with your hard-earned money.
Hold on....I'm taking a deep breath.

Yahoo has changed it's technical analysis link to "new charts".
- It now defaults to the price bar, not the line chart (about time).
-Hit the technical Indicators bar on top and enter 20,100-d ema
- You will now get the same chart as before

Keep an eye on the following stocks:

BTU
CCJ
QCOM

These are stocks that I have done quite well with in the past but then broke down. They are making a comeback and are close to getting back on my watch list.

Linda located the following stocks from this weeks IBD:

MTL (watch out for tomorrow's scheduled Earnings Report)
CPX
WHQ
SPN

I ran these through the "Multiple" tab page of the option calculator and printed out the results in the **attachment.**

Note that since the current market values are between strike prices (except SPN) the ROO's are not impressive but the upside potentials and downside protection are.

If I were deciding between these equities my first choice would be SPN which would give me a 1-month return of 3.6% or 43% annualized.
My second choice would be WHQ. ROO's on both the In-The-Money and Out-of-the Money are close to 2% and 22-23% annual returns. Depending on which option you chose, you would get a fabulous downside protection or upside potential.

I'll let you know when you can start using the "what now" tab.
Best Regards.
Alan

E-17   CHART #1 [60] - May 20, 2007

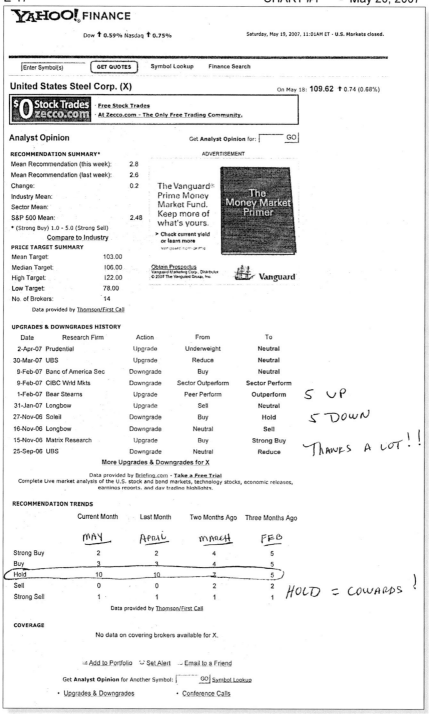

YAHOO! FINANCE

Dow ↑ 0.59% Nasdaq ↑ 0.75%   Saturday, May 19, 2007, 11:01AM ET - U.S. Markets closed.

| Enter Symbol(s) | **GET QUOTES** | Symbol Lookup | Finance Search |

United States Steel Corp. (X)
On May 18: **109.62** ↑ 0.74 (0.68%)

$0 Stock Trades zecco.com · Free Stock Trades · At Zecco.com - The Only Free Trading Community.

Analyst Opinion
Get **Analyst Opinion** for: [ ] **GO**

RECOMMENDATION SUMMARY*   ADVERTISEMENT

Mean Recommendation (this week):	2.8
Mean Recommendation (last week):	2.6
Change:	0.2
Industry Mean:	
Sector Mean:	
S&P 500 Mean:	2.48

* (Strong Buy) 1.0 - 5.0 (Strong Sell)

Compare to Industry

PRICE TARGET SUMMARY

Mean Target:	103.00
Median Target:	106.00
High Target:	122.00
Low Target:	78.00
No. of Brokers:	14

The Vanguard® Prime Money Market Fund. Keep more of what's yours.
The Money Market Primer
> Check current yield or learn more
vanguard.com-prime

Obtain Prospectus
Vanguard Marketing Corp., Distributor
© 2007 The Vanguard Group, Inc.
Vanguard

Data provided by Thomson/First Call

UPGRADES & DOWNGRADES HISTORY

Date	Research Firm	Action	From	To
2-Apr-07	Prudential	Upgrade	Underweight	Neutral
30-Mar-07	UBS	Upgrade	Reduce	Neutral
9-Feb-07	Banc of America Sec	Downgrade	Buy	Neutral
9-Feb-07	CIBC Wrld Mkts	Downgrade	Sector Outperform	Sector Perform
1-Feb-07	Bear Stearns	Upgrade	Peer Perform	Outperform
31-Jan-07	Longbow	Upgrade	Sell	Neutral
27-Nov-06	Soleil	Downgrade	Buy	Hold
16-Nov-06	Longbow	Downgrade	Neutral	Sell
15-Nov-06	Matrix Research	Upgrade	Buy	Strong Buy
25-Sep-06	UBS	Downgrade	Neutral	Reduce

5 UP
5 DOWN
THANKS A LOT!!

More Upgrades & Downgrades for X

Data provided by Briefing.com - Take a Free Trial
Complete Live market analysis of the U.S. stock and bond markets, technology stocks, economic releases, earnings reports, and day trading highlights.

RECOMMENDATION TRENDS

	Current Month	Last Month	Two Months Ago	Three Months Ago
	MAY	*APRIL*	*MARCH*	*FEB*
Strong Buy	2	2	4	5
Buy	3	3	4	5
Hold	10	10	7	5
Sell	0	0	2	2
Strong Sell	1	1	1	1

HOLD = COWARDS!

Data provided by Thomson/First Call

COVERAGE

No data on covering brokers available for X.

⊠ Add to Portfolio   ✎ Set Alert   ✉ Email to a Friend

Get **Analyst Opinion** for Another Symbol: [ ] **GO** Symbol Lookup

· Upgrades & Downgrades   · Conference Calls

E-18   CHART #2 - May 20, 2007

RETURN ON OPTION (ROO) CALCULATOR - MULTIPLE STOCKS

Stock Name or Symbol	Stock $/sh	Option $/sh	Strike $	Expires	Intrisic	Upside	ROO	Up Potential	Down Protect
mtl fg	$ 36.71	$ 2.05	$ 35.00	06/15/07	$ 1.71	$ -	1.0%	0.0%	4.7%
mtl fh	$ 36.71	$ 0.30	$ 40.00	6/15/2007	$ -	$ 3.29	0.8%	9.0%	0.0%
cpx fe	$ 26.72	$ 2.15	$ 25.00	06/15/07	$ 1.72	$ -	1.7%	0.0%	6.4%
cpx ff	$ 26.72	$ 0.20	$ 30.00	06/15/07	$ -	$ 3.28	0.7%	12.3%	0.0%
whq fl	$ 62.80	$ 3.90	$ 60.00	06/15/07	$ 2.80	$ -	1.6%	0.0%	4.5%
whq fm	$ 62.80	$ 1.20	$ 65.00	06/15/07	$ -	$ 2.20	1.9%	3.5%	0.0%
spn th	$ 39.99	$ 1.45	$ 40.00	06/15/07	$ -	$ 0.01	3.6%	0.0%	0.0%

2ND
1ST

Run: 5/20/2007 1:01 PM

May 25, 2007

Hi to all,
These last few days should remind you of the S&P 500 short term chart I showed you **twice**. I deliberately showed it twice to bring home the point that the market has short term volatility. That's just the nature of the market. You can't get emotionally sick over a downturn. History shows that it will come back and go up (long term chart).

I noticed today that one of the stocks on my watch list, **VIP** is up in price and volume. Makes me wonder what the "big boys" are up to. If we were to buy this stock today and sell the June $105 option we would get a 3-week return of 2.7% or 46% annualized.

Luck is the intersection of preparation and opportunity
For the last few months I have been selling options on **ICE** at a cost basis of $145/share. I have been generating profits of between 2-5% per month. Last Friday the stock closed at about 141. I had sold the May 145 so I was not assigned.
Monday it was up to 144. Should I sell the June 145 on Monday? A late emergency in my office and the next thing I knew the market was closed. But I knew to keep my eye on this one Tuesday morning.
Tuesday morning...BOOM! the stock jumps up $5.25 to 151. The June 145 call was selling for $11.20! In between patients I went online. A few clicks on the computer and $1113 was in my account. This for 1 contract! This represented an 8% 1-month return or 96% annualized.
You don't get returns like this every day but they do happen.
Was I lucky? Or was I prepared and able to take advantage of an opportunity? You decide.

This month (so far) I have generated $8000 into my account from the sale of options. This represents about a 3% return on my underlying stock investments. I am pleased with this return in that we are in a shortened option contract period. Here are a few more options that I sold this month with the underlying stock ticker:
CLF-FN (CLF)
X-FA (X)
TEX-FP (TEX)
CQL-FK (CENX)

On June 7th we will discuss stock splits (among other topics). Here are 3 stocks that may be on your watch list that will be splitting in the near future:

ESRX 2 for 1 on June 22nd
POT 3 for 1 on May 29th
CROX 2 for 1 on June 14th

Many investors (**not us!**) will buy a stock simply because of a stock split announcement. However, a split along with meeting all other system criteria should get our attention.

Finally, I wanted to clarify my new rule banning retail stocks reporting monthly same store sales. These companies are NOT required to report on a monthly basis. They chose to do so to appear "transparent" and stay in the good graces of the SEC. Two companies that recently decided to no longer report monthly same store sales are YUM and SBUX (YUM is the company that owns Pizza Hut, Kentucky Fried Chicked and Taco Bell; the other is Starbucks). I have not been able to think of any companies not on the list I gave you. If I do, I'll send it out on the next alert.

Linda and I wish you all a wonderful holiday weekend.
Alan

June 3, 2007

I can't believe we're down to our final seminar!

You are a very impressive audience. I can't wait to here about your success stories in the near future!

One stock I want to highlight is **FCX**. This is a metal mining company that has exploded the last few months.

It is solid both fundamentally and technically.

Institutional money flowing into this industry ranks in the top 98th percentile!

With the stock trading @ $79.50 we could do the following plays:

1- sell the June/80 (FCX FP) @ 1.80.

This would generate a 2-week return of 2.3% or 59% annualized (my choice).

2- sell the July/80 (FCX GP) @ 3.90

This would generate a 6-week return of 4.9% or 42% annualized.

These are close to at-the-money strike prices so there is negligible upside and no downside protection but great returns on a stock performing extremely well.

Please **see attached chart** which demonstrates the great performance of the equity since early March.

Thanks (again) to Brice Sheppard for finding this one for us: **SII**

This is a company in the Oil Service Industry. Institutional money flowing in to this industry ranks in the top 86%.

These type of companies are good plays due to the tight oil supply, Iranian issues, and the inability of oil refineries to increase production due to their old infrastructure.

With the stock trading @ $55.63, we could look at the July/55 in-the-money strike:

This would give us a 6-week return of 3.9% or 34% annualized.

We would also get about 1% downside protection.

Great find Brice! I've added it to my watch list.

Stocks I've added to my watch list this week with comments on the flow of institutional $ flowing into its industries:

GME- low but increasing, don't buy yet

CHE- Average

SSYS- low but increasing, don't buy yet

VOLV- Average

Advanced Workshop II alerted you to the risks involved in selling options through earnings reports. Here are a few stocks that may be on your watch list that are scheduled to report prior to the July 20th expiration:

RS

STLD

VOLV

AAPLis a company you have heard me speak of frequently.

Currently the computer manufacturing industry is not sound technically but AAPL is flying high (no surprise). This stock has definitely been my biggest money-maker the last few years (could change, but I've been saying that for a long time!).

AAPL is scheduled to report earning on July 18th. It is currently trading at $118.40.

Historically it will declare a stock split in the 80-90 range. Will it announce a split on July 18th? If it does and it has yet another great ER, the stock will go even higher.

I currently own AAPL and will not sell July calls. I do plan to hold on to my shares up to and perhaps through the ER. I've done this several times with AAPL and won every time!

Finally, thanks to Jesse Friedman for updating the Stock Analysis Combination Page.

Please see attachment for this update.

Looking foward to seeing you this Thursday.

Alan

E-19   CHART [61] - June 3, 2007

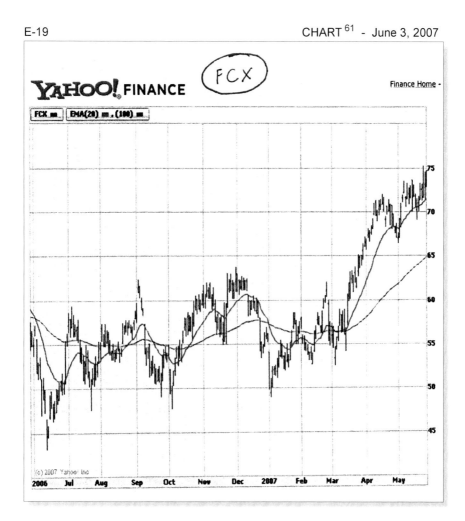

June 20, 2007

Jeanmarie,

Welcome back!

Please print out the attached chart.

You did not make a mistake purchasing this stock based on the ER coming up shortly after expiration. I do it all the time. What happened here is that BW pre-announced to soften the blow of a second straight poor ER (see the circled #1 on the chart to see what happened after the last ER). This rarely happens but when it does consider it unavoidable.

Now, that being said, **you should not have purchased this stock for the following reasons:**

1- It has a stock technical rating of B minus, falling short of our system criteria.

2- In early June, it breaks down technically:

    A- At #2 it drops below its 20-d EMA

    B- Similarly, at #3 MACD turns negative

    C- Finally, at # 4 the stochastic oscillator double dips below 80%

These 3 indicators are telling you to run for the hills! Couldn't be more negative.

At this point, I would sell all the shares and put my cash into an equity that meets all system criteria.

Keep paper trading until you feel like you've mastered all aspects of the system (should take a few months). It took me a long time to figure all this out but my mistakes cost me $$$$$$$$$$$$. You are way ahead of most and well on your way to being a successful options trader.

Best of luck

Alan

E-20

CHART [62] - June 20, 2007

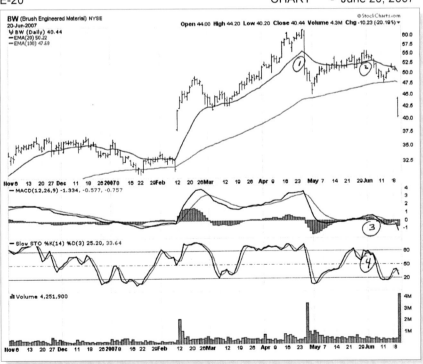

July 9, 2007

Subj:	**Re: Follow-up Seminar Question**
Date:	7/9/2007 7:11:29 PM Atlantic Daylight Time
From:	Agewen
To:	imandel@

M+A's

Hi Ira,

This is a rare, interesting situation that I did not discuss at the seminars because in the past it almost never came up.

However, with the extreme increase in mergers and acquisitions of late I may include it in the next series.

Here is what happened:

FCX merged with Phelps Dodge. Shareholders who owned PD received .67 shares of FCX for every share of PD plus $88 per share. Notice the first 3 letters of the contract are DPT, not FCX..

These contracts are conversions from those who sold (or bought) PD options before the merger.

To calculate the example you asked about, you would take the current price and multiply by .67 and add $88.

Your stock is worth $148 and you're selling the 100 strike, 48 in the money. Your option return barely covers that. Therefore this option makes no sense to consider and that is why you see no activity.

To get more info on mergers:

www.cboe.com
go to trading
go to tools
type in ticker

In general when something seems too good to be true, it probably is.
We have to settle for our 2-4%/month returns!
Best regards
Alan

Alan Eltoon here...
Want to read more e-alerts?
Then go to my BLOG Today!
www.thebluecollarinvestor.com/blog

THE BLUE COLLAR
INVESTOR

APPENDIX III
Stock Trading vs. Option Selling

Conventional Stock Market Investing:

1. Buy a stock and hope it goes up.
2. If the stock goes down and you sell, a loss is incurred.
3. If the stock goes up and you sell, a gain is realized.
4. If you do not sell your stock, you have neither a loss or a gain.
5. If, and when you have a gain, you can take your profits and re-invest it, thereby compounding your money.
6. Historically, the stock market appreciates about 1% per month.

Selling Covered Call Options:

1. Buy a stock and we are perfectly fine if it doesn't go up in value. We just don't want it to go down precipitously.
2. If the stock goes down in value, we may still make money. If we lose money, it will be less than if we didn't sell the option.
3. If the stock price goes up and we sell, we will make, in many cases, profit from the sale of the stock and the sale of the option.
4. If you do not sell your stock, you still make money.
5. The profit you generate from selling the option is in your account in seconds. This allows you to compound your money in seconds!
6. Under normal market conditions, returns of 2-4% is quite realistic.

APPENDIX IV

Testimonials

Certainly a very sensible technique, Alan. In fact, I will do some back testing (as much as is possible) with charts and my trading records to see how I might have fared doing it your way. Of course I can't really say at this point which stocks I would have chosen to replace at those points, but I'll play with it. Your way is simple, and I like simple. It frequently is the most effective. It is very possible to get too sophisticated in attempting to redirect a bad siuation, spending much time and energy to succeed, while simply cutting bait and finding a fatter fish would do a much more credible and less stressful job. I like it.

Your attitude on this reminds me of the advice I once received from a professional trader I used to speak with occasionally. He said he made his substantial money by nibbles, not gulps, and mostly by keeping what he had gained (limiting losses and keeping cash to use to play another day). That meant no attachment to a particular trade, but a x% loss before he just closed it. No matter what. I think your attitude is a hallmark of a good trader and I will see how it works for me. Another thing I might do if I believe in a stock but feel that an event (earnings) might damage my position temporarily, is to long some puts. It lowers my net credit (raises my debit), but in some circumstances might actually provide a better trading possibility while still allowing me to exit with a profit, no matter what.

I really love this stuff, Alan. I make my living at it, getting about the same returns you are, and working to improve my equity positions even while creating around 4% cash each month. SInce your first class, I have been much more careful with my fundamental due diligence and I'm not having to deal with nearly as many post expiration remanagement exercises :-).I'm geting a lot from you and I really appreciate your generosity and enthusiasm. I'm now into IBD and investors.com as well as quicken.com (go to portfolio, stock evaluator, and value indicator . . .very helpful).

Well, I love talking with you about this, but I better get to bed. We'll talk soon. Thanks again. I value your advice.

Bruce

On 2/11/07

Subj: **Re: STOCK OPTIONS SEMINAR- Course Outline- March 1, 2007**
Date: 2/26/2007 6:34:26 PM Atlantic Standard Time
From: bruce.fields█████████
To: A█████████
Sent from the Internet (Details)

Hi Alan - I'm endlessly impressed with the way your new career as Speaker/Guru is advancing and at the terrific job you are doing. Thanks for all the great updates. Communication is 90% of the game as far as I'm concerned.

Looking forward to Thursday.   -b-

On 2/26/07, A█████████ wrote:
  Hi to all,
  I've attached an outline with a few key definitions.
  Also, I've included a sample option log to help keep track of your monthly profits.
  You should all have previously received directions.

  Plainview Holiday Inn
  Thursday, March 1st
  7PM - 10 PM - **WILL START PROMPTLY @ 7 PM**

  Feel free to suggest stocks that we can evaluate together as a class. Looking foward to seeing you this Thursday.
  Alan

  ★★

--
Bruce Fields
bruce.fields█████████

Subj: **Thanks Alan**
Date: 3/23/2007 11:26:49 AM Atlantic Daylight Time
From: bruce.fields█████████████
To: a█████████████████
Sent from the Internet (Details)

Thank you, Alan. Another wonderful evening. I get a lot out of listening to you and appreciate your willingness to share your experience (faith and hope :-) with us.

I've been running some call calendars with AAPL, APR95/JUL95 (last month I did 90's) and am making over 25% each month!! so far on those trades. All I need to do to sink the company is to do more than a conservative 5 contracts. Only greed kills. Hard to remember, but crucial. Talk to you soon. -b-

--
Bruce Fields
bruce.fields█████████████████

April 1, 2007

I can't believe how BWLD has moved since I started using "the System" (I think it needs it needs a name, or do you already have one for the book??) $ 50 to $ 64.?!?! For chicken wings??? Must be really good!! Well can't argue w/ success and momentum!!

Thanks again for insight!!

Have a good week

Don

4/02/07

Alan,

Your course has been a dream answered.

I can actually see myself making a steady income stream to help support my family.

I joined the LIREIA hoping to learn how to earn with RE but instead found you and your

wonderful system for selling options.

Bless you for making the system available to me.

MarciaGrace

Subj: **Re: TELESEMINAR REPLAY- Alan Ellman**
Date: 4/13/2007 12:56:54 PM Atlantic Daylight Time
From: Marlins███
To: A███

Hi Alan: I enjoyed your presentation & look forward to the seminars.......you are becoming an
incredible capable internet monster!
Thanks,
Paul

-----Original Message-----
From: A███████████
Sent: Fri, 13 Apr 2007 11:27 AM
Subject: TELESEMINAR REPLAY- Alan Ellman

Fellow Investors,

TO ALL THOSE INTERESTED IN GENERATING MONTHLY CA$H PROFITS INTO YOUR ACCOUNT VIA THE
STOCK MARKET.

Here is a link to a replay of a teleseminar I conducted Thursday April 12th that will explain this strategy. It also
contains a link to a **registration form** to sign up for a seminar series I will be giving starting April 26th.

http://www.lireia.com/audioclub/ellmancallreplay.html

Wishing you all the best in investing.
Alan

Subj: **Re: Stock Options- Alan**
Date: 4/14/2007 12:01:45 AM Atlantic Daylight Time
From: OSARGENT
To: A█████████████

Like you, I love a standing ovation.

Seriously, all of the calculations that we have been doing are repetitious and tedious. That is precisely what Excel is for. I have a flair for using it because it is the most powerful tool I have as an accountant.

I have been investing in the stock market and options market for thirty years. It was always hit or miss for various reasons. I took your class, and I am glad I did, because you have developed a methodical, easy to follow set of investing rules. Hit or miss will always be hit or miss. Your rules, carefully followed, produce more winners than losers. That's how early (and comfortable) retirements are built.

So, thank you for sharing your experience with us. The least I can do is share some of mine.

Owen

TESTAMONIALS

STOCK OPTIONS SEMINARS

Alan Ellman / A-Line Properties Corp.

MEETING & "TRAINING" WITH ALAN HAS TRULY BEEN A LIFE CHANGING EXPERIENCE. FOR YEARS I HAVE BEEN DISSATISFIED WITH MY "BUY & HOLD" INVESTMENT STRATEGY I WAS A PASSIVE INVESTOR, WHO HOPED FOR STOCKS TO GO UP, BUT LACKED A STRATEGY TO DO ANYTHING BUT SELL, WHEN STOCKS WENT DOWN.

AFTER ATTENDING ALAN'S STOCK OPTION SEMINARS, AND SOME PERSONAL COACHING, I NOW HAVE THE TOOLS AND THE KNOWLEDGE TO BE AN ACTIVE & SUCCESSFUL INVESTOR. I HAVE BEEN ABLE TO TAKE CONTROL OF MY FINANCIAL ASSETS. USING ALAN'S SYSTEM I NOW SYSTEMATICALY CHOOSE MY STOCKS, GENERATE INCOME SELLING COVERED CALL OPTIONS, GENERATING AN AVERAGE RETURN OF 3%/MONTH OR 36% ANNUALLY AND I AM NOW ABLE TO EMPLOY ALAN'S EXIT STRATEGIES TO SOFTEN THE INEVITABLE MARKET DECLINES AND EVEN GENERATE PROFITS

DONALD EMPETT   CENTERPORT, NY
Your name   City, State

WHEN I WOULD HAVE NORMALLY BEEN PASSIVELY WATCHING MY LOSSES ACCUMULATE.

APRIL 2007

Subj: **Re: Multiple stock page**
Date: 4/24/2007 9:39:15 PM Atlantic Daylight Time
From: OSARGENT
To: A

I couldn't have done it without you. Your ROO sheet is simple and easy to understand. Putting those calculations on a spreadsheet was fairly easy once you showed us what you use.

I started out in architecture many years ago. I went to the Illinois Institute of Technology. The architecture department, and half of the school's buildings, was designed by Mies Van der Rogh. His motto was "Less is more."

In your own way you have shown that phrase is true. So many of the stock screens, filtering programs and books provide many ways to pick stocks. Your method is much less, but it produces much more. You don't find yourself overwhelmed with "noise" to the point you freeze and do nothing. That can be used to select stocks even if you're not selling options.

I will send you more cards. I think I'll send you some personal business cards. My firm can get pretty expensive. I would be honored to be in your book. I would also be willing to polish up the spreadsheets (like include e-mail address, name, etc) to be handed out on disk with the book. I'm almost done with the "What now?" page and I want to add a Schedule D spreadsheet that your students can use to attach to their tax returns.

Anyway, I've rambled on, and you have things to do, so I'll be in touch.

Thank you for sharing your experience. I wish I had met you years ago.

Owen

Subj:
Date: 4/27/2007 12:42:03 PM Atlantic Daylight Time
From: ablacker
To: A
Sent from the Internet (Details)

Hi Alan,
   I've got to hand it to you. You found your niche. You are an outstanding presenter, teacher and have the charisma to go along with it.
   Your Stock Option Seminar was easy to understand - sequential, clear and logical. It's not often I say this, but I can't wait to do my homework and study the materials!!!
   I was expecting to just participate in Part 1 of the series to acquaint myself with the concept of stock options. After last night, I intend to attend all four sessions because I am so highly motivated to continue to learn and have a handle on such a practical money-making opportunity.
   Please sign me up for the next three sessions!!
Amy Blacker

April 27, 2007

hi alan,
the seminar was great yesterday.
the simplicity with which you explained the concept and the steps to
identify the stocks and execute the options really worked for me.
looking keenly forward to the next three.

regards to linda and you

neeraj sharma

April 30, 2007

Thank you for the information above and your telephone call. I received
both.

I wanted to take this opportunity to mention how much I enjoyed the
first session of the Option class. It was very informative and as you
mentioned put me in the top 5-10% of the population. Thank you for this
opportunity to have my money work for me.

See you both on Thursday. Thanks.

Tress

April 30, 2007

Alan,

Here's a heartfelt testimonial to add to your list:

It is rare to find a teacher who can distill complex concepts into layman's terms with heart, humor and a sincere desire to share his own secrets of success. Alan has not only found a steady, repeatable method to beat Wall Street, he wants his fellow investors and students to achieve equally great results! Initially, it may seem too good to be true but when you take the course, you quickly realize that this generous mentor is the real deal!

Thanks again from both Terry and myself to you and Linda for your integrity, openness and hospitality.

Sincerely, Terry and Becky O'Brien

May 1, 2007

Alan & Linda, Guess what, I think we're getting it. I'm glad we decided to take the course again and because of your kindness it was easier for us. We have been working every night together and we seem to understand what we're doing. (hallaluia). Anyway - now it seems too easy. Is this possible. We still have alot to learn - we're slow learners - mainly because we haven't been too active in the stock market. But!!! we really have a positive outlook now. Last time we were really, really lost and we felt that we were over our heads. We still have some questions but i think we can do it. Thanks to you and Linda. See you Thursday. Janet and Stephen

May 4, 2007

hey alan,
once again, clear, concise and great information.
you are an excellent teacher.
looking forward to the next one-
best regards to Linda

neeraj

TESTAMONIALS

STOCK OPTIONS SEMINARS

Alan Ellman / A-Line Properties Corp.

ALAN has saved me so much heartache & money!
what an education. It would have taken me years
to learn what he has taught.

           Frank. P.

my husband convinced me to come to see Alan. It
was interesting and easy to understand. Thank you for ~~making~~ breaking
the "mystery" of the stock market

           Edie P.

_____   HUNTINGTON NY

Your name   City, State

MAY 2007

Fax :
May 27 04:21

Alan Ellman has an uncanny way of taking eight years of accumulated knowledge on a complex subject which details his acquired methodology of successfully picking stocks and selling covered call options while minimizing risk and maximizing profit utilizing creative exit strategies.

He is gifted in his ability to disseminate this information by simplifying the process in a 'step-by-step' procedure and by 'seeing it' through the eyes of a novice.

He is clear and concise with his communication as he teaches 'newcomers' in his four-part seminar series.

He is always open and honest, respectful of the participants and holds the highest values of integrity at the heart of his teaching.

Bruce Steifman
Innovative Property Investments LLC
Old Bethpage, NY

June 12, 2007

Hello, Alan

I'm the one to be glad—i got the benefit of your last class! I'm in the process of getting all my IRAs moved to USAA so i can start trading. Would you believe i already received the packet you sent!! Thank you so much, not only for a truly helpful seminar series but also for your enthusiasm, consistency and ethics.

In gratitude,

MarciaGrace

My name is Amy Blacker. I am a public school teacher in an elementary school. Always having had an entrepreneurial spirit and being somewhat of a "money-nerd", I have learned to manage my own finances fairly well. This pertains to making my investments work for me with my retirement objectives (Roth IRA, 403B) and personal investments which include mutual funds and real estate.

In April 2007, I enrolled in Alan Ellman's Stock Option course (Part 1) just to acquaint myself with how to analyze stocks and the concepts of stock options. To my surprise, the seminar was easy to understand – sequential, clear and logical. I learned a great deal in this session, in which time seemed to fly! After the session, I was eager to do my homework and study the materials.

I was so motivated to continue learning from Alan's presentation and materials, that I signed up for the additional 3 sessions! Each of the following three sessions were just as motivating as the first. Alan's sense of humor, charisma and down-to-earth approach made the process of learning the necessary tools and skills enjoyable as well as meaningful.

Since the sessions, I have followed through and practiced all that I have learned. It is now three months since the seminar and I have gotten into the routine and organization necessary to sell callable options. I now have the confidence to transition from paper-trading to actual trading. The method and skills I've learned are invaluable! I intend to do very well financially and am thrilled to be able to use this with my IRA account!

This seminar has been an excellent resource and a money-making opportunity for life. Thank you Alan and Linda for a wonderful learning experience and sharing your "wealth" of knowledge!

JUNE 2007

June 15, 2007

Alan,

This is Linda Simon's son, Hal writing.

As a novice, I was overwhelmed at first in the first session. By the end of that seminar I had a pretty good handle on what it was you are offering. The materials really helped me at home prepare and review for the second session. I was a lot more comfortable. The approach you have in the seminars is one that anyone can grasp the material. I really enjoyed the laid back style and confidence you exhibit. Business got in the way so I was unable to attend the final two seminars. Duty calls. I think I was most upset about not being there for the last class. I was looking forward to giving my testimonial to the production crew. I felt it would have been sincere and genuine especially coming from a novice like myself. Besides it would have been a way to express my gratitude toward you for giving me this opportunity.

I look forward to the release of the DVD so that I can complete my education. The tools you offer, I am sure will be a valuable lesson as I move forward and attempt to do some investing on behalf of my mother and myself.

Again, my many thanks to you for your kindness, knowledge and above all else, your friendship.

Yours truly,

Hal Simon

July 7, 2007

Hi alan,

hope linda and you are having a great summer.

just to let you know that im doing great with the paper trades and the watchlist.

what is even better is that my 12 year old son is doing even better than me![we both have a 5 stock 50,000 dollar paper portfolio]

am going to paper trade for another month and get into the real thing is september.

best regards

neeraj

APPENDIX V

Forms

THE BLUE COLLAR INVESTOR

The Blue Collar Investor Covered Call Stock Evaluation Worksheet

Option Month:　　　　By:　　　　Date:

Stock	Source of Selection	Fundam'tls				Technicals						Other				Comments
		Earnings Report Date In Current Month (No)	IBD-100 - SmartSelect Ratings. (6 Green)	MSN - StockScouter (5 min.)	Stock in Uptrending Channel (Y)	Price Above 20 EMA & 100 EMA (Y)	20 EMA Above 100 EMA (Y)	MACD Positive (>0, Uptrending)	Stochastics (Bet. 20 & 80, Uptrending)	Volume (>250K Sh. & 1.5+ Avg Vol.)						

Notes: (Will change depending on economy)
[1] No financial stocks
[2] No FDA impact related stocks
[3] No same store sales related stocks
[4] No housing or residential construction stocks

Source of Data: MSN Money, Google Finance, Yahoo Finance
IBD: www.investors.com/new
MSN: http://moneycentral.man.com/investor/StockRating/
Charts: http://stockcharts.com/
Earnings: www.earningswhispers.com
Key Financial Data: http://www.finviz.com

Full-sized, versions of all charts, graphs, forms, photos, and other images contained in this book are available at

www.thebluecollarinvestor.com/vip

THE BLUE COLLAR
INVESTOR

DATE	BTC ?	# contracts Premium/ option ticker	Account	month/strike price	Profit
20-Oct	-48	sell (4) GLW KX @ 1.60	45	NOV 22.50	254
24-Oct		sell (1) DVN KN @ 2.75	45	Nov-70	266
2-Nov		sell (4) glw kd @ .70	45	Nov.-20	266
20-Oct	-46	sell (2) AAO KU @ 2.10	500	NOV-37.50	
20-Oct		sell (2) AAO KH @ 1.00	500	Nov-40	431
24-Oct		sell (1) UCJ KF @ 1.35	500	30-Nov	127
24-Oct		sell (2) NUE KL @ 3.20	500	Nov-60	629
30-Oct		sell (2) ADS KL @ 1.90	500	Nov-60	369
30-Oct		sell (2) FLK KM @ 2.50 (FFIV)	500	Nov-65	489
30-Oct		sell (2) QAA KP @ 2.25 (AAPL)	500	Nov-80	439
31-Oct		sell (1) UW 45 (UARM) (	500	NOV_ 45	110
10-Nov		sell (3) ULP KI @ 1.23 (EZPW)	500	Nov-45	468
20-Oct		sell (3) KUO KE @ 1.55 (BEBE)	950	25-Nov	385
20-Oct		sell (2) DQI KJ @ 4.90 (DRIV)	950	Nov-50	348
27-Oct		sell (1) CRS KA @ 4.80	950	11/105	471
30-Oct		sell (1) RUP KD @ 3.30 (RIMM)	950	11/120	321
30-Oct		sell (2) ISE KK @ 1.05	950	Nov-55	199
30-Oct		sell (2) NSI KM @ 2.90 (NTRI)	950	Nov-65	569
30-Oct		sell (4) DSW KG @ 1.05	950	Nov-35	389
30-Oct		sell (6) QPM KW @ 1.01 (SMSI)	950	11/17.50	590
30-Oct		sell (2) AUE KH @ 1.40 (CRDN)	950	Nov-40	209
30-Oct		sell (1) SWF KJ @ 1.40 (SNDK)	950	Nov-50	132
30-Oct		sell (RQL KL @ 2.90 (STLD)	950	Nov-60	459
30-Oct		sell (2) ROG KN @ 1.70	950	Nov-70	329
31-Oct		sell (2) TNL KE @ 1.10	950	25-Nov	209
1-Nov		sell (2) GQR KI @ 1.60 (GRMN)	950	Nov-45	309
10-Nov		sell (2) ISE KJ @ .55	950	Nov-50	102

OPTION LOG NOVEMBER, 2006

Full-sized, versions of all charts, graphs, forms, photos,
and other images contained in this book are available at

www.thebluecollarinvestor.com/vip

FORM TO TAKE TO COMPUTER WHEN READY TO BUY OR SELL

TICKER	PRICE	BUY	OWN	OPTION TICKER	NUMBER OF CONTRACTS	OPTION PREMIUM

THE BLUE COLLAR INVESTOR

Full-sized versions of all charts, graphs, forms, photos, and other images contained in this book are available at

www.thebluecollarinvestor.com/vip

Stock Name or Symbol	Stock $sh	Option $sh	Strike $	Expires	Intrisic	Upside	ROO	Up Potential	Down Protect

RETURN ON OPTION (ROO) CALCULATOR - MULTIPLE STOCKS

THE BLUE COLLAR INVESTOR

Full-sized versions of all charts, graphs, forms, photos, and other images contained in this book are available at

www.thebluecollarinvestor.com/vip

APPENDIX VI

Commendation

Unsolicited, Unbiased, Unedited Unconditional
Unabridged, Unplugged, Unmatched, Unparalleled.

I am writing this letter of commendation for Alan Ellman, and I am particularly addressing those considering taking his seminars on stock options.

I have found that Alan is informative, articulate, easy to listen to, and delivers his material in a relaxed and easy to understand manner. His teaching style is professional, but with a sense of humor. I highly recommend Alan's seminars, and all associated learning materials.

With Genuine Regard,

Minnie Ellman
(Alan's mother)

APPENDIX VII

Master *Figure* List
of charts and graphs

APPENDIX VIII

Resource Center

Stock Research & Information - Free Web Sites:

1- The Blue Collar Investor: _www.thebluecollarinvestor.com

2- http://finance.yahoo.com/

3- www.cnbc.com/

4- http://money.cnn.com/

5- www.fool.com/

6- www.marketwatch.com/

7- http://moneycentral.msn.com/investor/StockRating/srsmain.asp

Stock Research & Information– Paid Sites:

1- www.investools.com/

2- www.investors.com/

Glossary/Definitions - Free Web Sites:

1- http://stockcharts.com/school/doku.php?id=chart_school:glossary_a

2- www.zacks.com/help/glossary/?id=v_z&PHPSESSID=c761

3- www.cboe.com/LearnCenter/Glossary.aspx

4- www.investopedia.com/terms/o/optionchain.asp

Technical Analysis Charts

1- http://stockcharts.com/index.html

2- http://finance.yahoo.com/charts

Earnings Reports Information:

1- http://biz.yahoo.com/research/earncal/today.html

2- www.earningswhispers.com/

Stock Split Information:

1- http://biz.yahoo.com/c/s.html

2- www.investmenthouse.com/

Stock Screens:

1- http://moneycentral.msn.com/investor/finder/predefstocks.aspx

2- http://screener.finance.yahoo.com/newscreener.html

Options Information:

1- www.cboe.com/

2- www.888options.com/

Online Brokerage Web Sites:

1- www.usaa.com

2- www.thinkorswim.com

3- www.tdameritrade.com/welcome1.html

4- www.optionsxpress.com

5- www.scottrade.com/

Financial Newspapers/Magazines:

1- Investors Business Daily: www.investors.com

2- Wall Street Journal: www.wallstreetjournal.com

3- Barron's Weekly: www.barrons.com

4- Forbes magazine: www.forbes.com

Bonds Online Account and Information:

1- www.treasurydirect.gov

Mutual Fund/Exchange-Traded Fund Information

1- www.vanguard.com

Books/Suggested Reading

1- *One Up On Wall Street,* Peter Lynch

2- *Common Sense on Mutual Funds,* John C. Bogle

3- *Jim Cramer's Real Money,* James J. Cramer

4- *Jim Cramer's Mad Money,* James J. Cramer

5- *The Road to Wealth,* Suze Orman

6- *Getting Started in Options,* Michael C. Thomsett

7- *New Insights on Covered Call Writing,* Richard Lehman and Lawrence G. McMillan

8- *Fundamentals of the Options Market,* Michael S. Williams and Amy Hoffman

Real Estate Information and Education:

1- Long Island REIA, Ltd. (LIREIA): www.lireia.com

2- The Deal Panel: www.thedealpanel.com

APPENDIX IX
Mean Analyst Rating (MAR)

The screening process for option-selling watchlists include fundamental analysis, technical analysis and common-sense screens. The BCI team is now adding a new screen the mean analyst rating (MAR) to replace the Scouter Rating we have been using for years. This will add an "institutional" component to our analysis.

What is MAR?

An investment analyst is a financial professional with expertise in evaluating financial and investment information, typically for making buy, sell and hold recommendations for securities. In order to reach an opinion and communicate the value and risk of a covered security, analysts research financial statements, listen in on conference-calls and talk to managers and the customers of a company, in an attempt to determine findings for a research report. Ultimately, the analyst decides whether the stock is a "buy," sell," or hold."

The Scale of Ratings

The analyst ratings scale is more involved than the traditional classifications of "buy, hold and sell." There are now various categories that include multiple terms for each of the ratings ("sell" is also known as "strong sell," "buy" can be labeled as "strong buy"), as well as a couple of new terms: underperform and outperform.

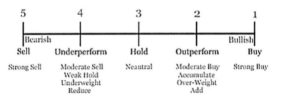

Figure E-21 - Stock recommendation Range

Additionally, not every firm adheres to the same ratings terminology: an "outperform" for one firm may be a "buy" for another and a "sell" for one may be a "market perform" for another. Thus, when using ratings, it is advisable to use a consensus figure like mean analyst rating.

The basics

Let's review the traditional ratings of "sell," "underperform," "hold," "outperform" and "buy".

- Buy: Also known as strong buy and "on the recommended list." This is a recommendation to purchase a specific security.

- Sell: Also known as strong sell, it's a recommendation to sell a security

- Hold: A hold recommendation is expected to perform at the same pace as comparable companies or in-line with the market moving forward.

- Underperform: A recommendation that means a stock is expected to do slightly worse than the overall stock market return. Underperform can also be expressed as "moderate sell," "weak hold" and "underweight."

Outperform: Also known as "moderate buy," "accumulate" and "overweight." Outperform is an analyst recommendation meaning a stock is expected to do slightly better than the market return.

It is best to view these recommendations as a consensus stat with at least 3 analyst reviews. These consensus stats should then be used in conjunction with other fundamental, technical and common-sense parameters when making our investment decisions.

Sample free site with MAR stats: finance.yahoo.com

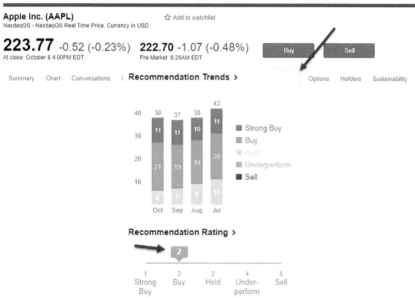

Figure E-22 - Locating MAR from finance.yahoo.com

Sample free site with MAR stats: finviz.com

Apple Inc.

Consumer Goods | Electronic Equipment |

Index	DJIA S&P500	P/E	19.41	EPS (ttm)	11.53	Insider Own	
Market Cap	1098.62B	Forward P/E	16.33	EPS next Y	13.71	Insider Trans	
Income	58.72B	PEG	1.81	EPS next Q	2.77	Inst Own	
Sales	255.27B	P/S	4.30	EPS this Y	10.80%	Inst Trans	
Book/sh	23.54	P/B	9.51	EPS next Y	16.38%	ROA	
Cash/sh	14.46	P/C	15.48	EPS next 5Y	10.75%	ROE	
Dividend	2.92	P/FCF	23.96	EPS past 5Y	7.90%	ROI	
Dividend %	1.30%	Quick Ratio	1.20	Sales past 5Y	7.90%	Gross Margin	
Employees	123000	Current Ratio	1.30	Sales Q/Q	17.30%	Oper. Margin	
Optionable	Yes	Debt/Eq	1.00	EPS Q/Q	40.40%	Profit Margin	
Shortable	Yes	LT Debt/Eq	0.84	Earnings	Nov 01 AMC	Payout	
Recom	2.00	SMA20	0.33%	SMA50	3.23%	SMA200	

Figure E-23 - Locating MAR from Finviz.com

Location of MAR stats in our Premium Stock reports

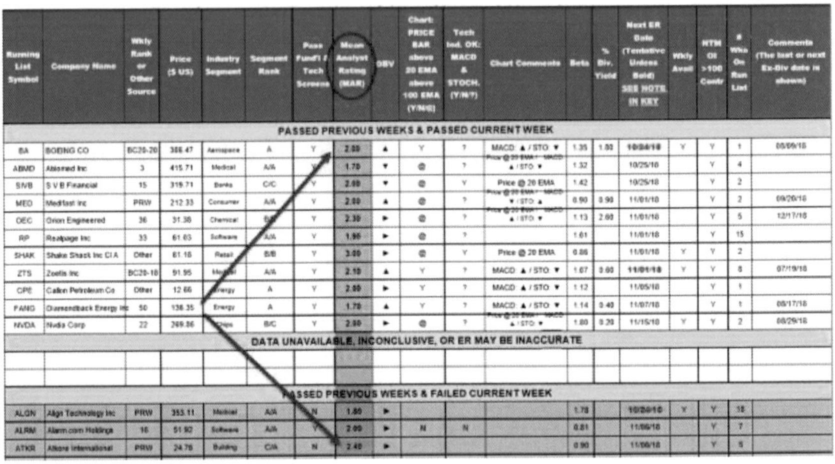

Running List Symbol	Company Name	Wkly Rank or Other Source	Price ($ US)	Industry Segment	Segment Rank	Pass Fund'l / Tech Screens	Mean Analyst Rating (MAR)	OBV	Chart: PRICE BAR above 20 EMA above 100 EMA (Y/N/@)	Tech Ind. OK: MACD & STOCH. (Y/N/?)	Chart Comments	Beta	% Div. Yield	Next ER Date (Tentative Unless Bold) SEE NOTE IN KEY	Wkly Avail	NTM OI >100 Contr	# Wks On Run List	Comments (The last or next Ex-Div date is shown)
PASSED PREVIOUS WEEKS & PASSED CURRENT WEEK																		
BA	BOEING CO	BC20-20	386.47	Aerospace	A	Y	2.00	▲	Y	?	MACD: ▲ / STO: ▼	1.35	1.80	**10/24/18**	Y	Y	1	08/09/18
ABMD	Abiomed Inc	3	415.71	Medical	A/A	Y	1.70	▼	@	?	Price @ 20 EMA / MACD ▲ / STO: ▼	1.32		10/25/18		Y	4	
SIVB	S V B Financial	15	319.71	Banks	C/C	Y	2.00	▼	@	Y	Price @ 20 EMA	1.42		10/25/18		Y	2	
MED	Medifast Inc	PRW	212.33	Consumer	A/A	Y	2.00	▲	@	?	Price @ 20 EMA / MACD ▼ / STO: ▲	0.90	0.90	11/01/18		Y	2	09/20/18
OEC	Orion Engineered	36	31.38	Chemical	B/B	Y	2.30	►	@	?	Price @ 20 EMA / MACD ▲ / STO: ▼	1.13	2.60	11/01/18		Y	5	12/17/18
RP	Realpage Inc	33	61.03	Software	A/A	Y	1.90	►	@	?		1.61		11/01/18		Y	15	
SHAK	Shake Shack Inc Cl A	Other	61.18	Retail	B/B	Y	3.00	►	@	Y	Price @ 20 EMA	0.86		11/01/18	Y	Y	2	
ZTS	Zoetis Inc	BC20-18	91.95	Medical	A/A	Y	2.10	▲	Y	?	MACD: ▲ / STO: ▼	1.07	0.60	**11/01/18**	Y	Y	8	07/19/18
CPE	Callon Petroleum Co	Other	12.66	Energy	A	Y	2.00	►	Y	?	MACD: ▲ / STO: ▼	1.12		11/05/18		Y	1	
FANG	Diamondback Energy Inc	50	138.35	Energy	A	Y	1.70	▲	Y	?	MACD: ▲ / STO: ▼	1.14	0.40	11/07/18		Y	1	08/17/18
NVDA	Nvidia Corp	22	269.86	Chips	B/C	Y	2.00	►	@	?	Price @ 20 EMA / MACD ▲ / STO: ▼	1.80	0.20	11/15/18	Y	Y	2	08/29/18
DATA UNAVAILABLE, INCONCLUSIVE, OR ER MAY BE INACCURATE																		
PASSED PREVIOUS WEEKS & FAILED CURRENT WEEK																		
ALGN	Align Technology Inc	PRW	353.11	Medical	A/A	N	1.80	►				1.78		**10/24/18**	Y	Y	18	
ALRM	Alarm.com Holdings	16	51.92	Software	A/A	Y	2.00	►	N	N		0.81		11/06/18		Y	7	
ATKR	Atkore International	PRW	24.78	Building	C/A	N	2.40	►				0.90		11/06/18		Y	5	

Figure E-24 - MAR Stats in Premium Stock report

The BCI team will eliminate all stocks with MAR Ratings higher than "3" For those securities remaining, we will publish the precise stats to assist our members in making the best investment decisions possible.

Discussion

Analysts' recommendations are the culmination of analyzing equity research reports and should be used in conjunction with thorough investment methodologies to make investment decisions. Additionally, "buy, hold and sell" recommendation meanings are not as cut-and-dry as they first appear; a series of terms and differences in meanings exist behind the basic terminology.

APPENDIX X

On Balance Volume (OBV)

Introduction

On Balance Volume (OBV) measures buying and selling pressure as a cumulative indicator that adds volume on up days and subtracts volume on down days. OBV was developed by Joe Granville and introduced in his 1963 book, "Granville's New Key to Stock Market Profits". It was one of the first indicators to measure positive and negative volume flow. Technical analysts can look for divergences between OBV and price to predict price movements or use OBV to confirm price trends.

OBV and the BCI Methodology

For years, the BCI methodology has stressed the significance of the institutional investors (the "big boys") in impacting stock performance. This explains why we require a minimum average stock trading volume and option open interest before entering our option-selling trades.

Volume is said to reflect the commitment on the part of traders. Because On-Balance Volume relates volume to price movements, many traders believe that it can offer great insights into the level of bullishness or bearishness that exists or is building among traders regarding a given stock or other asset.

By incorporating OBV, we are factoring in the trend of institutional interest or lack thereof in each security and adding another dimension to our stock screening process.

Calculation

The On Balance Volume (OBV) line is simply a running total of positive and negative volume. A period's volume is positive when the close is above the prior close. A period's volume is negative when the close is below the prior close. T

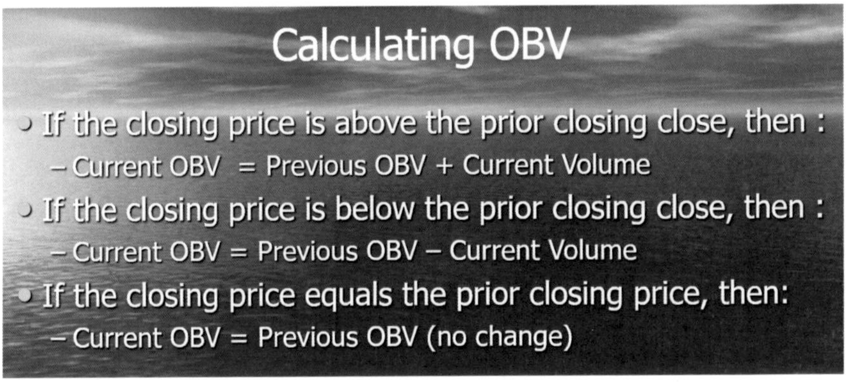

Figure E-25 - Calculating OBV

Interpretation

Granville theorized that volume precedes price. OBV rises when volume on up days outpaces volume on down days. OBV falls when volume on down days is stronger. A rising OBV reflects positive volume pressure that can lead to higher prices. Conversely, falling OBV reflects negative volume pressure that can foreshadow lower prices. Granville noted in his research that OBV would often move before price. Expect prices to move higher if OBV is rising while prices are either flat or moving down. Expect prices to move lower if OBV is falling while prices are either flat or moving up.

The absolute value of OBV is not important. Technical analysts should instead focus on the characteristics of the OBV line. First, define the trend for OBV. Second, determine if the current trend matches the trend for the underlying security. Third, look for potential support or resistance levels. Once broken, the trend for OBV will change and these breaks can be used to generate signals. Also, notice that OBV is based on closing prices. Therefore, closing prices should be considered when looking for divergences or support/resistance breaks. And finally, volume spikes can sometimes throw off the indicator by causing a sharp move that will require a settling period.

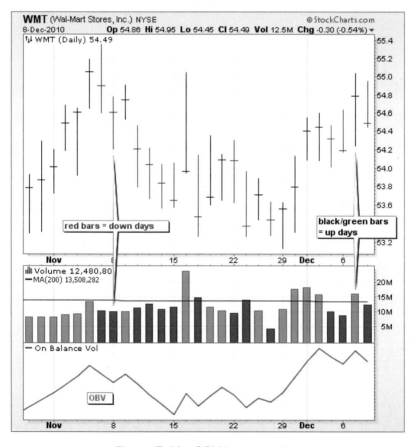

Figure E-26 - OBV Interpretation

OBV Location in Premium Reports

Running List Symbol	Company Name	Wkly Rank or Other Source	Price ($ US)	Industry Segment	Segment Rank	Pass Fund'l & Tech Screens	Mean Analyst Rating (MAR)	OBV	Chart: PRICE BAR above 20 EMA above 100 EMA (Y/N/?)	Tech Ind. OK: MACD & STOCH. (Y/N/?)	Chart Comments	Beta	% Div. Yield	Next ER Date (Tentative Unless Bold) SEE NOTE IN KEY	Wkly Avail	NTM OI >100 Contr	# Wks On Run List	Comments (The last er next Ex-Div date is shown)
						PASSED PREVIOUS WEEKS & PASSED CURRENT WEEK												
BA	BOEING CO	BC20-20	386.47	Aerospace	A	Y	2.00	▲	Y	?	MACD: ▲ / BTO: ▼	1.35	1.50	10/24/18	Y	Y	1	08/08/18
ASMD	Ablomed Inc	3	416.71	Medical	A/A	Y	1.70	▼	⊙	?	▲ / STO: ▼	1.32		10/25/18		Y	4	
BVB	B V B Financial	15	319.71	Banks	O/C	Y	2.00	▼	⊙	Y	Price ⊙ 20 EMA	1.42		10/25/18		Y	2	
MED	Medifast Inc	PRW	212.33	Consumer	A/A	Y	2.00	▲	⊙	?	▼ / STO: ▼	0.90	0.90	11/01/18		Y	2	08/20/18
OEC	Orion Engineered	36	31.38	Chemical	B/B	Y	2.30	►	⊙	?	▲ / STO: ▼	1.13	2.50	11/01/18		Y	6	12/17/18
RP	Realpage Inc	33	61.03	Software	A/A	Y	1.90	►	⊙	?		1.01		11/01/18		Y	15	
SHAK	Shake Shack Inc CI A	Other	61.18	Retail	B/B	Y	3.00	►	⊙	Y	Price ⊙ 20 EMA	0.86		11/01/18	Y	Y	2	
ZTS	Zoetis Inc	BC20-15	91.95	Medical	A/A	Y	2.10	▲	Y	?	MACD: ▲ / BTO: ▼	1.07	0.60	11/01/18	Y	Y	2	07/19/18
CPE	Callon Petroleum Co	Other	12.66	Energy	A	Y	2.00	►	Y	?	MACD: ▲ / BTO: ▼	1.12		11/08/18		Y	1	
FANG	Diamondback Energy Inc	90	136.36	Energy	A	Y	1.70	▲	Y	?	MACD: ▲ / BTO: ▼	1.14	0.40	11/07/18		Y	1	08/17/18
NVDA	Nvdia Corp	22	289.36	Chips	B/C	Y	2.00	►	⊙	?	▲ / STO: ▼	1.80	0.20	11/15/18	Y	Y	2	08/29/18
						DATA UNAVAILABLE, INCONCLUSIVE, OR ER MAY BE INACCURATE												
						PASSED PREVIOUS WEEKS & FAILED CURRENT WEEK												
ALGN	Align Technology Inc	PRW	353.11	Medical	A/A	N	1.80	►					1.78		10/24/18	Y	Y	18	
ALRM	Alarm.com Holdings	16	51.52	Software	A/A	Y	2.00	►		N	N			0.81	11/06/18		Y	7	

Figure E-27

Pass Fund'l & Tech Screens	Mean Analyst Rating (MAR)	OBV	Chart: PRICE BAR above 20 EMA above 100 EMA (Y/N/?)	Tech Ind. OK: MACD & STOCH. (Y/N/?)
SED PREVIOUS WEEKS & PASSED CU				
Y	2.00	▲	Y	?
Y	1.70	▼	⊙	?
Y	2.00	▼	⊙	Y
Y	2.00	▲	⊙	?
Y	2.30	►	⊙	?
Y	1.90	►	⊙	?
Y	3.00	►	⊙	Y
Y	2.10	▲	Y	?
Y	2.00	►	Y	?
Y	1.70	▲	Y	?
Y	2.00	►	⊙	?

Figure E-28

Trend is identified with up, down or sideways arrows (▲, ►, ▼).

Summary

- Cumulative indicator that adds volume on up days and subtracts volume on down days

- Look for divergences between OBV and price to predict price movements or use OBV to confirm price trends

- OBV rises when volume on up days outpaces volume on down days

- OBV falls when volume on down days is stronger

- A rising OBV reflects positive volume pressure that can lead to higher prices

- Falling OBV reflects negative volume pressure that can foreshadow lower prices

- Focus in on the OBV trend, not the actual number

- Look for bullish and bearish divergences with share price

- OBV can be used to confirm a price trend, upside breakout or downside break

Conclusions

On Balance Volume (OBV) is a simple indicator that uses volume and price to measure buying pressure and selling pressure. Buying pressure is evident when positive volume exceeds negative volume and the OBV line rises.

Selling pressure is present when negative volume exceeds positive volume and the OBV line falls. Technical analysts can use OBV to confirm the underlying trend or look for divergences that may foreshadow a price change. As with all indicators, it is important to use OBV in conjunction with other aspects of technical analysis. It is not a standalone indicator. OBV can be combined with basic pattern analysis or to confirm signals from momentum oscillators.

When we use OBV with the BCI methodology, we are looking at the trend of OBV, not the absolute value of the OBV. The relative direction (▲, ▶, ▼) of the indicator is what we are looking for. That is, we want to know if the institutions accumulating shares and supporting the stock (▲ & ▶) or are they exiting from the stock (▼) since they move the stock.

The OBV indicator can be found in most charting packages, including those that are free:

www.stockcharts.com
www.freestockcharts.com
www.barchart.com
www.tradingview.com

OBV is typically available in the charting packages provided by your broker as well.

For additional information, visit www.stockcharts.com and click on the "Chart School" tab (a free resource) on the command bar at the top of their home page.

***Some charts from www.stockcharts.com

Glossary

Accumulation: Buying of stock by institutional or professional investors over an extended period of time.

Acquisition: When one company purchases the majority interest in the acquired.

Actively Managed Mutual Funds: Shareholders, through a mutual fund manager, buy and sell stocks and bonds, within the fund, in an attempt to *beat the market.*

American Style Options: An option contract that may be exercised at any time between the date of purchase and the expiration date.

Assignment: The receipt of an exercise notice by an option seller that obligates him to sell (in the case of a call) or purchase (in the case of a put) the underlying security at the specified strike price.

At-the-money: An option is at-the-money if the strike price of the option is equal to the market price of the underlying security.

Bearish: Pessimistic investor sentiment that a particular security or market is headed downward.

Bullish: Optimistic investor sentiment that a particular equity or market will rise.

Buy down price of stock: Using the intrinsic value of an in-the-money option premium to reduce the cost of the stock purchase.

Buy to close: A term used by many brokerages to represent the closing of a short position in option transactions.

Call: An option contract giving the owner the right (but not the obligation) to buy a specified amount of an underlying security at a specified price within a specified time.

Cost basis: The original value of an asset. It is used to determine the capital gain, which is equal to the difference between the asset's cost basis and the current market value. Also: the amount of your original investment.

Covered call writing: A strategy in which one sells call options while simultaneously owning the underlying security.

Currency carry trade: A strategy in which an investor sells a certain currency with a relatively low interest rate and uses the funds to purchase a different currency yielding a higher interest rate. A trader using this strategy attempts to capture the difference between the rates, which can often be substantial, depending on the amount of leverage the investor chooses to use.

Dilution: A reduction in earnings per share of common stock that occurs through the issuance of additional shares. This is avoided with stock splits by reducing the current market value of a stock by a similar ratio as was the number of shares increased.

Distribution: the selling of stock by large institutions over an extending period of time.

Diversification: A risk management technique that mixes a wide variety of investments within a portfolio. The rationale behind this technique contends that a portfolio of different kinds of investments will, on average, yield higher returns and pose a lower risk than any individual investment found within the portfolio.

Dollar cost averaging: The technique of buying a fixed dollar amount of a particular investment on a regular schedule, regardless of the share price. More shares are purchased when prices are low, and fewer shares are bought when prices are high.

Downside protection: The intrinsic value portion of an in-the-money call option premium divided by the original cost basis. It is the percentage of your investment that can be lost without affecting the option return on your investment. The formula is as follows:

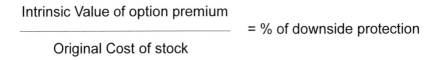

$$\frac{\text{Intrinsic Value of option premium}}{\text{Original Cost of stock}} = \% \text{ of downside protection}$$

Earnings estimate: An analyst's estimate for a company's future quarterly or annual earnings.

Earnings guidance: I nformation that a company provides as an indication or estimate of their future earnings.

Earnings report: A quarterly filing made by public companies to report their performance. Included in these reports are items such as net income, earnings per share, earnings from continuing operations, and net sales. These reports follow the end of each quarter. Most companies file in January, April, July, and October.

Earnings surprise: When the earnings reported in a companies quarterly or annual report are above or below analysts' earnings estimates.

ESOC: Ellman System Option Calculator which is an excel calculator used to compute option returns specifically for Alan Ellman's *Cashing In On Covered Calls* system.

ETFs: See exchange traded funds.

Exchange traded funds: A security that tracks an index, a commodity, or a basket of assets like an index fund, but trades like a stock on an exchange, thus experiencing price changes throughout the day as it is bought and sold.These securities provides the diversification of an index fund.

European Style Option: An option contract that can only be exercised on the expiration date.

Exit strategy: A plan in which a trader intends to get out of an investment position made in the past. It is a way of *cashing out* or *closing out a position.*

Expense ratio: A measure of what it costs an investment company to operate a mutual fund. It is determined through an annual calculation, where a fund's operating expenses are divided by the average dollar value of its managed assets Operating expenses are taken out of a fund's assets and lower the return to a fund's investors. Some funds have a marketing cost referred to as a 12b-1 fee, which would also be included in operating expenses. It is interesting that a fund's trading activity - the buying and selling of stock - is NOT included in the calculation of expense ratio.

Expiration date: The last day (in the case of an American-style) or the only day (in the case of European-style) on which an option may be exercised. For stock option, this date is the third Friday of the expiration month. If Friday is a holiday, the last trading day is the preceding Thursday.

Exponential moving average or EMA: A type of moving average that is similar to a simple moving average, except that more weight is given to the most recent data. It reacts faster to recent price changes than does a simple moving average. The 12- and 26-day EMA's are the most popular short-term averages, and they are used to create indicators like the MACD.

First call: A company that gathers research notes and earnings estimates from brokerage analysts and forms a consensus estimate. The estimate is compared to the actual earnings reports, and then the difference between the two is the earnings surprise. The other major player in this estimate game is **Zacks.**

Fundamental analysis: A method of analyzing the prospects of a security by observing the accepted accounting measures such as earnings, sales, and assets and so on.

Globalization: The tendency of investment funds and businesses to move beyond domestic and national markets to other markets around the globe, thereby increasing the interconnectedness of different markets. It has had the effect of increasing international trade and cultural exchange.

IBD 100: The Investor's Business Daily 100 is a computer-generated ranking of the leading companies trading in America. Rankings are based on a combination of each company's profit growth; IBD's Composite Rating, which includes key measures such as return on equity, sales growth and profit margins; and relative price strength in the past 12 months.

Index fund: A type of mutual fund with a portfolio constructed to mirror, or track, the components of a market index such as the S&P 500 Index. An index mutual fund is said to provide broad market exposure, low operating expenses and low portfolio turnover. *Indexing* is a passive form of fund management that has been successful in out-performing most actively managed mutual funds.

In-the-money: A term describing any option that has *intrinsic value*. A call option is in-the-money if the underlying security is higher than the strike price of the call.

Intrinsic value: The value of an option if it were to expire immediately with the underlying stock at its current price; the amount by which the stock is in-the-money. For call options, this is the positive difference between the stock price and the strike price.

Key economic indicator: Macroeconomic data that is used by investors to interpret current or future investment possibilities and judge the overall health of an economy. These are specific pieces of data released by the government and non-profit organizations. These include:

- The Consumer Price Index (CPI)
- Gross Domestic Product (GDP)
- Unemployment statistics
- The price of crude oil

Lagging indicator: A technical indicator that trails the price action of an underlying asset. It is used by traders to generate transaction signals or to confirm the strength of a given trend. Since these indicators lag the price of the asset, a significant move will generally occur before the indicator is able to provide a signal. It confirms long-term trends but does not predict them.

Large cap: An abbreviation for the term *large market capitalization.* Market capitalization is calculated by multiplying the number of a company's outstanding shares by its stock price per share. The expression *large cap* is used by the investment community as an indicator of a company's size. A large cap stock has a market-capitalization dollar value of over 10 billion.

Long (position): The buying of a security, such as a stock or options contract, with the expectation that the asset will rise in value.

MACD (Moving average convergence divergence): A trend-following momentum indicator that shows the relationship between two moving averages of prices. The MACD is calculated by subtracting the 26-day exponential moving average (EMA) from the 12-day EMA. A 9-day EMA of the MACD, called the *signal line,* is then plotted on top of the MACD, functioning as a trigger for buy and sell signals.

MACD Histogram: A common technical indicator that illustrates the difference between the MACD and the trigger line. This difference is then plotted on a chart in the form of a histogram to make it easy for a trader to determine a specific asset's momentum.

Market capitalization: The total dollar market value of all of a company's outstanding shares. It is calculated by multiplying a company's shares outstanding by the current market price of one share. The investment community uses this figure to determine a company's size, as opposed to sales or total asset figures. Also referred to as *market cap.*

Market consensus: The average earnings estimates made by brokers and security analysts. Also known as *earnings expectations.*

Mergers: A general term used to refer to the consolidation of companies. It is a combination of two companies to form a new company.

Momentum indicator: Designed to track momentum in the price of a security to help identify the enthusiasm of buyers and sellers involved in the price trend development. Some indicators compare the closing price with some historical price so many periods before, others construct trend lines like the *MACD*. Others, like *Stochastics,* is a ratio using the high, low, and close values on various days.

Momentum Oscillator: A technical analysis tool that is banded between two extreme values and built with the results from a trend indicator for discovering short-term overbought or oversold conditions. As the value of the oscillator approaches the upper extreme value the asset is deemed to be overbought, and as it approaches the lower extreme it is deemed to be oversold. This oscillator is most advantageous when a stock price is in a trading range (sideways). An example is the *stochastic oscillator.*

Money market securities: The securities market dealing in short-term debt and monetary instruments. These forms of debt mature in less than one year and are quite liquid. Treasury bills make up the bulk of the money market instruments. These securities are relatively risk-free.

Moving average: An indicator frequently used in technical analysis showing the average value of a securities price over a set period. Moving averages are generally used to measure momentum and define areas of possible support and resistance.

Nasdaq 100 index: An index composed of the 100 largest, most actively traded U.S. companies listed on the Nasdaq stock exchange. This index includes companies from a broad range of industries with the exception of those that operate in the financial industry, such as banks and investment companies.

OHLC (bar) chart: Short for *Open High, Low Close chart.* This type of chart is used to spot trends and view stock movements, particularly on a short term basis.

Option: A contract that gives the owner the right, if exercised, to buy or sell a security or basket of securities (index) at a specific price within a specific time limit. Stock option contracts are generally for the right to buy or sell 100 shares of the underlying stock.

Option chain: A way of quoting option prices through a list of all the options for a given security. For each underlying security, the option chain tells investors the various strike prices, expiration dates, and whether they are calls or puts.

Options contract: Represents 100 shares in the underlying stock. Information included consists of the underlying security, type of option (call or put), expiration month, strike price and premium.

Option premium: The price at which the contract trades. It is the price paid by the buyer to the writer, or seller, of the option. In return the writer of the call option is obligated to deliver the underlying security to an option buyer if the call is exercised or buy the underlying security if the put is exercised. The writer keeps the premium whether or not the option is exercised.

Out-of-the-money: A call option is out-of-the-money if the strike price is greater than market value of the underlying security.

Over-the-counter option (OTC): An option traded off-exchange, as opposed to a *listed* stock option. The OTC option has a direct link between buyer and seller, has no secondary market, and has no standardization of strike prices and expiration dates. This securities market is not geographically centralized like the trading floor of the NYSE. Trading takes place through a telephone and computer network.

Overbought: A technical condition that occurs when prices are considered too high and susceptible to decline. Overbought conditions can be classified by analyzing the chart pattern or with indicators such as the Stochastic Oscillator. Generally, a security is considered overbought when the Stochastic Oscillator exceeds 80. Overbought is not the same as being *bearish. It simply infers that the stock has risen too far too fast and might be due for a pullback.*

Oversold: A technical condition that occurs when prices are considered too low and ripe for a surge. Oversold conditions can be classified by analyzing the chart pattern or with indicators such as the Stochastic Oscillator. Generally, a security is considered oversold if the Stochastic Oscillator is less than 20. Oversold is not the same as being *bullish. It merely infers that the security has fallen too far too fast and may be due for a reaction rally.*

Paper trade: A hypothetical trade that does not involve any monetary transactions. It is a risk-free way to learn the ins and outs of the market.

Passive management (of mutual funds): An investment strategy that mirrors a market index and does not attempt to beat the market.

Portfolio management: The art and science of making decisions about investment mix and policy, matching investments to objectives, asset allocation, and balancing risk versus performance. *It requires organized lists of accurate information.*

Price bar: see *OHLC.*

Put: An option contract that gives the holder the right, but not the obligation, to sell the underlying security at a specified price for a certain fixed period of time.

QQQQ: This is the ticker symbol for the Nasdaq 100 Trust, which is an exchange traded fund (ETF) that trades on the Nasdaq. It offers broad exposure to the tech sector by tracking the Nasdaq 100 index, which consists of the 100 largest non-financial stocks on the Nasdaq. It is also known as the *quadruple-Qs.*

Resistance: The price level at which there is a large enough supply of a stock available to cause a halt in the upward trend and turn the trend down. Resistance levels indicate the price at which most investors feel that the prices will move lower.

Rolling down: Closing out options at one strike price and simultaneously opening another at a lower strike price.

Rolling out (forward): Closing out of an option contract at a near-term expiration date and opening a same strike option contract at a later date.

Rolling up: Close out options at a lower strike and open options at a higher strike.

ROO (return on option): The percent profit realized from the sale of a covered call option based on the cost basis of the underlying stock. If an in-the-money option was sold, the intrinsic value is deducted from the option premium before calculating the return.

Rule of 72: A rule stating that in order to find the number of years required to double your money at a given interest rate, you divide the compound return into 72. The result is the approximate number of years that it will take for your investment to double.

S&P 500 (Standard and Poor's 500): An index consisting of 500 stocks chosen for market size, liquidity, and industry grouping, among other factors. It is designed to be a leading indicator of U.S. equities and is meant to reflect the risk/return characteristics of the large-cap universe.

Sarbanes-Oxley Act of 2002 (SOX): An act passed by the U.S. Congress to protect investors from the possibility of fraudulent accounting activities by corporations. It includes the establishment of a *Public Company Accounting Oversight Board* where public companies must now be registered.

Securities and Exchange Commission (SEC): A government commission, created by Congress, established to regulate the securities markets and protect investors. It also monitors the corporate takeovers in the U.S. The SEC is composed of five commissions appointed by the U.S. President and approved by the Senate. The statutes administered by the SEC are designed to promote full public disclosure and to protect the investing public against fraudulent and manipulative practices in the securities markets. Generally, most issues of securities offered in interstate commerce, through the mail or on the internet, must be registered with the SEC.

Sell to open: A phrase used by many brokerages on the street to represent the opening of a short position in option transactions.

Short (or short position): The sale (also known as *writing*) of an options contract or a stock to open a position.

Simple moving average (SMA): A moving average that gives equal weight to each day's price data.

Stochastic Oscillator: A momentum indicator that measures the price of a security relative to the high/low range over a set period of time. The indicator oscillates between 0 and 100. Readings below 20 are considered oversold. Readings above 80 are considered overbought.

StockScouter Rating: MSN Monet Central's rating of stocks from 1 to 10, with 10 being the best. It uses a system of advanced mathematics to determine a stock's expected risk and return.

Stock split: A change in the number of shares outstanding (in circulation). The number of shares are adjusted by the split ratio, e.g. 2 to 1. In this case, 1000 shares splits to 2000 shares but the opening price and current price are cut in half. The overall effect is to maintain the same cost and current value of an investment while increasing the number of shares and lowering the per share price. This makes it easier for small investors to own the stock in round lots.

Street expectation: The average earnings estimates made by brokers and security analysts.

Strike price: The stated price per share for which the underlying security may be purchased (in the case of a call) or sold (in the case of a put) by the option holder upon exercise of the option contract.

Support: A price level at which there is sufficient demand for a stock to cause a halt in a downward trend and turn the trend up. Support levels indicate the price at which most investors feel that prices will move higher.

Technical analysis: The method of predicting future stock price movements based on observation of historical stock price movements.

Time decay: A term used to describe how the theoretical value of an option *erodes* or reduces with the passage of time.

Time value: The portion of the option premium that is attributable to the amount of time remaining until the expiration of the option contract. Time value is whatever value the option has in addition to its intrinsic value.

Trading range: The spread between the high and low prices traded during a period of time.

Treasury note (one of the *treasuries*): A marketable, U.S. government debt security with a fixed interest rate and a maturity between one and ten years. T-notes can be bought either directly from the U.S. Government or through a bank.

Trend analysis: An aspect of technical analysis that tries to predict the future movement of a stock based on past data. It is based on the idea that what has happened in the past gives traders an idea of what will happen in the future. The concept is that moving with trends will lead to profits for the investor.

Trigger line / signal: Usually an exponential or simple moving average of a technical indicator which serves as a frame of reference for positive and negative divergences.

For example, if the MACD indicator moves above its moving average, a bullish signal is produced.

Upside potential: Additional % of profit, as it relates to the underlying stock cost basis, that can be realized if the stock price reaches the strike price at expiration. It applies to out-of-the-money strike prices.

Velocity (of money): A term used to describe the rate at which money is exchanged from one transaction to another.

Volume: The number of trades in a security over a period of time. On a chart, volume is usually represented as a histogram (vertical bars) below the price chart. The NYSE and Nasdaq measure volume differently. For every buyer, there is a seller: 100 shares bought = 100 shares sold. The NYSE would count this as 100 shares of volume. However, the Nasdaq would count each side of the trade and as 200 shares volume.

Volume surge: An increase in the daily trading volume of an equity equal to at least 1.5 times its normal trading volume.

Watch list: A list of securities that are in consideration for investment buy/sell decisions.

Whisper number: The unofficial and unpublished earnings per share (EPS) forecasts that circulate among professionals on Wall Street. They were generally reserved for the favored (wealthy) clients of a brokerage.

Wilshire 5000 Total Stock Market Index: A market capitalization-weighted index composed of more than 6700 publicly traded companies. These companies must be headquarted in the U.S. and actively traded on an American stock exchange.

Yen carry trade: A strategy in which an investor sells the Japanese currency (yen) with a relatively low interest rate and uses the funds to purchase a different currency (dollar) yielding a higher interest rate. A trader using this strategy attempts to capture the difference between the rates-which can often be substantial, depending on the amount of leverage the investor chooses to use.

Index

X

Y

Z

About The Author

Dr. Alan Ellman wears many hats during the course of a typical day. He is a licensed general Dentist in the State of New York and the owner of a vitamin store called The Natural Vitamin and Herb Source of Long Island. In addition to these titles, Alan is also a licensed certified Personal Fitness Trainer and a licensed Real Estate salesperson.

Alan is also an avid Real Estate Investor, owning properties in Texas, Florida, Pennsylvania and New York. He has often been invited to speak in front of large groups of investors about his successful investment properties.

Of all the facets of his life, Alan has become most passionate about the Stock Market and Call Options in particular. He loves the challenge of beating the market and sharing his ideas and system with others. This has manifest itself in the form of seminars and 1-on-1 coaching classes. In particular, he wants to spread the word about selling call options to the blue collar investor. Alan is determined to assist the average investor get the returns normally reserved for the Wall Street insiders.

Not only does Alan want you to achieve successful results in your stock market investing, he wants you to be in total control of the process. To learn how to best accomplish these goals and become CEO of Your Own Money, please visit his web site at www.TheBlueCollarInvestor.com.

Dear Reader,

How is it possible that I have written a book about a subject that I am so passionate about... stock options?

I have friends who fish, play tennis, and golf... no books!

Others are passionate about gardening, pottery, scrape booking and woodworking... still no books!

Well, it all started back in the early 1990's when I decided to educate myself about the stock market. As I learned more and more, I became increasingly fascinated with the subject. I also was getting progressively wealthier and wealthier. Although I was reluctant to impose my ideas on others, I decided to share with some friends and relatives my impressive results. I was surprised and discouraged to discover that there was little or no interest in pursuing my formula.

I began to formulate a theory as to why people would react so negatively to the concept of self-investing in the stock market. As I thought about it, I realized that the answer lies in the fabric of decades of negative "brain-washing" we "blue collar investors" have been subjected to; such as:

> We shouldnt invest ourselves, we are not smart enough! We must hire a stock broker or a financial planner... they will lead us to the promised land of financial freedom.

> The stock market is much too complicated. It takes a Wall Street insider to truly understand the inner workings of this marketplace.

In addition to this negative indoctrination, the situation is exacerbated by the fact that we are not taught about the stock market while in school. Worse yet, it is in nobodys best interest to teach it to us after we graduate. As a result, the doctrine of "laissez-faire" lives on in the arena of blue collar stock investing.

I check my stock portfolio every day. I ask you: Which stockbroker or financial planner would do that for me?

OR YOU?

In August of 2006, I was asked to speak to a group of 250 investors about several successful real estate deals I had been involved in. During the course of my presentation, I mentioned that I purchased my first investment property with the profits I earned selling stock options. The response and interest to this "comment in passing" was overwhelming.

I learned that times have changed! People DO want to take control of their financial lives and become CEO of their money. This was truly an uplifting moment for me. It led me to write this book and create a DVD and CD series, also called "Cashing in on Covered Calls."

I don't fish, and I dont play tennis; but I am passionate about investing in the stock market. So, how is it possible that I have written a book about a subject that I am so enthusiastic about?

IT IS BECAUSE OF YOU, THE MOTIVATED BLUE COLLAR INVESTOR !

So, if you have a book club, investors group, REIA (real estate investors association), or similar organization, and plan to discuss investing ideas, please let me know. I'd be delighted to call your group and chat about "Cashing In On Covered Calls." I'd like to hear what the members of your group think about it... such feedback is always rewarding. If you are simply another blue collar investor like me and would just like to drop me a line, please do so. My email is Alan@TheBlueCollarInvestor.com.

I genuinely thank you for giving me the opportunity to share my experiences with you.

Sincerely,

Alan G. Ellman

FREE EXCEL OPTION CALCULATOR

I want all my fellow Blue Collar Investors to succeed!

That's why I'm offering you my Ellman System Option Calculator (ESOC) at absolutely no cost, whatsoever. An irreplaceable tool that unoquivically supports your success, the ESOC is used throughout this manual to quickly and accurately measure and manage risk and results. I use it everyday to calculate and track my transactions. Now, you can, too! And, its yours F R E E, as my gift to you.

Here's your recipe for success:

- READ THIS BOOK -

- WATCH THE DVDs -

- LISTEN TO THE CDs -

- USE THE ESOC -
and calculate *your* incredible returns

To get your copy of this valuable device, simply go to my website, www.thebluecollarinvestor.com/esoc, fill out a simple e-form, and the ESOC is yours! If you prefer to order it by mail, just complete the form below and mail it to MY ESOC, THE BLUE COLLAR INVESTOR, P.O. Box 266, Old Bethpage, NY 11804-0266. Within days upon receipt, we'll have your ESOC CD on its way home to you.

Name: _____

Home Address: _____

_____

City: _____

State: _____   Zip: _____

Email: _____

Ph: ☐ cell   ☐ home   ☐ work _____

Wishing you all the best as you begin Cashing In On Covered Calls.

Alan